OVERCOMING MURPHY'S LAW

OVERCOMING MURPHY'S LAW

William C. Waddell

A Division of American Management Associations

To Jim, Dick, Bill, and Leslie

Library of Congress Cataloging in Publication

Waddell, William C
    Overcoming Murphy's law.

    Includes index.
1. Management.   I. Title.
HD31.W235   658   80-65708
ISBN 0-8144-5628-6

First Printing

Preface

This is a book about how to manage. It does not present theories and schools of thought or address some timely topic or fad. Its purpose is to advance a practical and logically consistent approach to the task of managing the work of others in current times.

Although one might argue that the principles of management are timeless, the applications certainly are not. There have been great changes in the attitudes and aspirations of workers, even within the last ten years. Technology presents new challenges. It has the potential for causing feelings of disassociation and alienation among employees, but it also can break the chains that sometimes shackle people to boring and unrewarding work.

Changes in every aspect of the environment—social, demographic, political, legal, economic, and technological—have added greatly to the complexities of running an organization. As tasks become more difficult and intricate, the possibility of error increases. This phenomenon has led to common acceptance of Murphy's Law in organizational life: "If anything can go wrong, it will." The thesis of this book is that, far from being inevitable, Murphy's Law operates all too frequently because management does not apply some fundamental principles in the context of today's requirements.

One of the themes addressed early in the book is that good management of others starts with good management of self. In a culture where formal authority in all institutions is eroding, the leader cannot rely on a title to gain the cooperation of others. His influence is more dependent on his own personal qualifications for leadership.

The pervasive thesis throughout this book is that the leader should view his unit both as a subsystem of a higher-level system and as a unit that contains subsystems within it. The planning function is preeminent in linking these systems together toward common goals. But, on the other hand, without creating the kind of human strengths that are needed in the systems, good planning is not possible. There is, in other words, a circular relationship between good systems and good planning. The defense against Murphy's Law is good planning executed by people who have a deep understanding of what is desired and why. This book presents a management philosophy that is necessary to get that kind of performance and some step-by-step procedures for putting the philosophy into practice. In the last five chapters there is an especially strong emphasis on how to do it.

The job of management in organizations today is done by professionals, staff personnel, or what may be called knowledge workers, who manage by making recommendations which more often than not have the force of decisions. Furthermore, they are often called to lead others on a project or task which might cover months or last only as long as a meeting. Increased specialization in knowledge and greater complexity of organizations have blurred the lines that formerly were distinct between supervisory and nonsupervisory personnel. This phenomenon is recognized in the book. The cumbersomeness of repeatedly naming managers, professionals, and staff personnel is avoided by using one term or another. However, except where the meaning is expressly more pointed, these terms may be used interchangeably. The material in this book is relevant to anyone who makes or influences decisions regarding how people are to go about their work in organizations.

I am indebted to Mrs. Judy Getzin, who typed the manuscript and assisted in the editing, and to my friend Charlie Szymanski, whose perceptive comments on the manuscript have contributed to the clarity of syntax of the book.

WILLIAM C. WADDELL

Contents

1

Planning: the key to top performance

The business world today is a complicated set of systems and sub-systems that interlock and react on each other. Among the components of these systems are the competitors within an industry, the industries that compete with each other for certain applications (for example, glass vs. steel for architectural use), the many facets and levels of government, the universities, developments in technology, and so on.

Not only is business complex but it is dynamic, operating in a continually changing environment. Many practices that were once thought to be immutable and impervious to changing conditions have been discarded or radically modified. One example is the role of women in our society. Once the federal government stipulated that equal employment opportunity for women was a prerequisite to being awarded a government contract, women began to enter the workforce and higher-paying positions at an accelerated rate. Perhaps this trend could have been predicted, but not without a few surprises. Very few military men, ten to fifteen years ago, thought that women would ever be admitted into the service academies.

The shock of the oil embargo in 1973 uprooted the plans of the corporations of the Western world, but it did not produce a loss of interest in formal planning. To the contrary, there followed an increased emphasis on planning—particularly planning for contingencies. The need to be prepared for the unexpected was a lesson that was taken to heart.

While this lesson at the corporate level was dramatic and harsh, certainly managers at all levels have always been aware that their plans and their expectations are frequently unfulfilled. This has led to "Murphy's Law" becoming a familiar catchword. It occurs often enough not to be taken lightly.

Problems with Traditional Planning

Management attempts to create plans that are appropriate, realistic, and sufficiently detailed to be a guide for operations. Having done this, it expects the plans will be carried out, assuming that they are communicated properly and accurately and that the people charged with their implementation have the incentive or the dedication to do so. This is the traditional view of the management process, and although it is outdated, incomplete, and certainly very simplistic, it is a view still found today. But *the traditional approach to planning is doomed to failure.*

To demonstrate this crucial point, I will list a dozen reasons for why things go wrong, show how these problems relate to planning and execution, and finally argue that they will never be circumvented by traditional planning and problem solving.

If you were to ask yourself why things go wrong, you would probably compile a list similar to the one below.

Assumption that plans are not necessary. The manager believes that his personnel and all other parties will perform as he anticipates without any discussion or planning. When the expected results do not occur, he blames the incompetence of others. Actually the failure to plan may be a rationalization on the part of the executive who is busy with other matters or dislikes planning.

Change in competition. A major competitor may change his approach to the market or introduce new products. If the market reacts favorably to his innovation, your plans would have to be overhauled.

Change in laws. In an era of increasing government regulation, new laws and new regulations that interpret law frequently have the capability of upsetting current ways of doing business and future plans.

Change in styles and preferences. For a time it looked like a man's leisure suit would be a permanent part of his wardrobe. People in the industry say that the low prices and low quality of many of the lines were responsible for quick saturation of the market, followed by a dropoff in sales. The suits went out of style, leaving retailers with inventory that could not be sold.

Communication. Problems with communications are abundant and come in many forms. In general, they can be classified into three subheadings. One is the failure to provide any communication, usually through oversight. Second are the many varieties and sources of misunderstanding—what is said is not heard. The third is distortion, in which incorrect information is passed on.

Detrimental side effects. A course of action may have been taken which seems to be beneficial on paper and in fact does benefit the group originating the plan. However, other groups are affected adversely by what is taking place. An organization is a system, and what is done in part of the organization often has a ripple effect in other parts.

Diversion. It can be very disconcerting to a manager to find that instead of working in accordance with the plan, people are devoting their time to other work or to other facets of the project that are not planned for current work. This happens on occasion even when the people involved know that what they are doing does not comply with the plan.

Fear of planning. This is the ostrich syndrome—people do not look ahead because they prefer not to face the issues and problems of the future. They find it discouraging or discomforting to cope with the difficulties on the horizon, and they rationalize their position by believing that they can take whatever steps are necessary "when the time comes." It amounts to preferring to handle crises rather than to avoid them.

Indifference. What is to be done is known, but it is still not done or is done improperly because of lack of motivation.

Lack of knowledge. A plan may be communicated down the organization and not be properly executed because the people affected lack knowledge or understanding of the systems and procedures involved. For example, a directive to stop work on a contract that has been canceled may involve many transactions to make adjustments in inventory and work-in-process. People who are not thoroughly trained in the system for making adjustments are likely to make mistakes. A lack of knowledge about the functions and responsibilities of the divisions and departments of an organization can be the source of errors. One group may assume incorrectly that actions will be taken by another group. There can also be a lack of knowledge about what are the responsibilities of a company, or a department, to the public. A misconception about the policy of the company regarding returned merchandise, for example, could cause a major problem with a customer.

Underestimation of difficulty. Failing to correctly assess the difficulty or the scope of work is a problem that many companies live with daily. It is a risk that must be taken on new work produced on a fixed fee contract. The people who are estimating the cost of a job may not think of themselves as preparing a plan for execution, but that is what they are doing. The data that they use for estimating work presume that the scope of work will be performed in a particular way and within the expected time. Some people are unrealistically optimistic and hence invariably underestimate the amount of work involved in new work or new assignments that their department is given.

Vagueness of plans. Either the definition of the tasks is vague or the time schedule for their completion is ambiguous. The effect is that the plan is a poor guide for current actions and is also valueless for monitoring progress.

The twelve reasons for why things go wrong are probably not all-inclusive, but they demonstrate the scope of the problem. These manifestations of Murphy's Law can be boiled down to four types of problems:

1. Poor plan for the situation. The plan itself is logical and all parts are internally consistent but it will fail because there are misconceptions or a lack of knowledge of the situation or of the environment in which the plan is to operate.

2. Technically faulty plan. The plan is not specific, perhaps not much more than a vague expectation on someone's part, or it is not realistic or logical.

3. Ineffective communication of the plan.

4. Failure to carry out the plan. This can occur even when the plan is appropriate, realistic, sufficiently detailed, and communicated properly.

The correspondence between the cause and the type of problem is shown on the following page.

Problem	Cause
1. Poor plan for the situation	Change in competition
	Change in laws
	Change in styles and preferences
2. Technically faulty plan	Assumption that plans are not necessary
	Fear of planning
	Vagueness of plans
	Detrimental side effects
	Underestimating difficulty
3. Poor communications	Lack of communication
	Misunderstanding
	Distortion or incorrect information
4. Failure to carry out the plan	Diversion
	Indifference
	Lack of knowledge

Eight Steps in Planning

To stave off these problems, management has evolved a philosophy of planning and control buttressed with often complicated procedures. This philosophy and its procedures are generally good and frequently excellent. Furthermore, they are needed if the complex organizations of today are to operate with any degree of efficiency and profitability. Good conventional planning and control is a process, which for the purpose of explanation can be broken down into eight steps, although the steps as practiced are not discrete and not necessarily in the sequence presented.

Step 1. Planning begins with determining direction. In the case of a corporation, this might be called a grand design. The vision of being able to take a picture and have it developed on the spot is the procreator of Polaroid. MacDonald's owes its success to the grand design of a chain of restaurants offering economical food for the family in clean surroundings with no waiting.

The concept is as valid for a goup within a company as it is for a corporation. The sales manager should visualize how his organization should perform, given the goals of the company. His grand design encompasses not only the methods of selling that are effective and reinforce the image of the company, but also the emphasis that should be put on different product lines and the internal workings of the sales department to get the desired result. A supervisor of a department in a hospital, X-ray for example, should go through the same process. A broad look at a department, which otherwise might easily be dismissed as having the single purpose of taking X-rays, could yield some interesting results. Suppose that many facets of the role of the X-ray department were considered. Among them might be communication with doctors to ensure that errors were minimized by both parties. The ideal might include optimum utilization of equipment and training of personnel. Since patients frequently require other services in addition to X-ray, the vision for the X-ray department should include how its services can be coordinated with other types of health care in the interest of economy and the well-being of the patient.

The direction to be pursued or the grand design is formulated by a process of visualization which entails asking and answering questions that deal with the organization's reason for being. "What is the purpose of the company and the larger organization of which I am a part? What is the purpose of my group or my job? Within the charter of purpose, how can the greatest contribution be made?" What comes from questions such as these is a vision of what the organization should be and what it should do.

Solving a problem requires planning, and the same steps apply. Maybe the terms "ideal" and "grand design" sound a little grandiose for problem solving, but in reality there must be a vision of the ideal state. To illustrate this, consider a problem that a company had in failing, through oversight, to follow through on commitments made to its customers. First-rung managerial personnel frequently made these commitments which they were authorized to do. However, there was no reliable system for review or control by higher management to see that commitments were adhered to. The first step in solving the problem was to write a letter to the three executives who between them had surveillance over all the field offices. The memo gave a description of the problem, an evaluation of the extent of the problem, and the *desired state*. Their comments were solicited. Before spending time on a project like this, which had all the earmarks of an exercise in futility, it was essential to get agreement on (1) the extent of the problem, (2) the desirability of improvement, and (3) a description of the control system that would exist in the desired state. In this instance, the desired state was originally thought to be a more comprehensive control system. It turned out to be more control than was desirable. Realizing this the three executives settled for a vision of the desired state that was a tightening up of some procedures that were already in place.

Step 2. Goals and objectives should be set that define the state to be reached or the level of performance to be attained. Goals give substance to the grand design or to the definition of the problem. They are the criteria for evaluation of the possible actions that might be taken and the final results. Chapter 6 discusses these and related points fully.

Step 3. Gathering information is the next step. Of course, some information had to be gathered in order to establish the direction or define the problem and to set goals. These steps are not rigidly prescribed in sequence. Frequently they are overlapping (sometimes must be repeated) but they do follow the general sequence of this outline.

Gathering information can be tiresome but it has no substitute. A client company of mine, a small foundry, had a very weak production control function. Information was not readily available on actual and promised delivery dates. Before changes in production control and scheduling practices could be recommended, it was necessary to find out how long it took for an order to be produced, the average time for each operation, and how well the company was meeting its promise dates. This entailed compliling data from records of individual orders. This investigation startled the owner with the information that 60 percent of the shipments were late.

Step 4. Closely related to getting information is examining limitations and available resources. There are always constraints on what can be done. Time might be one. Solutions are limited by what can be done in three months, for example. Company policy can be a limitation. Policies such as buying from minority-owned businesses or promoting from within may have a bearing on what can be done.

A word of caution is in order here. Limitations should be verified and possibly tested. Don't assume that past practice comprises a policy. This will limit thinking and might cause the truly superlative and innovative solution to be completely overlooked.

Step 5. Alternative ways of solving the problem or reaching the goal should always be found. Of course, one alternative is to do nothing. Another is to decide not to decide. Chester Barnard has said that this may be the most important decision: "The fine art of executive decision consists in not deciding questions that are not now pertinent, in not deciding prematurely, in not making decisions that cannot be made effective, and in not making decisions that others should make."*

A person who proposes only one solution runs many risks. The foremost of these is that a better solution can easily be found. Identifying three solutions, for instance, more fully exposes the problem. If we find that a problem can be approached in three different ways, we find that we know more about the problem. We are able to see its many dimensions. The final solution might not be any of the three but still another or a combination.

In presenting recommendations for the approval of higher management, always include a discussion of alternatives. Failure to do so may cause your superior to believe that bias or laziness is behind your insistence on one solution. You have a stronger case if you can state that you have given careful consideration to solutions A and B but have rejected them in favor of solution C. Imagine how much weaker your case is if you go to your superior with a recommendation for C without mentioning A and B. Now he asks you if you have considered A and B. Immediately, you are on the defensive, trying to establish that you have but that you believe solution C to be superior.

Step 6. The final plan begins to take shape after you have made a choice. At this point you have evaluated the information and the alternative solutions and you have a clear idea as to how the goal will be reached or the problem solved. There is a risk that the plan will not work and you understand that all decisions of consequence involve risk. Knowing that there is risk and that it cannot be avoided allows you to make the decision. If you are waiting for a risk-free choice, you will no doubt become immobilized and make no choice at all when one is required.

You must be resolved to take the risk. I believe a person making such a decision does so both intellectually and emotionally. It is intellectual in that the numbers add up or that the plan is logically feasible or that the mathematical extent of the risk is commensurate with the return. However, a major decision is emotional as well. All the num-

---

* Chester Barnard, *The Functions of the Executive* (Cambridge: Harvard University Press, 1938), p. 194.

bers can add up but if there is some nagging unexplained doubt, the ultimate decision maker will not take the step. The popular expression is that the person "has no stomach for that." On the other hand, when the costs and profits of a proposal look quite ordinary, the decision maker might have a hunch that causes him to make the favorable decision.

There is nothing new about businessmen making decisions by hunch. In spite of the advances in information technology and models for decision making, thoughtful men have always agreed that there is a place for the decision made on intuition. The Appendix to Chester Barnard's *The Functions of the Executive* is an essay on what he calls nonlogical mental processes. Robert Ornstein, a research psychologist and author of *The Psychology of Consciousness,* * is among those scientists who believe that the two sides of the brain function differently. The left side is used for logical, linear, step-by-step processes, and the right side sees problems holistically, processing information in a more simultaneous and comprehensive way. Henry Mintzberg believes this explains the ability of top-level managers to make decisions without making a step-by-step analysis. John Mihalasky and E. Douglas Dean have conducted hundreds of experiments with people for precognition—the ability to predict the future. From a study of top executives in small manufacturing companies (chosen to ensure that the top man was in reality the key decision maker) they found that there was a statistically significant correlation between the performance of the company measured by the increase in profits over a period of five years and the score of the top executive on a precognition test.

Though the process may be intuitive, the rationale is nearly always presented analytically and logically. If for no other reason, this process is needed for explanation and to secure the support of others. It further substantiates my claim that the major decisions are made by bringing together the emotions and the intellect.

Step 7. Once a choice has been made between alternative solutions to the problem or alternative plans, the next step is implementation. This is the process of doing. Making the plans on paper come true is usually the most difficult step because change is often involved. Finding a way to cope with change and to introduce change has been a problem that has vexed management at least since the Industrial Rev-

* San Francisco, W. H. Freeman, 1975.

olution and has become more of a concern in the last 30 years, when change has been so rapid. Many of the more recent innovations in management such as organizational development (OD), the linking-pin concept, and the matrix organization are attempts to increase flexibility and coordination in the face of new circumstances. Industrial engineers (with the possible exception of those just out of school) have learned that finding new and improved methods is not nearly as difficult as installing the new method.

Step 8. The final step is to follow up on the implementation and progress. This entails getting feedback. At the time the plan is adopted, measures should be taken to ensure that material like financial data or production reports will be available if they are not produced routinely. At critical points in the plan, reports may not be adequate to warn you of impending problems. In that case, you will have to make it your business to get verbal information from knowledgeable sources. Your job is to know whether the plan is on track or not, and if it isn't, to get it back on course.

Why the Planning Process Fails

The planning process described in the eight steps above could not be faulted for not being thorough. Indeed, adherence to these steps would prevent a great deal of wasted time and delays. To make my point on the inadequacy of the planning process by itself, I have not painted the traditional planning process as a collection of trivial steps, full of flaws, which could then be compared with a "new brilliant" approach. Good planning, encompassing the eight elements outlined, is a necessary condition to getting good results, but it is far from being sufficient. Many problems will still occur with a frequency that is unacceptable to a manager with high standards of performance.

The persistence of problems and errors, seemingly a contradiction to good planning, is not attributable to a conceptual weakness in the eight-step process. The difficulties arise from poor execution. *Poor execution of planning principles will always be the result of a traditional approach which focuses on the process instead of on the system in which planning and doing are taking place.* Unless the system possesses required strengths and qualities, it is impossible to visualize an appropriate and rewarding grand design, impossible to select goals and objectives that satisfy needs and desires, impossible to properly carry out any phase of planning and doing. Attempts to improve the process of planning without addressing the underlying systems will always create gaps between what plans are produced and what should be produced to be truly appropriate, logical, and realistic. There will always be severe problems with outdated or incomplete information, and execution will be no better than planning.

In fact, the execution may be a good deal worse, because there is a systemic failure to fully understand the importance of the plan or the procedure. The key to these issues of poor planning and poor execution and the key difference between focusing on the process and focusing on the system lies in the feedback. The usual approach is to employ the feedback loop to make corrections in the plan, whereas what is needed is to make corrections in the system. The system itself must be dynamic. It must learn and benefit from its experiences. The system must find new ways of doing things and overcoming its deficiencies. This is a very crucial difference.

To think of the planning process merely as a process suggests that it takes place in a sequential manner. In fact, good planning and good doing in a system are all interacting at the same time. The key to success is the free flow of information. Feedback is the dominant element in the planning process and the first line of defense against Murphy's Law.

The Systems Concept

Figure 1 illustrates the planning and doing as they should occur in a system. At first glance it may seem that this diagram is not much different from what is found in all the textbooks on the subject. True, the similarity is there, but the differences, which may seem to be minor, are in fact substantial. In the first place the arrows go both ways, suggesting that the elements are not accomplished through a series of sequential and discrete steps. The concept of planning illustrated in Figure 1 recognizes that the plan must be appropriate instead of treating appropriateness as an unstated assumption. The traditional approach to planning takes the view that plans *must* be appropriate, because no sane person would deliberately devise one that was not. This presumes perfect knowledge on the part of the planner.

The importance of understanding within the full context of the situation is another aspect of planning that is often overlooked. The

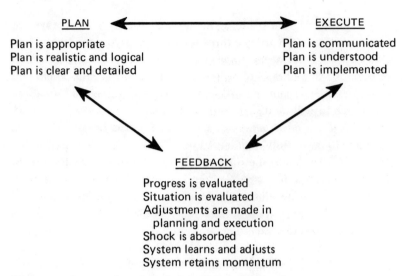

PLAN

Plan is appropriate
Plan is realistic and logical
Plan is clear and detailed

EXECUTE

Plan is communicated
Plan is understood
Plan is implemented

FEEDBACK

Progress is evaluated
Situation is evaluated
Adjustments are made in
  planning and execution
Shock is absorbed
System learns and adjusts
System retains momentum

Figure 1. System for planning and execution.

principle that is usually followed is to make sure that the plan itself is communicated and understood, in the belief that this is sufficient. Yet, procrastination and other faults in implementation can stem from failing to truly comprehend what effect the plan will have when implemented or to underrate its priority.

The concept of feedback is greatly expanded to include not only modifications in planning or in execution but also in the system itself. This broader definition of feedback is suggested by several phrases in the diagram.

Now, here are a few words about systems and the approach of this book. A system is composed of a number of parts which interact with each other, and the net effect of what the system accomplishes cannot be fully explained by a summation of what each part does. A well-functioning system produces much more than what could be produced by the parts working separately. Changes in one part of the system cause a ripple effect throughout the system, but the effect is not uniform. Some components may be radically changed by a change in another part, and others may, for all practical purposes, be unaffected.

The job of managing an organization which is in reality a system is further complicated by the fact that each system is a subsystem, or a component, of a larger system. This puts the manager in the position of trying to deal with at least three levels of systems at once. His fundamental task is trying to direct his system, that is, his organization, toward its goals and objectives. However, in selecting these goals and objectives he must have an understanding about the larger system of which he is a part. His goals and objectives, and his role, must take into account the needs and desires expressed in the larger system. At the level of a firm, this means understanding the market and other aspects of the environment such as fair employment, environmental protection, and the like. For the head of a functional department, this means that he must understand the needs of the larger organization.

The third level of systems of concern to the manager takes in the subsystems below his own system. Individual employees, groups of employees, and professional groupings are the essence of these systems. As formal or informal systems, they have aims that the manager must strive to satisfy. Failure to come to terms with these aims can produce apathy, militancy, and a distorted self-serving sense of professionalism which forsakes loyalty to the organization.

The chapters that follow are certainly not an academic treatise on systems theory. Rather, they deal with the practical aspects of managing organizations as systems and avoiding the difficulties that occur when this is not done. The topics do not follow the conventional sequence of planning and control steps because this would put the emphasis on the process. Instead, the arrangement of chapters and the underlying philosophy of the book are directed to what can be done to design a good system and strengthen an existing one.

2

What today's employee wants from you

Jean H., age 40, reentered the workforce two years ago as a supervisor of the serving kitchens in a suburban school district. Her bachelor's degree in home economics and previous experience qualify her for the position. But at this writing she is looking for another job in her field, because she is dissatisfied with her work environment. Although she would like more money, that is not the problem. Sometimes she feels that she shouldn't work "extra" hours, but at most this is only a minor annoyance. Furthermore, she genuinely likes working with the women in the 13 serving kitchens. What is the problem then?

Her management, specifically, her supervisor, is not meeting her needs as a professional. Moreover, to meet her needs doesn't take money; it doesn't require expenditures for new facilities or equipment; it doesn't involve a promotion or even a new title. In fact, all her needs could be satisfied by means available to her supervisor.

Jean feels that she is not growing professionally. For instance, she is frustrated in her attempts to become more involved in menu planning. For reasons known only to her supervisor (although the topic of much speculation) she has been systematically excluded from the menu planning discussions between her supervisor and one of her peers. In addition, the distinction between Jean's responsibilities and those of another supervisor has never been clearly defined. She feels powerless to take the steps that are needed to get better control of inventories and reduce pilferage. Nothing has come from her efforts with her supervisor to define the responsibilities so that she can take action to correct the deficiencies.

Steve S. has recently taken another job as the regional manager for a national collection agency. It is a big promotion for Steve. Reporting to him are the district managers from eight cities. In his previous job with a large company he performed financial studies and was a staff assistant for collection matters. Steve has a special problem—his legs are crippled from polio, and he walks with the aid of crutches and braces.

It seemed to Steve that his previous employer was "protecting" him from travel, thereby denying him the opportunity to meet the company's clients and broaden his knowledge of the business. The work he was doing had become boring and there was no challenge. Furthermore, he felt that he was being second-guessed in his recommendations and that management did not have confidence in him.

The contrast between his old job and his new one is as between night and day. Now his responsibilities cause him to travel much of the time. He feels that he is developing as a professional in the credit and collection field and he now manages other managers, a new experience for him. He is making headway with a combination of toughness and understanding, but knows he has much to learn. As a line manager, he thoroughly enjoys having profit and loss responsibility for his region. In short, he is proving to himself that he can do much more than in the prior job. He is *excited* and *challenged* by his new responsibilities.

Gary F., 29 years old, took an early interest in electronic funds transfer systems (EFTS) and the technology of what has been described as the cashless society. After receiving his degree in business, he went to work for a bank in the department responsible for work measurement. In a couple of years his reputation was such that he was transferred to a department that was in trouble and desperately needed talented personnel. The performance of the department, which was responsible for administering trusts for the California Savings and Loan League, was threatening to jeopardize the bank's relationship with the savings and loan industry. Gary was placed in charge of a group of 30 people, including systems analysts and computer specialists. Because of his ability to communicate well on sensitive subjects, and because his approach was direct and low key, he was able to build an effective group of people, many of whom had requested transfers from other departments to be on the project.

In his open manner, Gary advised his superiors of his aspirations for advancement, and he was promised a promotion. He expected that his candor and openness would be returned, but after some changes in management and realignment of responsibilities, Gary became convinced that the promised promotion would not be forthcoming although he was given a sizable raise in salary. Furthermore, he saw some of the gains that he had made being reversed by a new manager brought into the organization.

Gary resigned and worked part time for a family business for almost a year and, in addition, became very involved in work for a charity. He did not feel any immediate pressure to get his career started again. This period of reflection and regeneration was ended when he was recruited by a savings and loan company at a much higher salary than he had received at the bank.

The Professional Employee

Jean, Steve, and Gary are three very different people, but they have one thing in common: They have experienced job situations that do not meet their needs. Their management—the way they perceived themselves to be managed—caused the dissatisfaction. The point is that if you had been their superior, you could have turned disillusionment into optimism and toil into accomplishment.

You have all known individuals like these; perhaps their experiences parallel some you have had. More important, you are going to know many more in the future. Since 1950 the total labor force has increased 54 percent, but the number of persons classified as "professional, technical, and kindred" has increased 167 percent. Today this group plus the group designated "managers and administrators" account for nearly 26 percent of all workers. This is the segment of the workforce that is growing. *It is these people who make up the arena where you succeed or fail as a manager.*

Today's group of sophisticated employees expect to be managed in a professional manner. Their undergraduate and graduate training has primed them to approach problems analytically. They have been taught that decision making should be orderly and objective, and they understand the value of taking steps today to avert a problem tomorrow. After some years in the business world, they have come to understand that it is not always possible and probably not always desirable to manage according to the book, but they know better than to ignore the common sense advice that is found in books. Sometimes they see their own managers contributing to problems and magnifying them by poor planning. You have probably heard many good employees voice disenchantment with their organization because of the frequent crises that could be avoided with better management.

The groups and individuals under a manager have many needs in addition to the need for professional management, and meeting these needs is no trivial matter. Indeed, it demands high intellectual and creative effort. Failure to meet the needs of the people and groups under the manager will, of course, result in poor performance. It may cause people to withdraw or even engage in disruptive behavior.

No manager can afford to have people, especially talented ones, using only a small fraction of their ability. Not only does the day-to-day work suffer, but often, what is more serious, the manager loses collective effort in planning ahead and anticipating new circumstances. Overcoming Murphy's Law should be a group effort.

Special Needs of Women

The most significant change in the workforce in the last ten years is the number of working women attracted by opportunities for management positions and other higher-paying jobs. The U.S. Bureau of Statistics reports that in 1975, 19 percent of 8.9 million managers and administrators were female, compared with 16 percent in 1970. Currently, it is estimated that women hold 6 percent of the middle management jobs and only 1 percent of the vice-presidencies and higher positions. Dena Kaye writes that less than 1 percent of working women earn more than $25,000 per year.* Recognizing that the trend is for more and more women to get into higher management, we can expect to know much more about the special needs of women in the future. However, even at this stage we are beginning to see some attitudes and problems that, if not common, are at least felt by a large segment of ambitious women in business.

First, there is the matter of commitment. The few women who

* "The Headhunters: Breaking Down the All-Male Ghetto," *Mainliner*, April 1977, p. 21.

have made it to the top, such as General Electric Vice-President Marion S. Kellogg, have probably worked harder and for longer hours than most of their male counterparts. Ms. Kellogg describes herself as a "workaholic." Challis M. Lowe is a branch manager for Continental Bank in Chicago. She spends 12 hours a day on the job, is enrolled in an MBA program for executives, and often gets up at 4:00 A.M. to do homework.

Many women are not willing to make the type of sacrifice that is called for. Working mothers are making a difficult choice, one that is often hard psychologically for them to live with when they combine the roles of corporation executive and mother. Having a sick child at home and being required to attend a meeting or make a trip to a branch office poses a dilemma that is rare for the average male executive. Consequently, it is not at all uncommon to find capable women who are not interested in climbing the corporate ladder to a level which they view as being incompatible with their family responsibilities.

Even when children are not a factor, there is some evidence that women eschew management positions to avoid pressure. Janet Jones, chairman of Management Women, Inc., an executive search firm for women, is beseeched by companies who want her to find women who cannot possibly fail. Failing may be interpreted not merely as personal failure but as confirmation that a woman "cannot do the job." A study of children ages 9 to 17 shows that 65 percent of female children did not want to become managers, compared with 48 percent of males. The difference apparently does not stem from desire for a different type of career. Only 32 percent of the females stated that they wanted to do something else, compared with 41 percent of males. The significant differences were in the number who said that they did not like the idea of being boss (29 percent of females, compared with 10 percent of the males), and believed that being in management put them under too much pressure (29 percent female vs. 15 percent male).*

Another problem is that there is prejudice against women in responsible positions. Many people believe that prejudice does not exist—but not most of the professional women. With the requirements for affirmative action and equal opportunities, it is easy to see how the problem of prejudice can easily be dismissed. Personnel directors and top managers have been prodded by government agen-

* Rosalind C. Barnett and Renato Tagiuri, "What Young People Think About Managers," *Harvard Business Review,* May–June 1973, pp. 106–118.

cies and, fully aware of some of the precedent-setting lawsuits, are eager to have women represented in management. A personnel manager, speaking of the difficulties of the mother in management, says, "There's really no bias against mothers in management. The only restrictions they experience are the ones they put on themselves." But many women, especially in the middle management ranks, find barriers to acceptance in advancement. For example, a woman who was the only woman vice-president at a major company found that she was the only one who did not have a company car, that hers was the only office off the executive floor, and that her salary was 20 percent below the salaries of other vice-presidents.

An executive who puts a woman in a managerial position cannot help asking himself whether or not the men in the group will accept her. Suppose that some refuse to work for a woman, what does he do now? Whatever the solution, it is a problem he would rather avoid. Some years ago, Judith Frank, an executive for Twentieth Century-Fox, filed an EEOC complaint against an architectural firm that fired her after 30 days on the job because some of the men in the organization would not work for a woman.

Companies are eager to hire young women with MBAs, but advancing them into positions of management is a different story. Richard Ferry of Korn/Ferry International, an executive search firm, has said, "Many clients are flat-out not interested in any female candidate for a job over the $30,000 mark."* His reason is that reporting problems begin (or perhaps intensify) at higher levels of management.

Many men who work for female bosses and have a good working relationship would still prefer to work for a man because, as one put it, males hold the key to upward mobility. Since a woman is less likely to be promoted, her subordinates' prospects of moving into her job are reduced. Moreover, some men believe that the female boss doesn't have the clout to push subordinates up the corporate ladder. In one firm, a woman replacing a man as the chief purchasing officer received the title of director of materials, whereas her male predecessor had been the vice-president of purchasing. Following a storm of requests for transfers out of the department, a management consultant called in to investigate found that the problem was not based on per-

---

* "The Corporate Woman: How Men Adjust to a Female Boss," *Business Week*, September 5, 1977, p. 90.

sonal dislikes or opinions about her competence, but on a general belief that the department had been downgraded.

A third problem for executive women is that they lack a role model. A man can, if he chooses, learn from and pattern his behavior on a number of successful men whom he comes into contact with. A woman is left alone to deal with problems that range from when to call a higher executive by his first name to how to use power and authority and still retain her femininity.

It is much more difficult for a woman to become the protégée of a successful executive, a process that accounts for the advancement of many male executives. A man who has a woman as his protégée must be confident and secure enough to withstand the tendency of others to question whether or not the relationship is strictly business and to resist feeling threatened by the growing competence of a woman whose accomplishments might surpass his one day. Such a male executive is not common.

Organizations that have evolved stereotyped passive roles for women present a particularly difficult problem for women who refuse to model their behavior to what is expected. Without the type of guidance that should come from her superior she is likely to be very uncertain about how to conduct herself in one ambiguous situation after another. A young woman fresh from an MBA program was accused of entertaining men in her office on the third day on the job—a friend had visited her in her office after lunch for two minutes to see her new office, and the next day a trainee from another division came to her office to look at the sales analysis. Her conduct in meetings was criticized contradictorily—she was told that she was too assertive if she spoke up and not aggressive enough if she didn't say anything. In spite of the fact that she received good reports about her work she was fired after six months. She concluded that the organization was not ready for a woman who did not fill the role of the compliant female.

A fourth handicap to the progress of women into higher positions is that they often lack relevant knowledge and experience, especially in high-technology companies, where the top managers almost to a man have engineering or science backgrounds. Traditionally, women have not majored in these fields in college. As a consequence, when employed in a high-technology company, they are limited to running departments such as personnel or public relations.

A lack of managerial experience is frequently the stumbling block to advancement. Typically, women enter higher-paying jobs as professionals acting in a staff capacity. Advancement beyond this point means that they will be supervising others—a responsibility for which they have had no previous experience. Their male counterparts, on the other hand, have probably held several low-level supervisory jobs before being given major managerial responsibilities.

Being accepted in the social realm of the business world, or feeling accepted there, has been a fifth stumbling block for women. It has been said that they are not part of the "old boy networks." Not being invited to join the foursome for golf or being left out of the luncheon at the club is often their lot. On the other hand, women are not taking this type of exclusion without a strong, albeit very subtle, fight. They are finding that it is important to be informed on the ups and downs of their city's football, baseball, and basketball teams. But even this does not guarantee inclusion. Men, especially older executives, want to have their informal business contacts with people they feel comfortable with, and this frequently means no women.

Probably nothing is more devastating to the effectiveness of a female executive than a perception on her part and on the part of others that she has the position merely because of fair employment requirements. If she is viewed as a token to government regulations, her authority and power, to say nothing of her self-esteem, will amount to nothing.

The Need for Identification

Everyone needs to feel that "I am somebody." Many people find their jobs and the companies they work for to be a source of identification which gives some meaning to their lives.

The need of a professional employee to identify with an organization becomes more complicated than merely being associated with a Fortune 500 company. He is desirous of having his company thought of as a leader in the field. The professional engineer wants to be employed by a company that is well respected in engineering circles. Young executives with service at IBM, Xerox, or Procter & Gamble, to name a few, find that they are a desired commodity on the job market.

Volvo, the Swedish car manufacturer, believes that its employees should have fine physical surroundings. It demonstrates to the employees that the company values them as contributors to the success of the company and as human beings. In turn, the employees of Volvo can be proud to identify with the company.

The Need to Be Used

To be grossly underutilized is sheer hell. I know because for three seemingly endless months I experienced this while working for a large aerospace company. I was receiving more money than I had on my previous job and utilizing perhaps one-tenth of my talents. I was not alone; it is an old story. Niccolo Machiavelli had held the post of secretary to the Council of Ten for War for 14 years when Florence fell into the hands of the Medici. For over a decade he wrote and through his writings attempted to gain a position of influence in the government, all the time chafing at the bit to be back in politics. When the Medici were overthrown and the republic was restored in Florence, he joyfully applied for his old job. But his endeavors to ingratiate himself with the Medici made him unacceptable to the republicans. Will Durant writes:

> He did not long survive that blow. The vital spark of life and hope flickered out in him, and left the flesh spiritless. He fell ill, suffering violent spasms of the stomach. . . . He confessed to a priest and died, twelve days after his rejection.[*]

There are millions of managerial and professional employees who are not being used to an extent that comes close to their capacity. Many quit their jobs to find something more satisfying. Many more stick it out by rationalizing that the working conditions or fringe benefits are good. Their superiors complain that they are not motivated. Perhaps, but in reality they are not being used.

The story is much the same with young people entering the labor force. Many people graduating from colleges cannot find the type of work for which they have prepared. One recent graduate said, "What shocked me is the dearth of positions that require creativity or any of the analytical skills a good liberal arts education teaches you. They [openings] are either clerical or sort of mindless entry-level manage-

---

[*] Will Durant, *The Story of Civilization, Part Five: The Renaissance* (New York: Simon & Schuster, 1953), p. 555.

ment jobs. You're bred for high expectations, and then you find there is nothing for you."

You managers and supervisors of professionals for the most part have it within your power to meet the need of being used. It often takes some deep thought and some creativity, and like any worthwhile venture, it is not without its risks. Brooks McCormick, the chief executive officer of International Harvester, has said, "I'd rather run the risk of a little anarchy than be stultified, ossified, or mummified."

There are movements in all the industrialized nations to give the blue collar worker and the office worker a larger voice in how their work will be conducted. In Europe, worker participation in company policy making is called co-determination. In some countries, workers are required by law to sit on boards of directors.

In the United States, the trend to increase worker involvement is called the Quality of Working Life. The form of QWL varies from an exchange of information and views between upper management and the workers, as in the case of Dana Corp., to work groups that plan and organize their own tasks. General Motors, just one of many companies, is an advocate of QWL. One GM executive said that "to be competitive, we've got to tap human resources."

Not to use is to abuse. If you don't believe this, ask some of your underutilized subordinates.

The Need for Commitment

History teaches us that all great accomplishments have resulted from the total commitment of a single individual, sometimes supported by others who shared his commitment. Think of Florence Nightingale who gave body and soul to her work. In the Crimean War of 1854–56 she attended to the wounded up to 20 hours a day, continuing to administer to the sick after she herself was stricken with a fever. Michelangelo spent the better part of four years on his back painting the ceiling of the Sistine Chapel. In the world of business, as in many other fields of endeavor, there are too many to mention who have built large organizations from their own hard work and commitment.

Everyone agrees that an organization and a boss look for a degree of commitment in employees. Lester Korn, a founder of the prestigious executive search firm of Korn/Ferry, has said that he looks for people who are willing to give extra effort and occasionally extra time. Just as organizations need committed employees, so do employees need to be committed to organizations or to the work they are doing.

The average professional employee probably does not see commitment itself as a vital component of his satisfaction. But there are three needs that the professional will often declare and that together meet the deeper, often unexpressed strong desire for commitment. These are the needs for participation, challenging work, and professional growth. When these three needs are met, you have an employee who is committed to his work and probably to his organization. When they are not, you have an employee who complains about the lack of any one of these and who does not feel a sense of commitment.

A person, especially a knowledge worker or professional, may be employed to carry out assignments that are truly demanding and that extend his skills and knowledge to their limits, but that do not satisfy the need for participation. He wants to be involved and consulted in the definition of problems, the priorities of his work assignments, and the interfaces between his work and the work of others. He wants and needs to participate in the process called planning.

"I love tension," says Daniel B. Hicks, a 30-year-old president of the New England Division of Kaufman & Broad Homes, Inc. "You can accomplish much more when the adrenalin is running." *People enjoy being challenged.* And by being challenged they become committed. John J. Hagedorn, a vice-president of finance for Pacific Intermountain Express Company, at the age of 34 thinks that older executives put too much emphasis on loyalty to the company, but he believes that dedication to the job is what counts, and you get this by challenging employees. He selects talented people and then attempts to motivate them by telling them, "It's your baby, and you're going to have to sell it all the way to the top."*

Just as challenge leads to commitment, pride, and stimulation, so lack of challenge results in apathy and mediocrity. Edward Roseman, author of *Confronting Nonpromotability: How to Manage a Stalled Career,* observes that persons who are not promotable become "depersonalized members of a growing army of second-class citizens."

---

* "Young Top Management—The New Goals, Rewards, Lifestyles," *Business Week,* October 6, 1975, p. 60.

But there are many ways to challenge people besides promotion or the enticement of a future promotion. Roseman observes that many companies fail to provide such challenge with their managers and professional employees. Indeed, too often the unchallenged employee's perfunctory performance leads to management's giving less challenging assignments in the future, which in turn creates still less achievement and lower challenge.

Hard-working results-oriented people need challenge too. Chris A., a 27-year-old merchandise manager at a department store, is enthusiastic about her work but complains that her boss, although a capable administrator, knows little about merchandising. He lets her do what she wants, acceding to her views. She believes that he should question her and that he should make her substantiate her position. To be sure, she might lose a battle once in awhile, but to her the stimulation would be worth the risk. Why? Because to meet an intellectual challenge is to grow.

The need for growth as an element of commitment is my next point. Robert R. Dockson, chief executive officer of California Federal Savings and Loan Association, has said that a happy person is one who is constantly reaching out to use his intellectual capacity to its maximum. Peter Drucker has identified "continuous learning" as a requirement for a person to take responsibility for his work (to be committed, as I see it). Volvo recognizes the need for personal development for the assembly worker. Pehr G. Gyllenhammar, president of Aktievolaget Volvo, has said, "Volvo wants individuals to have a chance to learn more and to enhance their personal lives and careers through opportunities available with the company."

The need for professional development has two dimensions—the need and desire for greater depth in the area of one's specialty, and the need for more broadly based knowledge in one field, company, and industry. People differ in their desire for knowledge along these two dimensions. Some are only interested in gaining greater mastery over a narrow area of specialization. More prevalent is the professional who has ample expertise for his job but needs to broaden himself, perhaps in order to be considered for higher positions.

A speaker from an executive search firm spoke to a meeting of corporate planners, many of whom had spent most of their working lives in this type of work. The questions, by and large, were not on how they could advance in the planning ranks or on how they could find a better job as a planner, but on how they could leave the planning specialty and get into line or general management. In effect, they were saying that they wanted to grow but didn't want the type of growth that would leave them pigeonholed in a specialty. To illustrate, William J. Popejoy, the 39-year-old president of American Savings and Loan Association, took a personnel job early in his career with the Larwin Group. At the time, he told Larwin's founder and chairman that he wanted to learn the real estate business. He was promised the opportunity on the condition that he would first set up a personnel department. Eight months later he was made a vice-president in the Larwin mortgage banking subsidiary. Popejoy understood that achieving his aspirations depended on his acquiring knowledge of the entire business, not just the personnel function.

The Need for Autonomy

The employee's need for autonomy is a complicated subject, affecting people in different ways. To help you understand the need for autonomy, I am going to discuss it from three points of view.

First, there is the need for autonomy or independence in carrying out the job. You can tell a man what to do, or better yet, mutually agree on what to do, but there is danger in telling him how to do it. A successful executive once told me that it was his policy to give a man the means and the latitude to do the job, otherwise he would have a "crutch"—a reason for not doing the job. The point is that the employee's need for autonomy is in actuality a need the organization must meet as a condition of getting high performance.

Second, professionals need the autonomy to free themselves from the demands of the organization at intervals. This need does not conflict with the desire to be committed or the value of being identified with a well-regarded company. It does relate to the need for a person not to lose his identity in what is sometimes believed to be the depersonalizing forces within the modern corporation.

Nearly all executives today, regardless of level, have the yearning to get away for awhile, although at the higher levels it becomes more difficult. A special report by *Business Week* stresses the total dedication to the job that these exceptional young executives have, but it also notes that there are some differences between today's executive and the organization man of the 1950s. "Obviously, this is a new breed of Organization Man, exhibiting a commitment to the corporation that characterized the young executive in the 1950s, and at the same time, a rebelliousness of spirit that grew out of the 1960s."* According to one of the executives quoted in the article, loyalty is not so much to the company as to the task.

Jet travel is a part of many a top executive's life, affording even the busiest person an opportunity to mix in a little of his time with company time. He can often use weekend travel and layovers to sneak in a day of skiing, tennis, or skin diving. I know people who take a tennis racket as a part of the standard luggage for traveling. On trips, they work hard, often ignoring the clock—it loses its relevance anyway with changes in time zones. Then as if to say, "I owe myself one," they find the time to do what they want. They exercise their autonomy to separate themselves from the demands of the job without feeling the guilt that was true of an earlier generation. *It gives them the sense of being in control rather than being controlled by the company.*

I have been describing how top executives meet the need for autonomy and still cope with a monstrous work week. The desire is the same for lower-level professionals and the opportunity is greater. Vacations provide some of the opportunity, but the need really goes beyond what a vacation can offer. The vacation is a condition of employment, something the employee is entitled to. The need for autonomy that I am discussing is met, for example, when an employee takes time off during the work week to attend to personal business or to go fishing—time he will probably make up for. Or it is *his* decision to come to work at 6:00 A.M. and go home early.

Third, there are some employees who require the autonomy of complete independence. Having gotten to this stage, the person is either no longer working for the organization that has accounted for most of his career or he is in a very disgruntled state of mind. Like most of us, he has gotten up some morning and wondered, "Is it worth it?" Only instead of dismissing the thought, he answers the question with an emphatic "No!" He wants to be his own boss, or he wants a slower pace to life, or he wants to live in more rustic surroundings. He meets his need by making a drastic change in careers and in lifestyle, for example, by buying a hardware store in Maine. Hundreds of examples of people who have made fundamental changes in their lives

---

* "Young Top Management—The New Goals, Rewards, Lifestyles," *op. cit.,* p. 57.

have been reported in magazines and papers, and it is no longer a rarity.

Do the people who break with the past in this way do it because the job did not meet their need for a modicum of autonomy, so that they accumulate an increment of dissatisfaction each year until total frustration grips their minds? Or are they people who require so much freedom that the corporate way of life is inherently unsatisfactory? If the latter is the case, there is little you can do to create a stimulating environment for this type of employee.

Difficulties in Using Talented People

Prestige, position, and pay are the three Ps that go together in most organizations and determine, to a large extent, how much influence a person commands. To a degree, they put a boundary on what a person can accomplish. We deal with this fact of organizational life by giving the valuable employee a higher position, and normally this means putting him into management. Frequently, this is the wrong way to give him influence along with pay, position, and prestige.

In the first place, there are many people with special training and interests who want to be free of the burden of management. Some don't want the care of management—they would rather be responsible for their own work and not the work of others. Some believe, usually correctly, that their technical skills will atrophy if not used, and they see management as a diversion from their real interests. And others find that many of the tasks of a manager are onerous. My discussions with college seniors and MBA candidates reveal that nearly all would rather have a job where they are doing work they find interesting than be a first-line supervisor over clerical or factory workers. (Of course, many would like line positions at a higher level.)

Second, it is frequently in the best interest of the company to leave a talented employee unburdened with management responsibilities. When I was researching the planning function in conglomerate corporations some years ago, it was explained to me that it was more valuable to the corporation to have a brilliant planning executive make an individual contribution than to have him "manage" a corporate staff.

It is possible to give the individual contributor the position, pay, and prestige, and the power that goes with these, without putting him

into a management position. A frequent example is the planning executive, often with the title of vice-president of corporate development,
who operates with a very small staff. Some years ago, I met Orhan
Sadik-Kahn, who was the vice-president in charge of corporate planning for Norton Simon, Inc., a company in the billion-dollar class. He
had two assistants. Many years ago, Hughes Aircraft Co. created the
position of senior scientist to keep its top technical personnel working
in their fields without management responsibilities and still give them
the pay and perquisites that go with high corporate rank.

In today's business world, the talented employee is often a professional who owes most of his allegiance to his profession. That he is a
computer programmer or an electrical engineer means more to him
than being an employee of a particular company. When asked about
his job, he will cite his profession before his corporate affiliation. This
does not mean that he doesn't take pride in his company or enjoy
being identified with a particular company. But to take pride in his
company he must see that his company affiliation and his professional
career are mutually supporting. In fact, when the company has a reputation for leadership or unusual competence in his field, he will relish
being identified with the company. For example, Procter & Gamble
has a reputation for being a leader in marketing. An executive in marketing in that company knows that he is with the best and has to be
good to hold his position. In addition, he is likely to receive offers from
other companies that want to strengthen their marketing function.
AT&T, facing a new era of competition, has hired marketing personnel from Procter & Gamble and other marketing-oriented companies.

If the professional believes that his employment is not reinforcing
his career, or is a detriment to professional growth, he has a choice.
He can elect to remain with the company, with the thought of moving
upward and into positions outside of his profession, or he can seek new
employment. Many of today's professionals, and perhaps those that
are among the finest, will opt for the latter course.

Some companies have encountered difficulty in using PhDs in industry. Many managers believe that PhDs are too deliberate, conduct
too many expensive experiments to get to the point of decision, and do
not produce up to the standards of business in a corporate setting.
Other companies have found the opposite to be true, probably as a
result of selecting PhDs with the desired personal characteristics.

Another problem with specialized personnel who have been in

their fields for many years is that they tend to go stale. Peter Drucker, writing the *Chronicles of Higher Education,* observed that this is a malady that affects the majority of college professors after about 20 years of teaching. He recommends that they make a career change in their mid or late forties. Some of the organizational arrangements and task assignments that are the topics of chapters in this book offer ways of dealing with this problem.

The needs discussed in this chapter are not intended as an exhaustive list, for whole books have been written on the subject. Rather, it seems to me that these are among the needs that are often overlooked and sometimes entail some special effort to meet. Yet, as a general rule, they remain within the power of the boss to fulfill.

Two very important points emerge from this discussion of what today's employee wants from you. The first is that there are needs for which the employee is totally dependent upon the organizational setting and most specifically on you as his manager. In this regard, he is more dependent on you than you are on him because he has only one boss whereas you frequently can backstop his contribution, or lack of it, with the work of others. If you fail to create the environment in which these needs can be met, you prevent full utilization of the minds and bodies of the people who come to work for you every day. You and you alone hold the key to creating a climate for success.

The second point is that meeting the needs of subordinates is an essential step in building the qualities in an organization that are needed to cope with change and complexity. Unfortunately, many managers in the past, and still today, ignore the debilitating effects of not meeting the legitimate needs of the employees. These managers themselves need identification, autonomy, and opportunity to participate, but gloss over the identical needs of their subordinates. By managing as if these needs did not exist, they establish a work culture which encourages compliance but not much beyond that. Changing environments, new situations, new problems, new requirements for coordination demand an employee who is functioning at his full capacity. When employees are not operating at this level of performance, particularly under the taxing conditions encountered by growing companies, you get the result known as Murphy's Law. But this is not inevitable—you can meet the needs of the employees, the needs of the subsystems, in other words, while at the same time getting out the work to meet your own goals. In fact, the two go together.

3

How to take a position
of leadership

Running an organization requires deliberate cooperative effort, and wherever two or more people are involved, there is a need for leadership. One of the early and great writers on management, Chester Barnard, called it the "indispensable social essence" for cooperation.

Just as leadership is indispensable for cooperation, cooperation is indispensable for proper execution of planned actions. But even when all involved are fully cooperative, the person who is charged with leading a program will find many obstacles in his path if the system itself does not buttress his program and if the people on the program lack the depth of understanding that comes with a solid appreciation of the underlying values, the purposes, and the procedures for conducting business.

The image of the leader suggests many other concepts, such as power, authority, charisma, influence, and respect. It is difficult to say which of these comes first and which is the product of the others. I *believe that none of these is possible without healthy understanding of yourself and a self-image that demands the exercise of leadership.* Therefore, to take a position of leadership, start with your self-image.

Reinforcing Your Self-Image

The thoughts you hold about yourself can either be positive or negative, encouraging or discouraging, leading to success or leading to failure.

To begin, let us consider six aspects of the self-image. First, there is the "real I," only God knows what this is. Second, there is that "I that I think I am," which is the real self-image that I can do something about. The third aspect of self-image is the "I that I want to be," and the fourth is the "I that others see." The fifth is the "I that I think others see," which is the feedback that I get from others, although it never represents with complete accuracy just exactly what people think of me. The sixth is the "I that I want others to see."

I am going to eliminate some of these images from your active consideration. Since the "real I" is known only to God there is little we can do with it. Similarly, because the "I that others see" is really known only to them, it is not something that you can work with. Let's assume that the "I that you want others to see" is either the "I that you want to be," the "I that you think you are," or something in between. An "I that you want others to see" that is distinctly different from either of these two is deception—and deception is not a firm base for creating a career in management.

This leaves three to work with: the "I that you think you are," the "I that you want to be," and the "I that you think others see." The key to good mental health and to being a successful leader as well as a successful person is getting these images together. Think of each as a circle. If the three circles are practically concentric you have a self-concept that will work for you in all respects (Figure 2). Moreover, when this state of congruence occurs, you do not need to be directly concerned with the "I that you want others to see."

A person with very little overlap between the three circles is one who has poor mental health. To illustrate, if there is very little overlap between the "I that a person thinks he is" and the "I that he wants to be," he is in a position of liking himself a very small part of the time. He may be unrealistically too self-critical. Or he may be so defeated by life's trials that he has lost all faith in himself. The extreme example of this is the skid row derelict. Many women have low self-esteem because they cannot reconcile the new expectations of the woman's role with traditional occupations. They have difficulty in thinking of

GOOD MENTAL HEALTH

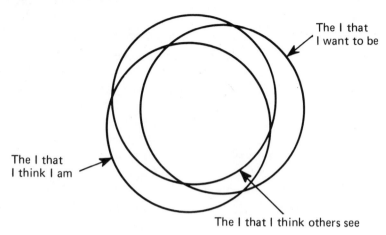

POOR MENTAL HEALTH

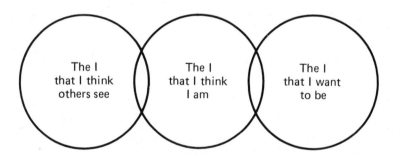

Figure 2. Self-concept and mental health.

themselves as successful persons in the role of housewife when their perception of how others (society) see them does not reinforce this image.

The secret in getting together the "I that you think you are" and the "I that you want to be" lies in establishing goals. If the goals are consistent with the "I that you want to be" and you are actively pursuing those goals, you will find that there is little gap between the two. In other words, you will be satisfied with what you are doing and can take justifiable pride in accomplishments along the way. This last thought is very important. Since you cannot always expect others to give you recognition for your accomplishments, you should learn the habit of rewarding yourself. Give yourself a pat on the back!

Although specific accomplishments that are important to you may go unnoticed by others or the difficulty of a single accomplishment may not be fully appreciated, much of the communication, verbal and nonverbal, that you receive carries a message that is either consistent or inconsistent with your self-concept. It is obvious that most of this must support the self-concept in order for a person to maintain a strong, healthy self-image of himself. For example, a person who considers himself to be witty and yet never receives a chuckle or a smile for his efforts is forced to make a change in either his humor or his image. Otherwise he is doomed to be the office and party bore that people try to avoid. The lesson is that an effective person gets positive reinforcement of his self-image (the "I that he believes he is" closely agrees with the "I that he wants to be") when the "I that he thinks others see" is supportive.

William S. Banowsky is a man who exudes self-confidence, has a strong self-image, and has been able to impart that image to the university he headed for over ten years. In 1967, he was urged to return to Pepperdine, where he had served as a philosophy professor, to assist in fund raising. At the time, Pepperdine had one location in south central Los Angeles, was faced with a bleak future of rising costs and being overshadowed by other major universities in the area such as USC, UCLA, Cal State LA, and Long Beach State. Its 30-year-old buildings, without much to commend the architecture in the first place, were located on a scant 32-acre plot in a deteriorating neighborhood. On top of that, as a private institution, it was expensive to attend in comparison to the state universities.

Ten years later, the assets of Pepperdine had grown from $6 million to $125 million. A beautiful new campus, designed by William L. Pereira, a noted architect, was built on 640 acres of hillside above Malibu overlooking the Pacific Ocean. The operating budget is now $40 million, compared with $4 million in 1967. In 1971 Banowsky was appointed president of the university, becoming at age 34 the youngest university president in the nation.

This "miracle at Malibu" has come to pass as a result of liberal contributions. Most of these come from the business community, but there are other contributors from the fields of sports, entertainment, and politics, along with some of the leading residents of Malibu. Banowsky says it is an appreciation of the ethic that binds diverse elements into supporting a common cause. But make no mistake, it took a Banowsky to orchestrate and activate this support. Over 80 percent of the contributions are attributable to him.

While at Pepperdine, Banowsky himself lived, breathed, and projected a personal image that was synonymous with that of the university during his tenure as president. He believes that the institutions that are in trouble are those that lack a clear sense of purpose. But Pepperdine, he says, stands for "conservative values, religiously, economically, ethically, and intellectually. We believe in the importance of the home as the building block of society. We try to invest . . . people with love of country, an appreciation for the free enterprise system, and the ideals of Western civilization."* He could be talking about himself. A leader like William Banowsky uses his self-image to serve as an example. By setting a tone of dedication and displaying a winning attitude, he inspires intense effort by others.

Your self-image also fine tunes your perception. If you think of yourself as a particularly good judge of character, for instance, you will find that you go through this mental exercise almost unconsciously when you meet others in your professional life and in your social life too. Have you ever noticed how some people can talk for hours on the "body" and "bouquet" of wines? Such a person cannot drink wine without being much more sensitive to the taste than the person who drinks wine occasionally with no particular thought about its relative merits.

In a similar manner, all the observations that you make are affected by your self-image. I have known businessmen who have had a great deal of experience in sales. Regardless of the responsibilities that they have in higher-level positions, they still fancy themselves as great salesmen (and often are). With this image of themselves, they remain acute observers of matters pertaining to sales.

Finally, you use your self-image as a stimulant by living up to it. A person who prides himself on his craftsmanship will not produce something that does not reflect his standards for quality. People who think of themselves as winners in everything that they do are often

---

* William J. Jeunesse, "Pepperdine University's William S. Banowsky," *The Executive of Los Angeles,* August 1978.

greatly distressed to lose a friendly game of tennis and will exert themselves tremendously to avoid a loss.

A desire to initiate ideas or to influence is often found in the person whose self-image reflects the predilection for leadership. Whether at a party or at a meeting he exhibits the quality that behavioral scientists call social ascendancy. Certainly a person with this attitude about himself can be offensive and overbearing if he does not temper his attitude with good judgment and consideration for others. But to take a position of leadership, you must have a self-concept that causes you to think of yourself, positively, as a leader.

Setting and Using Personal Goals

After you have given some thought to the "I that you think you are," the "I that you want to be," and the "I that you believe others see," the next logical step is to set some personal goals. This is a definitive outgrowth of your self-image. It is translating the thoughts you have about yourself into specific statements that will strongly influence your decisions and will ultimately lead to specific actions and programs—programs that totally reinforce your effectiveness as a leader and as a person. This is the power of goal setting. As Paul Meyer of Success Motivation Institute, Inc., has written, "When you set goals for yourself, they work in two ways: you work on them and they work on you."

Geo. T. Scharffenberger, chief executive officer of City Investing Co., has written to me:

> All too many businessmen are totally preoccupied with the setting of goals for their companies rather than for themselves. I don't think that it is at all immodest or improper for the businessman to set personal goals, provided that his personal goal setting does not turn into a zeal for personal growth which is at the expense of ethics, morality, and plain ordinary common sense.

In 1975, *Business Week* carried a special report on a group of young top managers.* Judging from the article it is difficult to conceive of a more committed and hard-working group. Long hours of work are the rule, taking precedence over social engagements and

* "Young Top Management—The New Goals, Rewards, Lifestyles," *Business Week*, October 6, 1975, p. 56.

time for the family. Yet a number of them are looking ahead to a period in their lives when they might be engaged in a different career. Some have aspirations of working in government, or teaching, which they believe can be done comfortably after they reach financial independence. We all have aspirations that are not a part of our daily jobs. If they are important, they should become personal goals.

I believe in setting goals to cover all aspects of your life. Although this may not be essential to becoming an effective leader, it must be regarded as contributing to the strength of a leader. Effective leadership rests very much on the leader's being an integrated and consistent human being, one who stands for something. If he or she does, he relates to others as a mature person. His values are evident by his actions in all walks of life. His subordinates, peers, and superiors know what kind of performance to expect. He is the kind of person that you can depend on in any situation. It is most difficult to build a leader without building the *whole person.*

Categories for goal setting can be useful thought joggers for writing goals that pertain to the full life experience. Eight that I use are:

1. Career and professional—the things I want to do in my professional life and the results I want to achieve.
2. Financial—objectives for earnings, savings, and investments.
3. Family and personal relations.
4. Social—goals that relate to my friendships and what I am doing about maintaining these friendships.
5. Spiritual.
6. Cultural—intellectual and cultural pursuits that are not connected with my profession, such as reading history books.
7. Physical—physical fitness.
8. Recreational.

Goals influence decision making, but before there are any results, the goals must be expressed in activities. That is, some type of tangible effort is required to link the goal with the desired result. The activities that are required may be so implied in the goal or so obvious that this takes place automatically, for example, as in the case of a goal of going to Europe. For other goals, it may be desirable to have both the activity and the objective expressed. If a long-range goal is financial independence, the specific objectives might be accumulating a specified amount of wealth by certain dates. The activities might include making payments into a savings plan, working a second job, or taking the time to carefully manage investments.

Goal setting is useful for any endeavor in life, but how is it especially useful in taking a position of leadership? Before answering that question directly, let me recap the train of thought that I have been following in this chapter: To become an effective leader, begin by including your role as a leader in your self-image. Then you write personal goals, supported by activities and specific objectives that are an extension of your self-image. There is a cycle of positive reinforcement between what you do and what you are, as illustrated by Figure 3.

The professional or career goals that you set for yourself are the ones most directly related to your success as a leader. In broad terms, they will contribute to your success in three ways. In the first place, you will set goals for achieving greater knowledge and competence in areas vital to your career. Often the process of setting goals will make you aware of what you need to do. Second, goal setting gives you some standards by which you can gauge your progress. When progress is not what it should be, goals become a spur for greater effort. Third, goal setting should be part of the style of management. A thesis of this book is that you obtain the full benefit of the knowledge and energy of people by involving them in the planning process. Certainly goal setting is an important part of planning. By incorporating personal goal set-

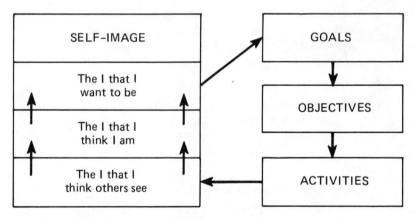

Figure 3. Cycle of positive reinforcement.

ting into your habits, even making it a component of your self-image, you find that organizational goal setting is natural and comfortable.

How to Get Started in Personal Goal Setting

Many people have a great deal of difficulty in writing personal goals. To be sure, it can be a self-wrenching experience, especially if it is the first time that you have ever seriously thought about what is important in your life. Here is a procedure that works for me and others who have used it.

Resolve to spend one hour—no more, no less—at a time when you can be completely uninterrupted, say early on a Saturday morning. With paper and pencil at hand, spend the time thinking about your own self-concept and how it relates to categories for goals (professional, financial, family, etc.). It will be tough work, but tell yourself that you can stand anything for an hour. Probably not much will get on the paper for the first 20 or 30 minutes. Then as the ideas begin to take form, you will no doubt find that an hour is not enough, and you will need at least two hours. But at this point, your frustration has turned to enthusiasm, and it no longer is a difficult chore. In the event that the whole hour passes without your having made any progress on the goals, stop and try the procedure again weeks or months later. By that time, your subconscious mind will probably have done some work on the subject and you will find that you are successful on the second effort.

Controlling Your Time

Time is your most precious asset and yet it is the one common denominator among men. Everybody has 24 hours per day. Obviously there are differences in how this time is used. You can let others control your use of time or you can gain control of it yourself. It is up to you, but without control of it you cannot be an effective leader because you will not have the time to do the things that *you* want and need to do.

I can suggest seven principles for planning and controlling time.

1. *Principle of visualization and goal setting.* This is the process of visualizing what you want to be and what you want to do. It is also the

process of putting these goals on paper as described in the section above. You should allow time for this; make it a part of the system.

2. *Principle of knowing where time is spent.* In order to plan your time and very likely make some change in your allocation of time, it is essential to know how you are currently spending your time. This will probably involve making a record of your activities for about two weeks. This is a procedure that I use about twice per year. For a daily record, I use a form with lines representing periods of 30 minutes (Figure 4). I briefly note my activities on the form, recording time in tenths of an hour (6 minutes). The daily form is summarized in a weekly form (Figure 5) which has categories of work in the lefthand column and a column for entering the time spent in that category each day of the week. At the end of the week, I can sum the amount of time spent by category and the total working time spent each day. (The categories on the Weekly Time Record are my own. Note that there are subtotals for major categories of work.)

3. *Principle of setting priorities.* The crucial distinction that needs to be made in setting priorities is identifying the urgent and the important. All activities can be classified as having either high or low urgency and high or low importance (Figure 6). Of course, these categories for the same activity can change. What is not urgent now may be later on. The trap to avoid is spending all the time on the urgent of both high and low importance. Setting priorities will uncover the work that is very important but not urgent. There lies the real opportunity to make a truly significant contribution to the effectiveness of the organization, yet there is no pressure to do it immediately or maybe no pressure to do it at all.

4. *Principle of making time.* This is the principle of planning and controlling time to create blocks of time that are needed to do important work. Some people are able to reserve a set time each week. Others will need to reserve time by scheduling on a week-to-week basis. It could be said that this principle is the purpose of all time planning. Without blocks of time, it is impossible to accomplish difficult tasks, which are often of high importance but of low urgency.

5. *Principle of scheduling work.* Most people keep lists of the things they have to do. Scheduling is the process of entering those activities on a daily or weekly calendar, together with the blocks of time you have reserved and the meetings and events that are a part of your normal weekly schedule. How frequently you schedule, say weekly or

Figure 4. Time analysis log.

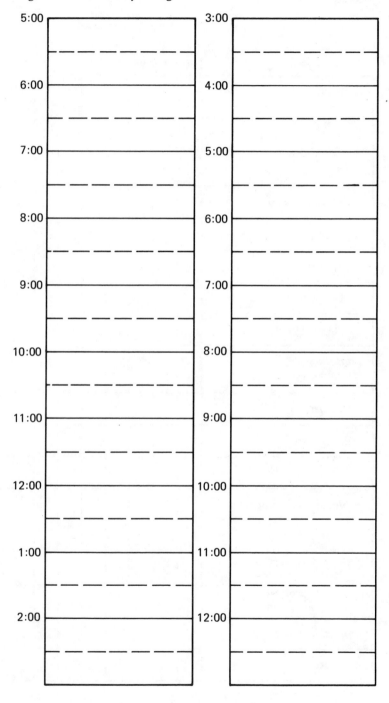

Figure 5. Weekly time record.

Week of _____

	M	T	W	T	F	S	S	TOTAL
Time planning								
Misc. work								
School Teaching								
Class preparation								
Grading								
Committees								
Misc. school								
Total school								
Consulting Company A								
Company B								
Promotion								
Total consulting								
Professional development Reading professional books and journals								
Attending meetings and conferences								
Total professional development								
Professional writing								
Total								

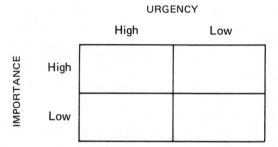

Figure 6. Four-way classification of urgency and importance.

daily, and how closely depends on what is required to get the desired results. In the first place some scheduling will be necessary to deal with urgent requirements or requirements that are becoming urgent. If a report requires eight hours of work and must be completed in two weeks, scheduling will reveal the times that you have in your busy schedule to get this done on time. Without scheduling, you can end up writing the report on the day it is due, doing a poor job, and perhaps letting other items that require your attention slip by. Scheduling ensures that the priorities you have set for work and the blocks of time that you have created will be used.

Scheduling by day can be a great aid in getting the best use of your time. After the events and blocks of time have been accounted for on the weekly or daily schedules, make an assessment of the urgency and importance of the other things on your "to do" list. Mark some of these for completion and give them an allotment of time on your schedule.

6. *Principle of flexibility.* Time planning can never be exact. There is always a need to allow for interruptions and unexpected happenings. (A major crisis will cause all prior plans to be disregarded, and there can be no planning for this.) Peter Drucker has observed that executives, in reality, have control over much less than half of their time. One of the reasons for finding out how you spend your time (principle 2) is to determine how much flexibility you must build into your time planning. You need enough so that the usual interruptions will not destroy the plan, causing your time and effort in planning to be wasted.

7. *Principle of being master of your own time.* This is a capstone

principle, embracing the previous six. It says that time management should be an objective in itself. It is a reminder that there is more to life than the professional side. If you have written goals that apply to all facets of your life, your use of time should reflect these goals. This is not easy to do; trying to do so makes us realize what a precious commodity time is.

Alan Lakein, author of *How to Get Control of Your Time and Your Life*,* notes that many people do a satisfactory job of planning for a time range of about a week but do a poor job in making use of the immediate small increments of time and do not incorporate long-range goals into their time planning. In other words, they do an adequate job in the middle of the time spectrum but a poor job at both ends.

The failure to make any progress on long-range goals is a result of procrastination. The principle of being master of your own time says that you will not let this happen, that you will make time to at least get a start on the project that you believe to be important, not urgent, either in your personal or professional life. If you have something that you have wanted to do for a long time, isn't it time to ask yourself if you are really serious about getting it done? What priority are you giving it? If you honestly want to get it done, the principle of being master of your own time says that your analysis of how time is spent (principle 2) will tell you what you need to do to make time (principle 4) to get it done.

The person who is in control of his time makes use of the five- and ten-minute intervals that are otherwise wasted. There are some kinds of work that can be done by working in short periods over a period of say two weeks. If you have a list of telephone calls that you would like to make, a short interval between meetings is a good time to get them out of the way. Carrying your reading material with you will eliminate the frustration of waiting time. The principle of being master of your own time says that you should always have something that you want to do to fill in the small chinks of time. You are in control when you have something to do that you want to do; you are not in control when you are waiting for someone else.

Finally, the principle means that you take time to relax and enjoy life. You can be overly conscious of how each minute is being spent and also be on the way to ulcers or a coronary.

* New York: New American Library, 1973.

A Different Checklist for Success

The process of examining your self-concept or image, setting goals that are consonant with it, and managing your time to carry out the goals is a winner in any field. A person who carries out this process will gain the respect of his associates so that he *can* become a leader, but the process does not of and by itself guarantee stepping into a position of leadership or being able to lead people. Incidentally, it is well known that there are people in supervisory or managerial positions who do not lead and there are people without formal authority who do lead. Certainly, other qualifications being about equal, people with a recognized capability for leadership have a better opportunity for advancement than those who do not.

How to apply your efforts and how to put into practice the process outlined above on attaining leadership involve most of the subjects addressed in later portions of this book. However, there are a few points that the aspiring leader could check that relate to goal setting and self-image.

Do you support organizational goals? A leader must thoroughly support organizational goals. This is not to say that he can never find fault with policies or tactics that are used by his company or his organization within the company. It is saying that fundamental organizational beliefs about quality, performance, and ways of dealing with people must be supported by the leader. Imagine how absurd it would be to put a person who had managed restaurants serving expensive dishes of high quality into a position of managing fast food outlets. If the person held to his former values, he would be a totally ineffective leader in the new position.

Are your personal goals and organizational goals mutually supporting? To support organizational goals, not just giving them lip service, requires a feeling that they are in harmony with your personal professional and financial goals. The best way to ensure that this occurs is to bring the question to your direct attention. If there is a high degree of congruence between the goals of your immediate organization and your personal goals, the work that you do should support both.

One of the best examples of a comparatively low-level job offering plenty of opportunity to meet personal goals is the account manager position in a client organization of mine. This man manages the accounts receivable program for a number of retail stores that are his clients. In addition to these ongoing responsibilities, he has a limited responsibility for marketing the service to prospective clients. He becomes very much involved with his retailers in matters pertaining to financial policies as they relate to accounts receivable and to revolving credit as a marketing tool. Much of his time is spent making visits to his clients in distant cities. As for personal goals, the account manager is challenged to understand the retail business. He is attempting to influence the retailer, who is often much older and certainly more experienced in retailing, to make decisions that are favorable to the company he represents and in the best interest of the retailer as well. If the account manager has set goals for himself that encompass learning more about business and being more effective in communication, to mention just two areas of development, he has a grand opportunity. But as a necessary condition for his being an effective representative of his own company to the retailer, he absolutely must be thoroughly convinced that the program for accounts receivable and the philosophy behind it is truly beneficial to the retailer. Otherwise he will be totally ineffective, realizing neither the goals of his organization nor his personal goals.

Is your self-image appropriate for the role? A key to mutually supportive personal and organizational goals is having the appropriate self-image for the role. The person who wants to be a leader must think of himself as being a leader. If he does, he will have no difficulty in establishing goals for himself that advance his own capabilities. In addition, the professional must also consider the function that he is performing and how this relates to his self-image. If the job calls for meticulous work and that fits his self-concept, all is well. On the other hand, as frequently happens, a person may be elevated to a higher position and not adopt a role or a self-image that is appropriate. A common example of this is the top sales executive who is given broader responsibilities and fails because he still thinks of himself as the only person who is able to close the "big deals."

This brings an interesting point to mind: Can you change your self-image? And if you can, should you? The truth is that you cannot avoid changing your self-concept. It has been changing throughout your life. If it didn't you would not be the kind of person you are today, but someone else who would be far less mature. Different and higher positions of responsibility call for different behavior. *Any sig-nificant change in behavior will only take place with a change in self-concept.* Therefore, changes in self-concept are not only inevitable but are necessary to make appropriate changes. Roy Ash, chairman of AM International and formerly president of Litton Industries, in speaking of the turnaround he is effecting at AM says that a change is needed in the "self-perception" of its managers. As an example, he explains, "Salesmen like to see themselves as offering costly, complex machines, not peddling supplies. We had to adjust their view, not of the company, but of themselves."*

What is to be avoided is a pattern of synthetic behavior that is merely acting, because it will be transparent and seen for what it is by others. Your real strength is the character and personality that you have developed over your life. Making profound changes in your attitude and your behavior is part of growing and gives strength. Assuming some facade for the occasion is weakness.

In addition to thinking of yourself as a leader, I believe that there are two other concepts that ought to be a part of your self-image. One is the idea of "being" not "going to be." Think of yourself as being a good reporter or a good designer or a good production planner or a good executive right now. You cannot long afford to be saying to yourself that someday you will be a good "whatever." Instead, by thinking of yourself as a *professional* in the present tense, you take the first step toward behaving as one.

The second idea is to think of yourself as an *achiever.* You may and should think of yourself as being many other things, but without the strong desire to get things done that stems from visualizing yourself as a person who gets things done, your ability to lead is severely curtailed. Business survives through results. All the studies and all the reports and all the discussions do not produce a dollar of revenue or subtract a dollar of cost unless put into action. The effective leader thinks of himself as an achiever who gets results. To illustrate, here are a couple of excerpts from a *Fortune* series on how chief executive officers have reached the top position.† Incidents in their careers demonstrate how they are achievers.

* Louis Kraar, "Roy Ash Is Having Fun at Addressogrief-Multigrief," *Fortune,* February 27, 1978.
† Arthur M. Louis, "An Awesome Mind Was Fletcher Byrom's Secret Weapon," *Fortune,* July 1976; "Charles Pilliod Was the Odd Man In at Goodyear," *Fortune,* May 1977.

Fletcher Byrom of Koppers Company:

"I would roam the plant," he recalls. "Here was a plant that hadn't been performing. I was asking people to do things they didn't think could be done, and sometimes I practically had to hold their hands. If a machine had been producing fourteen gallons of chemicals a minute, I would have the operator push it to twenty-one. The operators would say, 'Mr. Byrom, we can't do that!' and I would reply, 'Maybe we can. Why don't I stay here with you while you try it?' Most processes are susceptible to refinements and improvements—little changes here and there. You should never accept what you're doing as being the best you can do."

Charles Pilliod of Goodyear Tire & Rubber Co.:

In the spring of 1947, he was transferred to Panama as managing director of the company's subsidiary in that country. It consisted only of a sales operation and a decrepit retreading plant. It employed just about twenty people altogether and generated about a million dollars a year in revenues.

But Pilliod plunged into his job as though the entire future of the corporation depended on his efforts. He demanded that the retreading plant be restored to top condition, and he himself wielded paint brushes, hammers, and an acetylene torch to help to get the chore done.

How to Have the Power to Influence Others

Power is the ability to get people to do what you want them to do and, if desired by you, to get it done your way and on your schedule. From this simple definition, it is clear that no discussion of leadership is complete without some consideration of power. Power is not a pleasant topic to many people because the term has negative connotations. Some of the most despicable men in history have had great power and used it outrageously and reprehensibly. Attaining power can be a goal in itself that is pursued with deceit and strategies for manipulating people. Michael Korda has chronicled such tactics and strategies in his book *Power: How to Get It, How to Use it*. My own experience with persons who have a compulsion to seek power is that the very tactics which are often successful over the short range eventually lead to a loss of power and even to ridicule. Geo. T. Scharffenberger, in coming to a similar conclusion, has said: "Business managers who deliberately set out to use power will ultimately come to failure. Power is a result of effort and not the means of effort."*

The power of the position. For those who are managers or supervisors, the power of the position itself is perhaps the strongest source of influence they have over subordinates. There are many reasons for this. In the first place, a person in the managerial hierarchy has conferred, or formal, authority, which is understood by all to convey the right to give orders that subordinates will carry out. In our culture, this expectation has been nurtured since childhood.

The leader with formal authority can and should use unit and company goals to channel the efforts of subordinates. The leader who is seen as actively working toward organizational goals can anticipate getting solid support from others who are also committed to the goal.

Many first-line supervisors today feel that they are powerless in dealing with their subordinates. Often the procedures and policies of the organization make firing an employee virtually impossible. Sometimes even professional employees are represented by a union, making the task of terminating an employee or otherwise disciplining him even more difficult. It would be naive to say that these conditions don't impose severe limitations on the range of actions available to the supervisor. On the other hand, strong supervisors who grasp the strength of the sources of power that they do have can exert control and, yes, power over employees even under these conditions.

Conferred authority and use of organizational goals occasionally are not sufficient to motivate some employees, but fortunately, short of termination, there are many other avenues to exerting power. The basis for most of these is the opportunity that the supervisor has to meet the needs of his employees (discussed in Chapter 2). The dependence of the employee on the supervisor for meeting his needs gives the supervisor power and influence.

Among the prerogatives that you as a supervisor can use to advantage is the authority to make assignments. Some of these are seen by subordinates as more desirable than others and some may even be seen as objectionable. In giving an undesirable assignment you must of course not cast it in the light of a punishment. This would assure poor performance. However, you can make it known, directly or subtly,

* Personal communication.

that good performance on that job is a prerequisite to getting choice assignments in the future.

Rewarding excellence is another tool of yours. Letting a person know he has done commendable work is a principle of leadership that is found in every book on the subject but that, in spite of its value, is often overlooked. Excellence can be rewarded in many ways that have tremendous significance for the person being rewarded. A few lines in a column in the house organ can give an individual recognition. Other ways are to encourage the employee to take the results of his work to a higher level or another unit of the organization in person, to include him in higher-level meetings, or to solicit his opinions on topics related to his assignments is another way. Most professional employees feel highly regarded and complimented by being sent to an all-expense-paid professional conference—still another way.

Often you as supervisor hold the key to access to others. A subordinate may consider this valuable for several reasons. He may relate the opportunity of meeting with others, and making a good impression in the process, to his chances for advancement, or he may find that a broad range of contacts helps him to be more successful. Indirectly or directly, such access may result in getting needed approvals or it may give him a broader view of the problem he is trying to solve. It may also open the doors to more knowledge and to higher professional development.

The employee looks to the supervisor to give him the resources and assistance that he needs. For you to deliberately handicap an employee in performing his work would be self-defeating, so it may seem at first that his ability offers little opportunity to be used on a discretionary basis. Insofar as the essential resources are concerned, this is true. However, there are some resources that you can convey that are not truly essential. In varying degrees, office space, office location, furnishings, and privacy are in this category. Ease of access to a computer terminal could be in this category but it might also be essential.

The amount of time that you give to a subordinate and how this time is spent is totally at your discretion and can be used to influence and motivate. You can make yourself available only as needed to give the information and guidance that is necessary to get the tasks finished, or you can take the time to impart your broader knowledge to the individual. You can coach. In this way you are helping the employee to grow and develop into a more capable person and into a more effective supervisor in his own right. Of course, you cannot afford to invest all your time with employees solely as a form of reward. This use of time must be balanced with other needs and tempered with good sense.

Finally, just as you in a supervisory position can reward good performance, you can use the power of your position to penalize poor performance. Short of dismissal, these penalties range from a mild rebuke to putting a letter of reprimand in a personal file. Writing such a letter is very strong action. Sometimes supervisors who do not have the authority to fire or transfer a poorly performing employee fail to grasp the power that they actually do have through their authority to report poor performance in writing.

The one rule that is paramount in applying negative sanctions is that the supervisor should anticipate the results that will follow. A sensitive employee who receives a letter of reprimand is very likely to have doubts, a feeling of insecurity, a loss of confidence, and a dislike for his job and his supervisor. This might lead to a self-reevaluation producing a change in behavior, or it might lead the employee to be less effective than he was because he may avoid making decisions or taking risks. Of course, there is a high probability that he will seek another job, believing that his present one holds no future. The supervisor cannot predict with certainty what the effect will be, but he must be ready to accept and plan for the results of what is likely to happen.

How to appeal to the self-image of others. The need for recognition is one of the strongest, so much so that top professionals in a field will travel thousands of miles to speak to a convention for no reimbursement whatsoever, not even travel money in some cases. Recognition is a form of reinforcement, encouraging still more of the type of behavior recognized. All theories of human behavior incorporate this concept. B. F. Skinner has built his theory of behavior modification around it. Transactional analysis, a popular model of human behavior, uses the term "strokes." Recognition, special attention, compliments—all are forms of strokes.

Recognition is most effective when it relates to the recipient's self-concept, particularly that area of the self-concept described as the "I that I want to be." For the mentally healthy person this is the slight extension of the "I that I think I am" that produces self-improvement.

Let me give you an example of how giving recognition can work to motivate people and put you in a position of leadership whether or not you are in a position of formal authority. A friend of mine, whom I will call Jack, is a division manager for a national company. Frequently he is involved in personal selling. His self-concept is that he is a very good salesman and that his success depends to a great degree on how well he has prepared himself with all the details of the sale and the relevant details of the prospective customer's business. He considers himself to be organized and methodical in getting this preparation done. Although he is not as well organized as he wants to be and may not always have all the details at hand that he would like, he has gotten recognition from his superior for his thorough preparation and he perceives that the "I that others see" matches the "I that he thinks he is" and the "I that he wants to be." This self-image, reinforced as it is, has become a reputation that Jack has to protect. He has no alternative but to continue to be fully prepared for a sales presentation, and his actions become a model for others to follow.

Supporting the subordinate's desire for growth is a powerful way of relating to his self-image. In some of the management training sessions that I have conducted for clients, I ask participants to prepare a one- or two-hour presentation on a designated subject that is related to the business but is not a part of their everyday work. The topic assigned gives them a broader view of their company and the industry it is in, and people who see themselves as knowledgeable professionals easily see the value of this type of assignment. From the beginning, most participants are warmly receptive to the assignment. They spend 15 to 30 hours in preparation, arrive at the seminar with flip charts and graphs, look forward to their time at the podium, and are ready to enjoy and absorb the presentations of the other participants.

The type of leader who does not appeal to the positive self-image of others is rarely in a business where teamwork and the ability to delegate responsibility are essential. According to Harry Levinson, a noted psychologist, such persons may have penetrating insight but it is often vitiated by a condescending manner, a lack of diplomacy, and an insensitivity to other people's feelings. I have seen many instances where a person with a healthy desire for personal development will not tolerate being subjected to this style of leadership for long.

Probably the greatest compliment you can pay a person is to have total confidence in him to live up to his self-concept. Making this confidence known to the person in countless little ways is a tremendous force for getting the job done and exercisng leadership. First there must be a clear understanding about what is going to be done. Then you assume that it *is* being done and rely on normal channels of feedback to report completion. Continually checking demonstrates a lack of confidence and is not using, is in fact gradually destroying, the strong self-image that a person may have as an achiever.

Dealing with people on a personal basis. What are the advantages and disadvantages of personal involvement with employees? Through personal involvement, you can create a sense of obligation on the part of your subordinates, or you can lose respect and power.

An executive vice-president who is a close friend of mine has built up a fierce loyalty among his subordinates because of his personal style of leadership. They know that he can be counted on to give them help when they need it. For example, he is generous in giving employees time off when needed to handle a personal problem—invariably, this time is repaid several fold. He has counseled with some of his people on their personal finances, has worked out an investment plan with a retiring employee, and he has even loaned money to employees, a step that is universally frowned upon by the experts in management. He makes it a practice to meet socially with his top people and their wives, saying "I believe that it is important to know something about a person's private life. This helps me to give him assignments (the type of work and the geographical location) that fits him. It is getting the round peg into a round hole, which is hard enough even when you know something about the person."

The pitfall here is that such a leader may come to be seen as one who is unable to exercise the formal authority of his or her position. Instead of increasing the power of the position, personal involvement with employees has detracted from it. This is a real danger; it can happen to any supervisor who will let it.

How much distance there should be between superior and subordinate cannot be answered categorically. It depends mostly on the superior and somewhat on the type of subordinates and the situation. The rule to follow is that personal involvement can never be allowed to detract from, distort, or divert the superior-subordinate relationship. That is, nothing must take away from the boss's being the boss. The boss who has dinner with an employee at night must be able to reprove him in the office the next morning. If this power is lost, his effective leadership is over.

It takes a rare person to be able to deal with people on a very personal basis and still retain the unquestioned position of leadership and authority. When it can be done, the leader greatly increases his power to influence the decisions and actions of those around him. In reflecting on the danger of dealing with employees on a very personal basis, it is probably prudent for the new supervisor to move cautiously in this area in spite of the high rewards when it is done effectively.

Personal power. Tom Wilcox, a Citicorp alumnus, is putting his stamp of personal leadership on Crocker National Corp., the twelfth largest bank in the country. Mr. Wilcox, who has been portrayed as the epitome of drive and ambition, pushes himself and others to the limit and demands both high dedication and high performacne from his subordinates. Some associates describe him as a person who considers people as fine pieces of machinery that can be fitted together, but others describe him as a sparkplug, a motivator, a charismatic person, one who generates loyalty and makes work exciting.* Above all, he is a man who sets the example.

Setting the example is probably the most important basis for personal power. Those who lead in this way have a strong self-concept that is appropriate for the situation. They invariably set goals, though these may be more implicit than explicit, and their actions, which are consistent with their self-concept and their goals, create an atmosphere for expected high professional performance.

According to some people, territory is another key to personal power. Robert Ardrey, author of *Territorial Imperative* and *African Genesis,* has analyzed the territorial instincts of wild animals and suggests that man has an "instinct" for territory. Michael Korda, author of *Power,* gives several examples of how personal power is enhanced by laying claim to "territory" such as files and bulletin boards. He cites an example of how a female magazine editor has furnished her office to make it clearly "hers" and to give her every advantage in any discussion that is held there. He writes, "From the moment they [male executives] entered her office, their one thought was to get out as soon as possible, and return to the safety of their own offices. . . . If they could have forced her to move to *their* floor, she would have been powerless."

* "Crocker's Tom Wilcox: Tough Management for a Stodgy Bank," *Business Week,* August 11, 1975, p. 41.

Another source of personal power is access to a resource, such as a person of influence who is valued, feared, or respected by the organization. Exposure to the media can be very helpful or highly damaging, and a person who has established friendly relationships with the media will be accorded personal power. Relatives of high-ranking officials are often thought to have or do have influence or power.

Expertise is still another source of personal power, because others believe in the opinions and the recommendations of those credited with expert knowledge, especially professionals in a technical area. For years, experts in data processing were probably given too much power because of their expertise and the fact that management was not able to challenge their recommendations. But it is not always the technical expert who has such power. The line executive with a track record of solid accomplishment is also a person whose opinions are respected and whose power stems from a reputation for success.

How to Use Power

Power, the force that causes one person to influence the plans and actions of another, is a pervasive and integral part of leadership and supervision. The leader is constantly using power and, in the process, building values. His daily acts of supervision create or reinforce the values of his unit, the organization as a whole, and, to a great extent, his personal values. Values are a set of attitudes about what is good or bad, desirable or undesirable. Supervisors and nonsupervising professionals should use their power to establish and maintain two essential values—high standards of performance, and an effective working environment.

Bill Graham, a rock concert promoter, and Tom Wilcox, chairman of Crocker National Corp., are probably as dissimilar in outward appearance as any two individuals you could find. But they have at least one thing in common: they set high standards. Bill Graham has been described as a perfectionist. A competitor, Jack Boyle, says of him, "He makes sound financial transactions and merchandises his product better than anyone else in the business. He's the very best at staging outdoor shows." *Business Week* has this to say about Wilcox:

> In just 15 months as CEO, Wilcox, who works 14-hour days and thinks his subordinates should do the same, has dumped two-thirds of

Crocker's senior and middle management, trimmed the payroll by 10 percent, skirmished with bigger rivals on the marketing front, and made it clear that he wants nothing to do with the slow-growth approach being followed by Crocker's most formidable competitor, Bank of America.*

In making the managerial replacements, Wilcox has hired young aggressive managers who share his yearning for growth. They come from the big banks in New York and Chicago and from management consulting firms.

Regardless of the level of professionalism of his staff, standards of performance will not be high unless the supervisor insists that they be kept high. This responsibility is central to his job. Sometimes this very basic principle of management is confused by studies and theories that supposedly demonstrate that the supervisor who shows concern for his personnel is more effective than the one who is task-oriented. Taking this conclusion at face value could be very detrimental to a supervisor's ability to lead, because the leader may lose sight of the goal, which is to get the job done.

A standard of performance, whether it be quantitatively measured or a pervasive desire to excel, must be accepted by the performers in order to have any effect. The leader of the group may at times find that he is wheedling, cajoling, selling, campaigning, and threatening to put his point across. And sometimes he has to compromise—temporarily. Suppose that he endeavors to get the acceptance of his group that output can be increased. The current level is 50 and he is certain that 100 is attainable. After a thorough discussion with the group there is general acceptance that 80 is realistic. The supervisor should adopt the goal of 80, reach it, and then raise the question with the group again about what can be done to get performance to 100.

Methods vary, but the real key to acceptance of high standards is understanding. People will not be committed to high standards unless they believe in what they are doing. The plan they are following or the function they are performing must be seen as appropriate to the needs of their immediate organization or to the organization at a higher level. Although the words should be chosen to fit the audience, the concept to be put across is that they are part of a system that is an integral part of a higher system. What they do should be seen as con-

---

* "Crocker's Tom Wilcox: Tough Management for a Stodgy Bank," *op. cit.*, p. 41.

tributing to the operation of their own system, which in turn enables it to better serve the higher-level system.

Along with giving meaning to what is being done, the leader needs to give an understanding of what is a high standard of performance in the context of the requirements of the system. There can be high standards of performance for producing garments priced in the $10 to $20 range just as there are for a high-fashion design of a similar garment costing $100. In both cases, it is the job of the leader or manager to establish a standard of performance that considers both the quality of the garment and the cost, and in both cases the standards of performance can be set at a point that is not easily reached. For thinking people to accept fully a standard of performance, they need to know *why* it has been set and what the effect will be—on their company, on their organization, on their leadership, and on their jobs—if the standard is not met.

The second essential use of power by a leader is to elevate the effectiveness of the working environment, which entails creating and maintaining an environment that is physically efficient and mentally stimulating. Concretely, this means providing the right tools and the physical surroundings conducive to doing the work. If there is any aspect of the working environment that hampers the work or is a genuine irritant to personnel, the supervisor must do all he can to correct the condition. If it is a problem that is not under his direct control, he should use the full force of his personal power with his superior and peers to get action.

It is not uncommon, especially in mature organizations, to find bureaucratic trappings of reports and procedures that detract from productive work. Sometimes the need for such reports has long passed, yet they remain a burden under which the industrious subordinate attempts to apply his talents. Engineers who find that they spend a large part of their time in administration rather than engineering work or top salespersons bogged down by paperwork are examples of this organizational plague. And I cannot resist citing the situation of the professor who wants to teach but whose efforts are diluted by incessant committee meetings that have little or nothing to do with his performance in the classroom.

Other manifestations of an unproductive working environment are a gross overlap in responsibilities and ill-defined assignments. These conditions were so prevalent in a large aerospace company that they were utterly debilitating and frustrating to the engineers and professionals from other disciplines. To execute one of this company's responsibilities, the installation of test equipment at Cape Kennedy, the monitoring and planning of test installations was done by seven departments.

Beyond overcoming negative forces in the environment, an effective working situation requires taking positive steps to improve interaction between the people in the group and between other groups and levels. While there are many very important reasons for actively reaching for the goal and value of interaction, I shall state only one at this point: feedback. Good interaction facilitates good communication between individuals and groups of individuals. It is through feedback that the group, its systems, and its role in a larger system learn and adjust. Learning is the basis for making needed changes and for retaining the momentum that is inevitably generated by sensing success. New and open lines of communication to people in an organization who have been intellectually deprived by the narrowness of their outlook can be exhilarating and exciting to them. Furthermore, this is happening with greater frequency than ever before in new operating and organizational arrangements under such labels as quality circles and the quality of working life. The people in these programs are getting new information and new insights that are stimulating them and equipping them to be more effective.

In creating an effective working environment, the leader must use his power in ways that are perceived as fair. Mention has been made in this chapter of using power to reward the excellent performer in a variety of ways such as asking him to join meetings with higher-ups. These tactics, if employed without careful consideration, can result in inspiring one person while disenchanting all others. To counter any tendency of this nature, the supervisor should make it obvious to the group that the reward is earned. In fact, having a subordinate attend an important meeting should not be presented as a reward in the eyes of others but as a normal part of the job for those who make a large contribution.

The best way to ensure that fairness is perceived is to treat all personnel as star performers to the extent that it is warranted. The effective supervisor avoids being seen as playing favorites and finds a way to reward every solid performer even though he may not really be a star.

Avoiding a Loss of Power

Power is a living force and like all living organisms or institutions it will atrophy if it is not used. In other words, as long as the leader is leading, he is using his power; it is impossible to do otherwise.

This does not mean, however, that power should be flaunted or abused, for that can only lead to resentment and in time even to a loss of power. The wise leader uses his power sparingly and indirectly. Bob Dockson, chief executive officer of California Federal, a large federally chartered savings and loan company, says that there is no question that the CEO of the company carries a great deal of power. But he explains, "If the person understands that the power rests with him, then he has no concern and he is usually delighted to give credit to others for making the recommendation or even the decision." It is a paradox but true, the more powerful a person is, the less use he has to make of overt power. This is as it should be and it is the condition the leader should strive to attain.

Successful results and effective performance reinforce the personal power of a leader. The opposite leads to a loss of power. In other words, it helps if you are right and your plans are carried out to completion. The leader who establishes plans and goals which are never met loses power through a loss of credibility. Those around him eventually do not take him seriously. Even by commanding the power of his position in the formal organization chart, he is only able to induce a mediocre effort toward pursuits that others believe will ultimately fail.

True leadership gives meaning to what might otherwise seem to be the humdrum of endless activities. In so doing, it enhances the vision of all involved of their organization, their mission, and their capabilities as professionals. Leadership of this type is never lost.

4

Being a builder

I like building for the future," says Robert C. Wilson, chief executive officer of Memorex. He has done just that since being brought into the company, which was hovering on the brink of financial disaster in 1974. The company had lost $90 million in 1973 after a venture into the mainframe computer business failed. Its stock was delisted from the New York Stock Exchange. The profits on its bread and butter lines of peripheral computer equipment had been reduced when IBM lowered its prices on the same equipment. In 1977 trading was resumed on the New York Stock Exchange and the company earned $56 million for the year. The tangible assets of Memorex have increased to the point where it now has a positive net worth, and its long-term debt, which was once about $300 million, has been cut by half. The intangible assets have grown also. The engineering staff has been increased by 40 percent and the sales program has been completely revamped. Like all successful executives, Robert Wilson is a builder.

Conceptually, building in an organization may be compared to the job of building a wall with bricks. One row of bricks is put into place at a time. If the completed row is square and true, it becomes a solid base for the next row. The bricklayer no longer has to be concerned with the completed row: he knows it will hold.

Building is the heart of the manager's job. It means increasing the assets of the firm. For most managers, more often than not, the opportunity for building lies with the intangible assets rather than with the tangible. In fact, the effective manager or the professional employee in a decision-making role adds value to the intangible assets daily.

Increasing the intangible worth of an organization is achieved by both improving an attribute and establishing its value. For instance, if steps are to be taken to increase knowledge or to improve teamwork, the value of these attributes must also be evident. Moreover, when the importance of the attribute is recognized by precedent-setting decisions, regularly reinforced, the attribute becomes a value in itself. It enters that class of acts, customs, and beliefs that are accorded special intrinsic merit. For example, on a national scale, the Constitution of the United States embodies many values, each reinforced many times over and each having great worth, but totally incapable of being priced in dollars and cents.

The manager and the professional are faced with the decision of what values to inculcate and how to implant them. They know that eventually the values of the organization, good or bad, facilitating or limiting, will become imbedded by consistently repeated actions. Effective managers are aware that they have a great opportunity to build strength and value. They can take full advantage of the opportunity by thinking seriously about what to build and how to do it.

A Look at the Nonbuilder

Before going into more detail on the "what" and "how" of building, let us briefly address the question of "why." The answer to this question becomes obvious by looking at the many people in managerial positions who are not builders. Of course, it is difficult to have a position of leadership in the formal organization and not build anything, but there are a vast number of people who approach this nihilistic level.

Actually the nonbuilder may be quite effective on routine matters. In this vein, he probably handles the paperwork and administrative chores of his ongoing operation quite efficiently. There are many who make no lasting contribution to their job; all that can be said is that they perform in the job and keep the seats of their chairs warm. There is no noticeable difference in the performance of their office or department from the day they start until the day they leave.

This is exposure, not achievement. It is the basis for saying that a person doesn't have ten years' experience, but one year's experience ten times over. This is a far cry from the builder who puts one row of bricks into place so that he can put another one on top of that.

The builder is able to point to a record of accomplishment largely through establishing values that last.

Walter Hoving, the guiding hand at Tiffany, the epitome of prestige in jewelry stores, has steadfastly ingrained his taste into the value system of the organization. Shortly after taking control of the firm in 1955, he sold all the items that he considered to be gaudy or vulgar in one massive sale. His impact on his organization is seen from this excerpt:

> In retailing circles, where today's fads are tomorrow's nostalgia, and where success so often hangs on the ability to divine the next big trend, Walter Hoving stands serenely above the fray. In the 20 years that he has been chairman and chief executive of Tiffany, he has combined impeccable taste with business acumen to make the chain of six stores synonymous with classic, if sometimes stodgy, elegance. And if the very, very chic look elsewhere for the last word in hip pizzazz, the Social Register set can always be depended upon to snap up the oh-so-correct sterling flatware and the 18-carat-gold charm bracelets.*

David Packard and William Hewlett started the Hewlett-Packard Company in 1938. Its sales have grown to be in excess of the $1 billion mark. The company has always had a sense of purpose and a value system that reflect those of its founders. In 1957, the first statement of corporate objectives was written. It has been modified from time to time since, but the basic precepts have not changed. One of these is that the company would concentrate its efforts in a specific field. Growth, as desirable as it may be, would not be sought if it meant going beyond the company's area of expertise. The company's objectives state that broadening of its product lines will take place only as the company has the technical, manufacturing, and marketing skills that are required to be successful.

Nine Areas for Building

Hewlett-Packard and other prosperous organizations owe their success to the strength of their human systems whose actions and interactions propel the organization forward. These systems operate in ways which essentially fulfill their own needs but also create output which is a reliable and productive component to other, higher and adjoining systems. What might be simply described as cooperation between well-trained and sophisticated individuals and groups is, in reality,

* Stanley H. Slom, "Walter Hoving Makes His Impeccable Taste a Tiffany Trademark," *The Wall Street Journal*, October 27, 1975.

synchronization of finely tuned, interlocking, support systems. The characteristics of such systems for planning, executing, and making adjustments were described in Chapter 1 and summarized in Figure 1.

How are we to build systems that exhibit the drive and imagination needed to succeed in a dynamic environment? What qualities are needed and how do we get them? There are nine primary areas for building, and a leader in an organization should consciously strive to build these nine values and qualities into his organization, periodically making an evaluation of how well this is being done.

1. *Knowledge.* I put this first because it encompasses everything else and is the most important resource that a firm has. When firms talk about having good people, to a large extent this means knowledgeable people. Chapter 5 deals with knowledge in greater detail than can be accorded here.

2. *Confidence and trust.* One of the interesting and somewhat unexpected conclusions in a study of conglomerate corporations that I made in the late 1960s was the importance of establishing confidence and trust between the divisions and the corporate headquarters. At the time it seemed to some that a conglomerate was created by a rash of acquisitions and managed by a system of financial plans and reports. Indeed, the formal reports were vital in supplying information consistently and automatically. However, truly effective management could not exist without mutual trust between corporate and division levels of management, because reliance on financial reporting alone creates too much temptation to seek short-term results at the expense of larger long-term gains. Division management that is trusted will be in a better position to convince corporate headquarters to take risks for a more profitable future at the expense of reduced short-term earnings.

Trust also comes very much into play when an operating division encounters problems. The corporation must have the confidence that division executives are presenting the facts correctly and will be candid in asking for needed assistance. False pride which prevents dealing with problems openly is detrimental to building confidence and trust. The president of one of the largest conglomerates in the United States told me that the division presidents who had the trust of corporate management actually had more autonomy than those who did not.

The lesson to be learned here is that in spite of the formal planning, paperwork, and emphasis on the proverbial bottom line, management still ends up being a relationship between people. The supervisor has essentially the same problems with his subordinates as does the chief executive officer of a corporation with his division presidents. He must be able to deal with problems openly, working out solutions jointly with his people.

Building confidence and trust is more than a two-way street. You need to work on the relationships in all directions, up, down, and sideways. Confidence and trust are needed in all transactions and relationships. It is an area for building that requires your direct attention.

You may suppose that these two attributes occur naturally in the course of business if people deal with each other honestly. While there is no question that dishonesty will destroy trust, there is certainly no guarantee that honesty alone will create it. Keys to trust are dependability, competence, consistency, and understanding. You would not trust someone who could not perform because of a lack of ability or the lack of effort in using his ability. Consistent performance is evidence of dependability. But understanding is also necessary. It becomes much more difficult to have confidence in what someone does if you have no understanding of the process. Would you accept the assurance that a research department will have a new drug available by a certain date if you knew nothing about the process, even if past performance showed that the department had met its goals? Possibly— but you would have more confidence if you knew what the department had to do. Certainly, before a record of dependable performance can be demonstrated, your best opportunity to build confidence is through having others understand your function and the type of problems that you encounter.

3. *Responsibility.* Commitment to an ideal or purpose is the basis for responsibility. In this sense responsibility goes far beyond being "responsible" for carrying out a set of prescribed steps. It is a concept which is covered more fully in Chapter 6.

4. *Team organization.* A good baseball team knows that wearing a uniform does not make a team. Furthermore, players who perform well as individuals but do not become part of the team effort will never build a great team. Teamwork in all endeavors calls for a dedication to common goals and cooperative effort to meet those goals.

The comeback at Lehman Associates, the investment banking firm, is powerful evidence of the value of teamwork. All Wall Street firms would like to forget 1973, but it was an especially devastating year for Lehman, with losses of about $9 million. Getting back on the road to profitability required making several changes and economies.

Probably none was more profound than the change in attitude. Prior to 1973 partners were fiercely competitive and secretive. They guarded their relationships with clients from each other as they would from a rival firm. It was even impossible to compile a centralized file of information on client transactions.

In 1973, Peter G. Peterson, a man known for his leadership qualities, was installed as chairman. At age 27 he had been put in charge of the Chicago office of McCann-Erickson, Inc., became the head of Bell & Howell Co. at 34, and was appointed to be the United States Secretary of Commerce at 45. At Lehman, he has created an environment in which the partners are now working for the firm instead of for themselves. They have actually gotten to like each other. No longer is it impossible for one partner to entertain the client of another. Peterson has set the example for this by being completely agreeable to having his own clients lunch with other partners. There is a new spirit of cooperation and trust at Lehman Associates.

One of Peterson's first steps was to install a system of business planning. In analyzing the firm's business lines, four questions are asked: (1) What is the profitability of this particular business? (2) Is this a business in which we can differentiate what we offer from what competitors offer? (3) Is it a business that is central to Lehman as a firm? (4) Do we have the capital? Planning and asking questions of this type cannot be done in isolation. The process requires discussion and involvement among the top officers, and these are team-building activities. The business plan is a key document, and going through the intellectual processes of understanding a business and formulating its strategy for the future binds people together. Discussion makes the common goals more relevant to an individualistic partner and discloses the frailities of the basic underpinning of the business wherever they exist.

Planning alone will not prevent the errors and oversights that stand in the way of achievement and effectiveness. Rather, performance ultimately depends on the strength of the underlying system, and planning is a means of building a better system and a better team.

5. *Effectiveness.* For the manager or the professional, doing the right thing is more important than the ease, speed, or alacrity with which it is done. The first concern is that the car is being driven down the right road; the second, that it is going at the proper speed.

To build effectiveness, you first must ensure that goals are understood and become the basis for priorities. The broad plans of individuals and groups should be known and discussed. As a manager, you need to reinforce these ideas continually. There are several ways for doing this.

I have prepared "priority games" for a client which deal with priorities and goals in a very practical way. The game is a little like the "in basket" exercise, in that the players are asked to cope with emergencies as they come up. Each player is given a calendar for the week with some duties and appointments already blocked out. Then the group members simulate a week of work and interruptions by recording on the calendar what they are doing to handle their normal work, special assignments, and meetings. As the simulated week progresses, they are given new information. For example, a subordinate calls in sick one morning, or the need to discuss a client problem suddenly comes up.

This type of exercise raises many questions about what is important, what is urgent, what are the correct priorities, what are the goals, and what activities are building activities that add strength to the organization. Managers can get some of the same benefit of such an exercise by discussing real and hypothetical situations in meetings. To emphasize the point again, people must know what the goals and priorities are as a first condition of being effective performers.

In addition to knowing the goals and priorities, people must have the climate that gives them the freedom or autonomy to carry out their tasks effectively. The work of people making the greatest contribution is not highly structured and may have practically no structure at all. An attempt on the part of higher-level personnel to dictate how each task is to be performed or to stipulate a sequence of work that satisfies all conditions will assure low levels of effectiveness, because it presumes that the higher-level manager knows more about the work of qualified employees than they do themselves. If subordinates are truly professional this cannot and should not be.

6. *Efficiency.* If you are supervising people doing routine work, you should be vitally concerned with efficiency. To a large extent, though not totally, efficiency has been or should have been taken care of by the design of the job. The prescribed duties of the job should further the aims of the organization and the system of which it is a part.

The dominant philosophy in progressive companies today is that the worker should be more formally involved in the design of his job. The net effect is that efficiency is now achieved more through human means than through technical means. To elaborate, if management finds it less appropriate to break down work into a set of steps and motions which are assigned to workers, it then must focus its efforts on establishing the structure and creating the conditions which will yield efficiency through the confluence of knowledge at the worker and management levels. With highly skilled and professional employees, this has always been the approach to getting greater efficiency. Now there is less difference between the routes to efficiency for the average worker and the professional, but for professionals, effectiveness remains the more important goal. Both efficiency and effectiveness can be increased through various types of organizational arrangements, productivity programs, goal setting, and management by objectives— all discussed in following chapters.

7. *Flexibility and creativity.* These attributes, although different, are highly interrelated and have a common denominator. Both require change. You should create an atmosphere in which change is acceptable and in which people can fail. Fletcher Byrom, chairman of the board of Koppers Co., has put it this way: "Our management style is one of as much lack of structure as we can possibly have. We attempt to eliminate rigidities and the tendency to introduce bureaucracy into large organizations. We don't demand that people always be right; we expect people to make mistakes and we accept the probability of error."*

Much of the lack of innovation in American industry today has been attributed to an overly cautious management philosophy, an emphasis on succeeding with the tried and true rather than trying something new. John R. Rockwell, who heads the venture-management arm of the consulting firm Booz, Allen & Hamilton, has summed up the situation by saying that innovation is best encouraged by "an environment that recognizes the right to fail." The idea that nobody can afford a failure must somehow be changed in the years ahead.† It is the job of a manager to build creativity and flexibility into the way people think, act, and work.

8. *External relations.* Establishing lines of communication and friendships with people outside the organization can be of great importance. It is, of course, essential to cultivate good relations with customers, potential customers, distributors, and all those involved in the sales and distribution of your products. Next in importance for most

---

* Remarks made in an interview with Dr. John F. Steiner, director of the Center for the Study of Business in Society, California State University at Los Angeles, on August 3, 1977.
† "The Breakdown of U.S. Innovation," *Business Week*, February 16, 1976, p. 56.

companies are financial relationships. There is certainly great value in having good communication with your sources of capital.

Beyond these obvious ones, there are varying degrees of value in outside relationships. Sometimes people you know, who are not your customers, have the opportunity to recommend your product or service to potential customers, for example, to a company selling a complementary line of products, or a company selling a service such as legal advice, accounting, or management consulting.

For most managers and professional employees, external relations are valuable as a source of information, moral support, and professional development. Professional and trade associations are helpful in these ways. Being able to discuss a problem with your counterpart in another organization, perhaps a problem that he has successfully overcome, can often help you to plan a strategy and give you confidence that your strategy will work. Sometimes you may face a problem that you are unwilling to discuss with anyone inside your company. Then an outside contact is very much appreciated.

9. *Winning attitude.* I am tempted to say that each of these values is the most important because as I ponder over each one, it seems to be preeminent at the time. So it is with the winning attitude. What could be more vital! Successful people are called winners, and losers are disparaged.

If a person is a football coach it is easy to decide whether he is a winner or loser by merely checking the record. For a salesman, it is about as easy, although depending on the circumstances the results might not be quite as apparent. For managers and important individuals in many functions such as production, engineering, and purchasing, the record does not so clearly show who is a winner and who is not.

With a little thought there are ways of defining success and identifying superior performance. The engineering department that consistently designs products that have better than average acceptance in the marketplace is a winner. The personnel department that is able to recruit people with outstanding qualifications is a winner. And the production department which holds to cost and quality standards in getting its shipments out the door on time is a winner. In all these instances, the success of a department does not come solely from its own efforts. For example, if the product design is superb but its marketing is poor it will probably not sell. Consequently, for most people and groups in organizations succeeding depends on fulfilling a role in conjunction with others. Winning in this context is winning confidence and respect. When others know that you will perform in your designated capacity to the high standards that you have set for yourself, that you will take strenuous steps to overcome impediments in the way of success, that your efforts will result in attaining the goal except when faced with clearly unsurmountable obstacles, then you are a winner.

How do you become a winner? The same way you become a builder.

How to Be a Builder

Have the attitude of a builder and a winner. This is the first step in being a builder. You should make this part of your self-image and think about building in everything you do. Henry Kaiser believed this. He said, "I'm a builder, and if you call yourself a builder you ought to be able to build anything." What he built was organizations—winners mostly.

Focus on contribution and accomplishment. John Hanley, currently the chief executive officer of Monsanto, describes how he and another executive worked together to promote Tide when he was at Procter & Gamble. "I didn't say to Ed Harness, 'Come up to my office.' I'd go down to his. He never gave a damn about who was boss, and neither did I; just get the work done. We did a hell of a job with Tide."[*]

Sometimes in organizations there is undue emphasis on position, perquisites, and other trappings which often have very little to do with accomplishing the job, but which lead to rampant political infighting. The cure for this often is trimming the staff to the point where there is no time to do anything but the work itself. In growing organizations, there is less of a tendency for politics and one-upmanship to take hold. Geo. T. Scharffenberger has described the task of building City Investing into a $5 billion company as just too immense for any activities not aimed at accomplishment and contribution. In mature companies, there is a greater risk of key executives not working for results. The antidote is a management philosophy stressing contribution and accomplishment.

At lower and middle levels of management, procedures and sys-

---

[*] "Jack Hanley Got There by Selling Harder," *Fortune,* November 1976, p. 166.

tems can be an end in themselves, thereby distracting from accomplishment. Certainly, procedures are needed, and the builder is a person who creates and installs procedures. But the crucial question is: are the procedures truly aiding in the accomplishment of work or have they become an anachronism?

Expect success. You should treat success at the *normal* condition. Indeed, it is to be recognized; indeed, it is to be rewarded; but above all it is to be *expected.* Organizations that are able to put this attitude into practice find that success breeds more success until it becomes habitual. Then people take justifiable pride in their accomplishments and their affiliation with a winning organization.

The major public accounting and consulting firms make the most of this principle. They recruit graduates and undergraduates from the top of the class. The new additions to the staff know that they have been selected to join a group of people noted for achievement and intelligence. Although their initial assignments are not without coaching and support, it is assumed that they will be effective professional performers from the start.

Maintain standards. You can make no accommodation with failure or shoddy performance. When it occurs, you must react vigorously. Apologizing for failure or attempting to sweep it under the rug erodes the dedication to results that marks the winner and builder and severely undermines his or her credibility. Take vigorous, positive actions to ensure that unsatisfactory performance will not be repeated. Sanctions, reprimands, or other negative actions are justified if they are used to improve *future* performance. They are not building actions if their primary aim is to chastise or retaliate.

Use the 80/20 rule. The 80/20 rule, also called Pareto's Law, has been applied to many aspects of management, most frequently to sales and customers and to inventories. For example, in sales it would mean that 80 percent of the business is accounted for by 20 percent of the customers. There is nothing scientific about the rule, and the numbers do not have to conform exactly to 80 and 20. However, practical experience confirms that the numbers are approximately correct for many situations.

As a professional or as a manager of professionals you can use it to make you aware that 80 percent of your accomplishments will come from about 20 percent of your time and effort. Indeed, the 20 percent may be high. The significance of this is to plan well for the 20 percent. You should recognize what is likely to have lasting consequences and put effort into those things. These are the precedent-setting and building actions.

The manager who uses the 80/20 rule distinguishes himself from the ineffective perfectionist, who strives for the ultimate in everything he does, no matter how trivial. I have heard of bosses so dedicated to high-quality writing that the most inconsequential memo had to be edited and approved with great care. This type of effort should be reserved for the 20 percent or so of the written communications that are truly important.

At one time, I became general manager of a small company that was having difficulty coping with its increased business. The company had two crucial shortcomings. The first was that, for all practical purposes, there was no production control system. My first task was to get one installed. Within a week, all incoming orders were put on the new system. The other problem was that there was no information on the profitability of the various service and product lines, information essential for pricing and making some fundamental decisions about the direction of the business. My second project was to get cost and profit data by operation and product/service line. I consider both of these to be building activities, and they were done within 20 percent of the total time on the job.

Have a track record. Having a track record means having a record of proven successful performance. Chief executive officers and frequently division heads are in positions where they automatically establish track records. The growth and profits of their units are a testimony to their success or at least they are interpreted as such. Unfortunately, most people in the business world are not in positions where their contributions are a matter of public record or even visible to any except close associates. But all professionals can have a track record with a little effort.

You establish a track record by first setting tangible goals or objectives that can be measured. Achieving the goals and recording the results produces a track record. It might be, for example, the number of people or the percentage of the workforce that eat lunch in the cafeteria, if you are its manager. This, you may believe, is a good barometer of the quality of the food and service. Granted, since you are part of a system, poor results may be caused by other parts of the system or outside forces, but you need to take responsibility (as defined in Chapter 6) for getting good results if it is humanly possible.

I once had the assignment of setting time standards and improving methods in a shipping department, working with an assistant supervisor in charge of about 15 people in one of the four sections in the department. He was a young man who, until my arrival, saw his job as getting out the day's work, nothing more and nothing less. He and I collaborated to make more than 20 small methods changes, such as reorganizing the work so that the shipping papers needed to go to the office only once for typing, rearranging the workplace to reduce walking time, and setting up a simple filing system for stencils used to mark crates. None of these by themselves amounted to much but taken in total there was a considerable reduction in time. Months after I left, when I would run into him in the plant, he would tell me about some new improvement in method that he had installed. Here were the ingredients for a great track record.

A person cannot have a written track record without being a builder. The two are synonymous. Therefore, I urge everyone to take the pains to have a track record, because it is a device that forces building.

Make before and after comparisons. This is the way that you can generate a track record for the parts of your job that are routine but important nevertheless. Think about the quality of the work, the cost, and the elapsed time for processing or getting it done. Ask yourself if an improvement in any of these would make a large contribution to the organization. I found that the elapsed time to handle certain types of production control transactions was critical in an organization I once managed. It was more important than the cost of processing the transactions because of the effect delays had on production. Prior to my management of this department, the time had stretched out because of backlogs and an acceptance of a time span norm that was, in reality, intolerable. After a few months we succeeded in reducing the elapsed time to less than half of what it had been.

Make use of management newsletters and reports. Make it a point to get into print an item that helps to build values or reports accomplishment. It should give credit to the people in your department and those in other departments whose cooperation was essential or helpful. This is a powerful tool both for recording ideas and facts that you want to point out and for motivating your subordinates. Moreover, by giving credit to other departments, such an item paves the way for good relations and more cooperation in the future.

If no newsletter exists, then consider starting one for your unit. If it is done with some grace and modesty, people will not think you are presumptuous. The time it will take will be worth it. To the objection that there is nothing to write about on a regular basis, there is only one answer: the supervisor who is building will find many things to write about. Each brick that is put into place is a topic, and certainly a new brick should be added regularly.

Use pride. Pride is a cause as well as a result of accomplishment. Everyone has an ego. Everyone wants to feel that he or she is important. You can appeal to the personal pride that people take in their skill, profession, or competence to build a winning attitude and an achieving organization.

Although there have been some noteworthy departures in recent years from the stereotyped pattern of assembly lines in the automobile industry, a high percentage of the older workers in that industry have spent their lives in narrowly structured jobs. Perhaps the most frequently heard criticism of assembly line work is that the workers do not take pride in their work. Assuming this to be true, you would expect them to have less interest in their work and not experience the motivation that comes with being in a winning organization. Statistics from companies that have introduced flexible retirement plans, now that the mandatory age for retirement has been changed by U.S. law to age 70, show this to be the case. Only 7 percent of automobile workers reaching age 65 take advantage of the opportunity of working additional years. This may be compared to at least 50 percent of the workers who remain on the job at Sears, Polaroid, and several insurance companies.*

The inference from this example is that there is a closed circle of pride and accomplishment. You can appeal to a person's pride, but you must also establish the working conditions which focus on accomplishment. Accomplishment, in turn, begets more pride.

Be opportunistic in using situations and in making decisions to build valuable precedents and make needed changes. Peter Drucker has pointed out that there are very few problems that are a special case. Typically, problems fall into classes and have common solutions. They can be treated generically. Treating each problem as a special case is often treating symptoms and does not get down to the root cause. The builder looks for the underlying causes that will not only solve the problem at hand but will prevent others like it from occur-

---

* Jeffrey Sonnenfeld, "Dealing with the Aging Work Force," *Harvard Business Review*, November–December 1978, p. 82.

ring. Or if the problem cannot be prevented, the approach to resolving it becomes a precedent for handling all similar problems. You must be careful, however, to establish a good precedent, one that is effective and efficient. Your credibility and authority as a leader will surely be diminished if the procedure you have proclaimed does not achieve its intended results. There is a temptation for some people in a position of authority to "shoot from the hip." What they say becomes a precedent or a procedure for others to follow. If it doesn't work well, the unit is stuck with an ineffective procedure, or the question of how to handle the problem is raised again. This is not solving problems generically.

Beyond solving the obvious problems properly, you can look for problems, even welcome problems. They often give you the opportunity to do what could not be accomplished otherwise. The principle is much the same as the one used by the Supreme Court. Not only does a decision reached on a particular case become a precedent for all others of that type, but also the court on many occasions has used the case to make decisions that go beyond the scope of the case. As you know, these rulings have the force of the law of the land.

You can make this method of managing work for you by having in mind what you want to accomplish. Your goal may be a needed organizational change that you'll have difficulty in implementing because of personalities, or the abandonment of an old product line that is no longer competitive, or instituting changes in the management information system. Frequently, you cannot make the changes that you would like to make because "the timing is not right," that is, there is not enough support within the organization to effect a change successfully. Perhaps others do not share your perception of the need, or they believe that the benefits are not worth the cost of transition, or they have a vested interest in the status quo. In any case, your only course of action may be to wait until conditions change and seize upon the new conditions as both the reason for making a change and the proof that it is necessary.

This is such a commonplace tactic of management and one that can be executed with such finesse that many people do not see that what was done was actually the product of a carefully laid-out strategy that may have been conceived years before. In one aerospace company, the shift from large production runs to smaller production orders coming from more sources and with different types of contractual arrangements triggered a major change in the organization of manufacturing. In the process, one manager with longevity—a person who many thought contributed little under the old arrangement—was reorganized out of a job. Was this the opportunity that management was waiting for? Another situation in this company gave the industrial engineering department the opportunity to have the data processing department placed under its control. The IE department really didn't want the burden of supervising the day-to-day operations of data processing, and demonstrated this by its eagerness to sever its direct control sometime afterward. However, in the interval, industrial engineering made good use of the opportunity to introduce some changes.

Auditors and outside consultants are often the forces that tip the scale to make an opportunity. Criticism of an inventory control system, for example, may give the champions of a new system the opening they are looking for. The threat of sanctions from a standard-setting association may also provoke needed changes. For example, the American Assembly of Collegiate Schools of Business, during its review of a California university, found that the school was deficient in one area. The school responded by introducing a new course that is now required for all business students. The course had been needed for a long time, but without the threat of sanctions from the AACSB, it is very doubtful that the chairmen of the finance, management, and other departments would have agreed to give up one of their courses so that all business students could take the new course.

An extreme example of opportunism was the case of an aluminum company. Finding that it could meet demand for aluminum extrusions during a recessionary period without one of its plants, the company shut down the plant and did not reopen it until any right of recall by the laid-off workers had lapsed. The plant had had a history of very troublesome labor relations and this was the chance for a new start.

Make room for creativity. "Creativity" conveys notions of originality, imagination, inventiveness, newness, and freshness. It may be defined as the power to create or, in the context of this chapter, the power to build. All actions begin with ideas, and building, whether it be of precedents and values or of brick and mortar, takes action. But not all ideas are creative as we normally use the term, and not all building is done creatively or even in keeping with the changing times. To cite a few examples, American Locomotive Company and Baldwin Locomotive Works, manufacturers of steam locomotives, did nothing to adjust to the threat of the diesel-electric locomotive introduced by General Motors. The ballpoint pen was first put on the market by Reynolds, a new company. Eversharp, Inc., a fountain pen maker, followed six months later, but Parker Pen Co. waited *nine years* to get into the ballpoint market.

I doubt that you needed to read these few examples to come to the conclusion that creativity is needed in organizations. The question is: How do you get it?

Probably the most important thing you can do is to make sure that there are as few impediments to creative behavior as possible. So much can be gained merely by removing roadblocks that you should give this the highest priority before deliberately taking steps to stimulate creativity.

Creativity is inhibited by a number of forces and attitudes. Two are fear and anxiety, which can be caused by a style of supervision that is essentially punitive—the type used by the manager who believes strongly in the "carrot and the stick." Of course, this type of management is counterproductive, especially with professional employees, but that doesn't mean it doesn't exist. People working under these circumstances are too concerned with carrying out orders, thereby avoiding "pain," to have the time or inclination to put their creative talents to work.

Perceived instability is another inhibiting factor. If your organization is going through, or people believe it is about to go through, the trauma of being reorganized or consolidated with another organization, creativity will be low.

Some of the forces in the working environment that can be used to stimulate creativity are goals, deadlines, freedom, autonomy, and support. Consider support. Creative output will be low if there are no rewards or recognition. Composers and writers are eager to get their works published for the recognition it brings as well as the monetary gain. You can encourage creativity in the future by demonstrating your appreciation of past creative efforts.

It is a misconception to believe that high levels of productivity occur in completely relaxed atmospheres. They do not. Tension can be a strong stimulant and cause productive, creative work to take place. Writers frequently work better under a deadline. Mozart completed his great opera *Don Giovanni* by working through the night before its premier performance. The goal of putting a man on the moon by 1970 inspired many to extend themselves in seeking answers to questions that had never been asked before.

To encourage creativity in your organization, your leadership must set goals and deadlines that cause people to stretch their talents fully believing that goals will be reached. Structure can be provided through meetings with agendas and formats designed to bring out creative ideas, unobstructed by past policies and actions. Brainstorming is an example.

Building creativity is essential to you as a manager of professionals. You encourage creativity by setting the environment, the policies, and the structure that are conducive to it.

How to Have the Self-confidence You Need to Be a Builder

All people who have progressed up the corporate ladder have at times been put in charge of organizational units in which there were many people who had a good deal more technical knowledge than they had. You have had or will have the same experience some day. Can you be a builder under these circumstances?

Of course, the answer is yes. But you have to believe it. In order to believe that you really can make a large contribution to the group and be a builder you have to believe in yourself. Believing in yourself is what self-confidence is all about.

Confidence is not only required when coming into a new situation but is vital to your success in any situation. Large doses (but not to the point of arrogance) are needed by the person who sets out to leave his mark on the organization. Installing new systems and new ideas and developing and launching new products require a tough self-confidence and unswerving faith that success will be attained. The best that can be hoped for from the timid and the fearful is that they can manage as the nonbuilder described at the beginning of this chapter.

The builder is confident that he will overcome the hurdles, and this confidence infects others. He treats the task as if there are no probabilities. He rarely thinks about the odds that he may fail once the undertaking has been started and never allows himself to reveal to his staff any lingering doubts that might still flash through his mind on rare occasions. This is the type of confidence that is vital if the commitment and dedicated efforts of others are to be enlisted. Can you imagine Winston Churchill telling the British in World War II that he hoped the war would turn out all right but he couldn't be sure? What he said on June 4, 1940, after the evacuation of the British army at Dunkirk was:

We shall not flag or fail. We shall go on to the end. We shall fight in France, we shall fight on the seas and oceans, we shall fight with growing confidence and growing strength in the air, we shall defend our island, whatever the cost may be, we shall fight on the beaches, we shall fight on the landing grounds, we shall fight in the fields and in the street, we shall fight in the hills; we shall never surrender.

One barrier to self-confidence is fear. In dealing with fear, the first question to ask is whether the fear is rational or irrational. There are rational fears that we would be foolhardy to dismiss from our minds. For example, we can place ourselves in situations where we face physical danger. The manager of a baseball team may know that if his team does not finish with more wins than losses, he will be fired. These are rational fears. They cannot be dismissed; you must take realistic steps to succeed, thereby avoiding the negative consequences you fear. Taking positive actions will cause you to concentrate on the desired result and put the fears in the background.

Often the more insidious and paralyzing fears for a manager are the irrational ones, like an unreasonable fear of failure which curtails new ideas and stymies creative people in your organization. It may be the fear of presenting a new proposal to higher managers because they might not think well of it, or it may be the fear of hiring a top performer because he might find things wrong with your organization and put you in a bad light with higher management. Generally, fears of this type are greatly exaggerated in your mind. Moreover, a person must have the opportunity to fail, and failure can be handled so that it becomes at least a partial success. The learning experience may give the organization strength for the future. Sometimes even when the main objective is not reached, by-products are produced, either tangible or intangible, in the form of better ways of doing business.

Cynicism is another attitude that destroys self-confidence. You have heard the person who can always be counted on to come up with a witty comment which depreciates and belittles the organization. Mistakes are the grist of his humor mill. This type of person can be very humorous, but he is not a builder.

If your style of humor runs to cynicism you are essentially a negative thinker and not a builder. The cynic looks for failure. He looks for opportunities to ridicule others. That's his material, and if he doesn't continually find new material he loses his audience. Cynicism may be fine for building a career as a critic or as a comedian but it has no place in the repertoire of a manager. Without exception, I have never known a chief executive officer who was a cynic.

The Secret to Having Self-confidence

Everybody knows that success is the foundation for self-confidence, but sometimes we learn the wrong lessons from our successes. Suppose, for example, that you have planned and installed a new incentive plan for salesmen. This may have been your first assignment in any aspect of wage and salary administration. After completing the task, the lesson that you may have taken from this experience is that you now know how to handle wage and salary assignments and would be successful in a similar undertaking in the future.

This is the wrong lesson. The right lesson is that *you have done something that you have never done before and have done it successfully.* The distinction is crucial. The builder must go into new areas. He must feel confident that he can succeed in doing what he has never done before. Otherwise he is not a builder but a person who has one year's experience over and over again.

This is not to suggest that everything is possible. I could not write a symphony or design an atomic submarine. But no one is going to ask me to do these things, and I certainly would have no reason to do them on my own. Instead, I am constantly asked to do things which are related to what I have done in the past but nevertheless mean extending my knowledge and breaking new ground.

In a consulting assignment I had quite a few years ago I was to find the best market for remote data processing services to serve small companies. The questions concerned the type of application (inventory control, cost accounting, and the like), the type of company (SIC Code), and location of concentrated markets. After about a week, the president of the firm asked me to give him a plan for my research. I replied that if I were to give him one right then I would probably have to make several changes in it later on, but if I waited for about a week or two, I could give him a firm schedule and plan. A more truthful answer might have been the thoughts that were really in mind as I answered his request, "I don't know what in hell I am doing right now, but in ten days I will." I had been in many new situations before, and I had learned that I always found a way to get the job done.

5

Building knowledge

Most management philosophies and systems, such as having good human relations, using management by objectives, and following a formal planning procedure, deal with the problem of *using* knowledge. They are intended to increase the ability and the desire of personnel to put their knowledge to work and to focus properly the application of knowledge to areas of opportunity and concern. Knowledge is not only a strength, it is an *asset*. As with any asset it must be managed.

Managing an asset has two highly interrelated aspects: controlling the value or size of the asset, and using the asset. It is important to make the distinction between the qualities of the asset itself and its application, because the distinction is a prelude to developing strategies for managing the value of the firm's most important asset—knowledge. Unlike most assets, knowledge doesn't wear out but improves with usage. When unused it has a limited "shelf life."

Every professional employee or knowledge worker is a part of the composite knowledge of the firm. He brings knowledge with him when he is hired and his knowledge grows on the job. Through hiring practices and the various avenues of development on the job, management determines to what extent knowledge is home grown and to what extent it is purchased in the labor market. A large diversified corporation, starting a formal planning system about five years ago, needed a corporate planner. Management decided to put a young man from one of the divisions in the post. He had knowledge of the corporation and an academic background which included an MBA. Having never been in a planning position before, he had to learn much about the function he had to perform. In this instance the corporation chose the alternative of "growing" the planning knowledge. Another choice would have been to hire an experienced corporate planner, who would then have to accumulate knowledge about the corporation and its businesses.

What Knowledge Is Important

Aside from the mental capabilities that any educated person should have, such as the ability to communicate, there are four areas of knowledge that directly relate to the decision-making capability of the manager or the professional. To be an effective decision maker, he or she must have competence in all four areas, although the relative importance of each varies according to business circumstances, the level of decision making, and the function.

Knowledge of human behavior. Occasionally you hear about a person who is apparently able to give directions to subordinates without any necessity for first thinking about how his orders will be received. This is a highly authoritarian style of leadership, and its viability rests on getting people who can produce under such circumstances. Even then, you could argue that there is knowledge about human behavior and that the manager has deliberately created the condition suitable to his style of management for his own personal reasons.

Far more typical is the manager who must fully employ the talents of his subordinates. He continually needs to create stimulation and motivation. He wants his employees to stretch their capacity for work and to increase their abilities. He realizes that his own contribution will be achieved largely by working through people.

Management principles. This is knowledge of administration, the manager's role, and the functions of management, which are variously defined as planning, organizing, directing, and controlling. Two of the nation's largest airlines at the time of this writing have chief executive officers who came from other industries. United Air Lines' Edward Carlson had been in charge of Western International Hotels, one of United's acquisitions, before he was nominated to replace a man in the number one spot who was steeped in airline experience. American Airlines chose Albert Casey, who had been president of Times Mirror Company. It is a safe bet that the boards of these two airlines rated both of these gentlemen very high in their ability to manage, to include their practical knowledge of the principles of management. Industry knowledge, as important as it is, was viewed to be of secondary importance in these two instances.

Industry knowledge. This area of knowledge is essential if a manager is to become a competent decision maker. According to *The Wall Street Journal,* one of the weaknesses of International Paper Company was a lack of industry knowledge among its top executives. Quoting industry analysts, the *Journal* says, "The result . . . has been to give short shrift to pulp and paper—to the point that untimely pricing decisions are routine, market shares have been lost, and management expertise in paper is sorely lacking at the highest levels."* J. Stanford Smith, chairman of the board, hails from General Electric, a company that is so well recognized for good management that its alumni are often sought after by other companies. Mr. Smith, believing that a good executive will function well in any business, has brought in a number of people from other industries. Only two of the four executive vice-presidents are considered to have a working knowledge of the paper industry. In spite of professional management, the lack of industry knowledge has been judged to be detrimental, at least for the present.

The importance of industry knowledge of a technical nature is especially evident in first-line supervisory positions. There is little opportunity for first-line supervisors to move from company to company to begin with, but when that opportunity exists, it is almost invariably open to only those who have had prior technical experience that closely parallels the requirements of the new job. Only after this qualification has been confirmed are abilities for managing and handling people considered.

Moreover, it is not always true that a good salesman can be successful in any industry. The technical aspects of the product or service, as well as the special needs and concerns of the customers, must be thoroughly understood. If the salesman has the qualities needed for success in sales but, whether through inexperience or intellectual limitation, he does not have the knowledge of his products, its uses, and his customers' needs, he will not be able to sell.

Business knowledge. Cutting across industry lines, business knowl-

---

* Susan Margolies, "Despite Vast Assets, International Paper Co. Fails to Lead Industry," *The Wall Street Journal,* August 30, 1977.

edge takes in such fields as accounting, computer systems, statistics, and principles of economics. The manager or the professional does not necessarily need to have detailed knowledge in these areas, unless he is responsible for a technical function drawing on these disciplines. What is required to varying degrees, depending on the position, is a general knowledge of the tools of business. It is important to understand the concepts and to be able to talk the language.

How to Plan for Knowledge

These four knowledge categories—human behavior, management principles, industry knowledge, and business knowledge—are a good starting point for evaluating the state of knowledge in an organization. However, a more detailed breakdown is needed as the basis for managing and building knowledge. Answers to the following four questions suggest the steps required in planning for knowledge:

What knowledge is needed now?
What knowledge is on hand?
What knowledge is needed for the future?
What has to be done to meet present and future needs?

All managers who consider themselves builders should answer these questions. The four-step procedure drawn from the answers to these questions can be applied at every level. It is not designed for the sole use of top management or the personnel department.

Step 1. Develop a list of knowledge success dimensions by analyzing the knowledge that is a prerequisite to success in your organization. What do you know that accounts for your organization's successes? What is it that your organization doesn't know or know well enough which causes failure and problems? How would strength in certain areas of knowledge lead to immediate improvements? In developing this breakdown use the four areas of knowledge discussed above as a guide, but don't be constrained by the idea that every point must fall into one of these four categories. Identifying the dimensions of knowledge is the prime purpose, not preparing a logically and neatly arranged list.

Some of the knowledge success dimensions may bear little resemblance to the divisions of subject matter in textbooks. To a company that owes its success to distributing paperbacks and magazines to retail outlets and local distributors, knowledge of truck transportation may be a vital element to its success. Knowledge of fabrics could be important to the profitability of an apparel manufacturer. Use the list below to prepare the dimensions of knowledge that are required for success in your organization.

Management
- Strategic planning
- Planning and control systems
- Time management
- Management by objectives
- Motivation and leadership
- Communication
- Conflict resolution
- Performance appraisal

Marketing
- Market planning
- Customers and market segments
- Merchandising
- Distribution systems, domestic and international
- Relative market share
- Advertising and promotion
- Sales and sales administration
- Market research
- Target customer

Competition
- Pricing policies
- Product/service
- Market penetration

Product/Service
- Technical characteristics
- Applications
- Customer appeal

Research and Development
- Electronics
- Physics
- Metallurgy, etc.

Engineering Design
- Mechanical engineering
- Electrical engineering, etc.

Manufacturing/Operations
- Manufacturing engineering
- Industrial engineering
- Production planning and control
- Inventory control
- Quality control
- Materials handling
- Facilities engineering and maintenance
- Cost control
- Industrial relations
- Numerical controlled equipment
- Micro-processors

Purchasing
- Sources of supply
- Commodity markets

Business Systems
- Data processing and transmission
- Word processing
- Internal control
- Management audit

Personnel
- Selection and recruitment
- Training
- Personnel services
- Wage and salary

Finance/Accounting
- Financial planning
- Budgeting and control
- Source of capital
- Cash management
- Cost accounting
- Credit management
- Insurance
- Real estate management
- Tax administration

Step 2. Survey the knowledge that is presently in the organization. This survey should not be based on a system operated by personnel that puts the formal education and history of job assignments on a computer, although this might be valuable as one source of information. The kind of a survey I am advocating must be done by those that have firsthand exposure to the capabilities of their subordinates and associates. The maximum number of people that one person might know sufficiently well would probably be in the range of 10 to 20.

The procedure for probing the extent of knowledge in the organization is to rate personnel by each knowledge success dimension on a scale of zero or blank to 3. A blank indicates that the person does not have enough knowledge to converse with professionals in the field without a tremendous amount of explanation. A one (1) shows that the person has general knowledge, two (2) that the person has a working knowledge of the field adequate for nearly all day-to-day situations, and three (3) that the person has great depth in the subject and can handle complex situations that are out of the ordinary. With these ratings you can compile a knowledge profile, such as the one shown in partial form in Figure 7.

This procedure is designed primarily to assist the manager to evaluate the knowledge in his organization going down one or two levels. It presumes that the manager is the decision maker and that, equipped with this knowledge, he can make decisions that build knowledge—or acquire it. If the critical infusion of knowledge through recruitment occurs at a level far below the manager who has completed a knowledge profile, then the people who will be the strength of the organization in the future are not rated on his knowledge profile because they are several rungs down the organizational hierarchy. The solution to this is to require that the lower-level manager also make a knowledge profile and that a summary of it be forwarded up the organization.

Step 3. Looking five or ten years ahead, repeat steps one and two. The results should be incorporated in the long-range strategic planning system that every company should have or be an adjunct to it. Strategic planning answers the question of what the company will be like in the future, taking into consideration all aspects of the business environment as they are anticipated for the future. From this process emerge strategies for new products, new markets, additional capabilities, growth in existing markets, retrenchment in some areas, and ways of coping with contingencies. But in well-run organizations, the stra-

	Davis	Smith	Jones
Management	2	2	2
Strategic planning	1	2	3
Planning and control systems	2	2	3
Time management	2	2	2
Management by objectives	1	1	2
Motivation and leadership	2	2	2
Communication	2	2	2
Conflict resolution	2	2	2
Performance appraisal	2	3	2
Marketing	1	3	1
Market planning		3	1
Customers and market segments		3	2
Merchandising	1	2	1
Etc.			

Figure 7. Knowledge profile (in partial form).

tegic planning process does not stop there. It also addresses the matter of what types and numbers of people will be needed—in other words, what dimensions of knowledge will be required.

I am familiar with a company that has a shortcoming at present in financial knowledge. There are a few people who are very astute in finance and have had the benefit of years of experience in solving knotty, high-level financial problems, and there are many others who have a good understanding of finance. But there is no one except the top two or three people in the organization with the knowledge to handle a major financial problem. This is a deficiency today. In the future it will be more of a liability, since it can be expected that this kind of business and the market it is in will see more complex financial problems in the future. This example illustrates the value of rating personnel in knowledge to identify the present and future capability of the organization for solving problems.

Technology is a good place to begin for taking a look at the future. All businesses are affected by technological change although the pace of technological change varies widely from industry to industry and is never at a constant rate. When a company is able to foresee that the impact of a new technology is, say, five years away, the time to start staffing for technological change is now. Although it is usually possible to hire the engineers and technicians when the need arises, it is not possible to provide effective management of new technology overnight. This requires people who understand the company and are able to integrate the work of technical people into the mainstream of the company's operations. It calls for an understanding of the business and the company and for the ability to coordinate.

The experiences of operations research or management science organizations within corporations illustrate this point very well. In March 1970, at a symposium on corporation simulation models, some 25 papers were presented. Repeatedly, the speakers reported that the first attempt to install an operations research group in their organizations had failed and that all the personnel had been discharged. Second attempts to resurrect operations research often failed also. However, the third attempt was generally successful. The successful groups had succeeded in creating corporate models that achieved good results and were being used by top management. Although there is no proof, I suspect that a major cause for the failure of the first groups was not incompetence in a technical sense but was perhaps largely attributable to a lack of understanding between them and management. And although their dismissal was no doubt looked upon as a failure, they did succeed in raising the knowledge level for their particular type of technology. This paved the way for the second or third groups, whom management no doubt welcomed as people who were "practical" and people to whom they could relate.

Taking a hard look at technology can uncover shifts in the fundamental nature of the business. One of the best examples of this is the effect of the widespread use of complex data processing systems on public accounting firms, which now have to be alert for computer fraud, estimated to be as much as $300 million annually. Traditional knowledge of accounting principles and practices is no longer adequate. New dimensions of knowledge are currently required and will be even more so in the future. To meet the need, accounting firms are hiring computer specialists and training their auditing staffs in computer technology.

Step 4. Make an evaluation and a plan for what has to be done to meet present and future needs. Putting together a list of knowledge success dimensions and a knowledge profile is the only rational basis for planning recruitment and training. Unfortunately, it is rarely done well. Managers are sometimes tempted to do what one personnel director of a large retailing chain says is the tendency in the industry—to hire in "their own image."

As important as it is, recruitment is only one of three general approaches to building knowledge. The others are training and using people. Training refers to all the programs for classes, coaching, rotating new employees through several departments, workshops, and so on. Usually these programs are formally identified and under the surveillance of the training or personnel department.

Using people might be called on-the-job training, although people given new assignments often do not view them as training, and in fact, commonly lament that they are being thrown into a new situation without adequate preparation. Moreoever, their superiors are looking primarily for performance in the job and frequently give the training that occurs a low secondary priority, if it is considered at all. However, the knowledge-building value of being thrown into a new assignment, if the person survives the first six months, may be very great.

Determining what knowledge is needed and what is available and then planning what to do about it should be part of the management process at every level. Furthermore, it is a process that lends itself very well to group involvement. What dimensions of knowledge are essential to success is something that is of interest to all employees, and a better list may be compiled with participation. What should be done to train and use people to build knowledge is likewise a topic of vital concern to most employees. Discussions on this topic, you can be assured, will increase the awareness of the strengths and weaknesses of the group in addition to stimulating all persons to gain more knowledge. Meetings of this type can be used to increase motivation as well as to lay plans for the future. In addition, when the present staff sees that they cannot overcome gaps in knowledge by themselves, they will be much more receptive to bringing new highly qualified persons into the group.

What You and Your Subordinates Should Know About Your Jobs

The job holder must be the resident expert in that job. This is a standard that all managers should insist upon without exception. It means that the person in the job is required to know more about that job than anyone else.

Being the expert in the job carries with it a responsibility for knowing how the job relates to other positions, other functions, and other departments. Often the objection is raised that the person in the job cannot be expected to know how his job fits into the larger picture since this is the responsibility of his supervisor. Robert Dockson, chairman of the board of California Federal, does not subscribe to this notion. He says, "I know there are companies where divisions really build Chinese walls between themselves. For example, a president might very well say to a personnel director, 'I want you to handle personnel only, and not get involved in the problems of the loan division, banking division, the controller's division, or what not.' "* Mr. Dockson believes that when there are rigid separations between company divisions, profit goals cannot be obtained. Instead, people with different responsibilities and functions have to work together, with each having an understanding of the roles of the others. There is no arguing with the fact that the higher-level manager should have a *greater* understanding of how the various functions fit together and how to achieve the needed coordination between them. This, after all, is one aspect of his job and he is expected to be the resident expert in *his* job, but that does not preclude a general understanding at lower levels.

The requirements for job knowledge can be portrayed by using the concept of the T profile. A person should be deep in his specialty and his job, and broad in other dimensions of knowledge. The concept of the T profile is so illustrative and powerful that it should be ingrained into the thinking of all professional and supervisory personnel. According to the T concept, which is related to knowledge success dimensions, people should have general knowledge (a rating of 1) in many areas of knowledge that relate to the business, and for knowledge required for their jobs they should be at the 2 or 3 level.

The importance of the T profile is easily seen by looking at people who are deficient in either depth or breadth. We have all known people who were experts in everything from the abacus to zoos but who have never shown more than a superficial knowledge of their jobs. They may not lack the ability to discuss business in general, or theories of motivation, and there is nothing wrong with their mental

* Personal communication, November 3, 1977.

capacity, but they have never invested the time and the effort to become the resident expert in their jobs. Regarding the knowledge related to their jobs, they are barely at the 2 level. To varying degrees there are people like this in every organization. Usually they perform well enough on the work they are given to remain on the payroll, but they are passed over for the really tough assignments, and may require more direction than should be the case on routine tasks. More often than not they realize they have not been putting their best effort into their work, which allows them to take a philosophical attitude when they see others going up the corporate ladder.

The person who is exceedingly strong in his specialty but has no breadth is a more serious case and can become a detriment to the organization. This is the man or woman who is recognized by all as a real expert in the field. When there is any problem relating to his knowledge or the function of his office, his advice is sought. He knows that he is good and so do others.

His strength can become a weakness for the organization as time passes. He sees others, less qualified than he, in his opinion, advancing to higher positions. At first he may shrug this off as an oversight on the part of higher management, believing that his turn will soon come. When it doesn't, he becomes disgruntled and often conducts his own function with an inward-looking, technical singlemindedness that reduces its and his value to the organization.

From his viewpoint, having proved to one and all that he can do the job he has been assigned, he should be given the chance to prove he can do the next higher job. But unfortunately for him, management doesn't look at his qualifications quite the same way. When there is a need to fill an important position, management looks to those who are most likely to succeed in the *new* position, not necessarily to those who are most successful in their present positions. What they are looking for is the person with the T profile, the person who has demonstrated ability to perform superbly in his present job and also has the breadth of knowledge to adjust quickly to new demands and to add new specialized job knowledge.

Accumulating breadth of knowledge has been the tenet of Robert Wilson, chief executive officer of Memorex Corporation, and one of the factors that account for his success. Early in his career he made moves from engineering, to marketing, to international operations. During his 28 years at General Electric, he worked in 20 different businesses. He set out to learn all phases of the business fully aware of the risks. He has said that if he had failed to perform anywhere along the line, he would have been out—after investing that much time, it would have been difficult to start over again.

It has been said many times that it is not *what* you know but *who* you know that counts. Although not totally false, the saying obfuscates the real truth. The fact is that the person who may know people at high levels who are in a position to elevate him will most assuredly not be promoted in any well-run organization unless he is also perceived to be a highly competent person. On the other hand, those who have an outstanding record of performance often become visible to higher management. Who you know still counts, but for most people it is what you know that affords the opportunity to be recognized.

How to Grow Knowledge

Establish the principle. Establishing the standard that each person is expected to be the resident expert in his own job is perhaps the biggest step a company can take toward building the collective pool of knowledge. This is a standard that should be applied to all jobs which require judgment and discretion.

To see how this principle works, consider the manager of a production control department who has a supervisor of scheduling as one of his subordinates. The production control manager is correct to insist that his supervisor of schedules know more thoroughly than anyone else the system for scheduling orders in the factory, have general knowledge of the schedules that are in effect, and be knowledgeable about scheduling systems in general used in similar manufacturing operations.

The last point is worth reemphasizing because it is here that so many people fall short. The true professional is not content to know the workings of his own scheduling system but understands other options available. He knows the advantages and disadvantages of each as well as his own; he has good reasons for choosing his present system. He is open to new developments and is prepared to make changes for the better. This is the professional scheduler who is recognized by his superior, the manager of production control, as being the expert in scheduling. As for his T profile, the supervisor of scheduling has greater depth, and is expected to have greater depth, than anyone else in all matters related to scheduling. His knowledge is at the 3 level.

Create a learning environment. Another important step toward building knowledge is creating a learning environment within the work setting. One way to do this is by arranging situations that cause people to learn from each other. Meetings with well-planned agendas can be used for this purpose. This can even be carried to the point of having professional development sessions conducted by the personnel themselves. The participants can be asked to give a presentation on a preassigned topic. I have been privileged to witness some superb reports complete with visual aids that relatively low-level employees have made in sessions of this type.

Work in groups. Organizing work that puts two or more people working together is an excellent way of stimulating the growth of knowledge. Project and task teams have this advantage.

Be receptive to ideas. Probably the most important underpinning of a learning environment is the receptivity of the boss to new ideas. If the boss never has time to listen to the ideas of his subordinates, the effect is stultifying. If he feels that the status quo will produce permanent excellence and is impatient with new ideas and new knowledge, the effect is worse than stultifying. On the other hand, when the boss shows he is eager to learn himself, this creates a challenging and exciting atmosphere. Furthermore, a well-informed boss puts still more pressure on his subordinates to gain still greater knowledge to retain the resident-expert status in their jobs.

Join professional organizations. Encouraging your subordinates to join professional organizations and to attend seminars and university classes is another step that builds knowledge.

Reward knowledge. Those persons who have accumulated knowledge and are the resident experts in their jobs should receive the reward of recognition.. As a supervisor you do this by consulting with them and bringing them into meetings with more senior management. If there is a problem with a vendor of sufficient magnitude to involve senior management, bring the buyer or the purchasing agent who is best informed to the meeting. If you are this person's superior, your bringing him into the meeting should be looked at with favor by the others present. It will not detract from your reputation. On the contrary, to any but the most dissentious or insecure management group, your action would be interpreted for what it is: tapping the source of the most detailed and up-to-date knowledge plus a move that builds strong subordinates. You become recognized as a builder.

Assign challenging work. Difficult assignments are both a reward and a challenge. The person who has demonstrated capability on previous assignments is obviously a candidate for more difficult tasks, providing further opportunity to acquire more knowledge.

Difficult assignments should be treated as a reward. They often provide a person with exposure to higher management and add to his or her reputation for accomplishment. It is, of course, important that you emphasize your belief that challenging work is an opportunity and a reward instead of a problem and a penalty or something to be avoided.

Knowledge-Building Work

It is no doubt true that all but highly repetitive work contributes to knowledge to some degree. But there are assignments that, by their very nature, are knowledge building, such as those involved in problem solving or planning.

Aside from minor differences, numerous authorities and authors have identified the steps in analytical problem solving as (1) defining the problem, (2) gathering information, (3) analyzing the data, (4) formulating alternative solutions, (5) making a choice, and (6) implementing the solution, including following up. If you assign a person or persons to tackle a problem and these steps are followed it is virtually guaranteed that there will be a substantial addition to their knowledge. They will have to look at the problem from all perspectives—for example, how it affects morale, the work itself, the linkages with other groups or organizations—in order to define it properly in the first place and to proceed through the rest of the steps. In other words, a systems approach should be used. If one part of the system is changed, the effect on the remainder of the system should be understood and evaluated.

Not all thinking takes place by what may be thought of as logical processes. Creative or intuitive problem solving is another route. No doubt there are wide differences in the creative abilities of people. Being creative or analytical is not an either-or proposition. In fact, if we treat creativity as a gift that only the very talented have, we are making a serious mistake that limits our own capabilities.

Although the processes of logical problem solving and creative problem solving may seem to be dissimilar at first glance, they have much in common. Contrary to what some may imagine, productive creative thinking does not occur only in a totally detached environment. Instead, the creative juices are much more likely to flow when the problem is defined and the subconscious mind is left to work on it.

Gathering information is an essential step in both processes. A goal-oriented creative thinker will immerse himself in facts and information relative to his subject. He lets this information incubate over a period of time; his subconscious is working on the problem. Finally, solutions appear. Admiral Elmer T. Westfall, who achieved a reputation in the Navy for his success in managing shipyards, has said that when a good solution to a difficult problem is not forthcoming, he puts all his information in the desk drawer for several days. When he takes it out again, he has never failed to find the right solution that escaped him on the first try.

Another great knowledge-building assignment is accumulating external information about the market and all dimensions of the business environment. Such information is needed for strategic and tactical planning, is vital to market planning, and is generally required in the planning for any specialized function. Just what information should be obtained and how it should be obtained are topics of large scope. Since it would be impossible to cover all situations, I shall offer a few general principles and examples to shed some light on how an assignment for gathering information might be carried out.

Begin by looking at the market or the potential market and the four sectors of the total business environment, which are economic, technical, social/demographic, and political/legal. For an industrial product or service, the economic study includes getting information on the structure of the industries to be served, in addition to giving consideration to the national and local economy. This means answering the questions of how many customers there are, where they are located, and what their needs are. For a consumer service or product, it may be helpful to know something about the economic condition of the typical target customer. The entire advertising campaign of Glendale Federal Savings, a California savings and loan company, is directed toward older people ("for a better second half") simply because this is the group that has money to put into a savings account.

Second in importance to knowing more about the market is knowing more about the potential and actual competition for the market. Data on this topic might include the pricing policies of major competitors, the quality and extent of the service offered, the geographical penetration, the market segments that are the targets of particular competitors, and their share of the market.

Technological change can and does affect the market itself. But often it affects how a market is served or the product produced. It is imperative that firms keep up with changing technology that relates to their businesses. Technology in data processing and data transmission is undergoing rapid change. Assigning a person to dig into how your company might benefit from advances in data processing is the type of knowledge-building assignment I refer to.

The social/demographic sector covers attitudes reflected in many forms such as environmental concerns, lifestyles, position on abortion. Government regulations, court decisions, legislation that is in effect or has the potential of becoming law comprise the legal and political sector.

A single knowledge-building assignment does not necessarily cover all the sectors outlined above. As a practical illustration of how information-gathering work builds knowledge and contributes to the planning process, take the case of a medium-size company that is considering investing in mini-computer-controlled machine tools. The company might feel that the switch is inevitable, but the real question is the timing. A medium-size company usually cannot afford to be a leader in installing advanced machine tooling. There are too many start-up problems as both the vendor and its initiating customers go through a learning process.

To help answer this problem of timing, three engineers are selected to evaluate the costs and benefits of the equipment as they exist today and as they are likely to be in the future. The three-man team will have to codify the benefits and the features of the equipment. Their first task is to assure themselves that they know what types of products they can expect to be producing in the future. In other words, the assignment starts with an understanding of the markets that will be served.

Next the three-man team will have to analyze the benefits and the features of the equipment. In this regard, they will be exploring its versatility, cost, expected production rates, and precision. The study will require establishing unambiguous definitions for these dimensions. Then the team will have to arrive at a means for measuring each of these dimensions so that comparisons can be made.

The team would then research the past to identify as accurately as possible what has been the trend for each of these dimensions. Costs should be put on a real dollar basis. History will probably show that tolerances have improved, speeds have increased, and that more operations of greater complexity can be performed by a single machine. Furthermore, it will no doubt be true that the real cost of these benefits will have gone down. From such a study of the past, some projections of future costs and benefits may be made. Opinions may be solicited from manufacturers of the equipment and from others who have made purchases.

The end product of the study by the three-man engineering team would be recommendations for the planned conversion to automated equipment based on an engineering evaluation. Before acting, the company would need to verify that the recommendations are consistent with marketing plans and that they meet financial criteria for acceptance.

To take another example, suppose a collection agency is planning to open an office in another state. Whether or not this expansion will be made depends on whether the expected revenues will meet the goals for profit margins and return on investment. To make the decision, the company must know something about the potential markets in the new state. Perhaps this is a collection agency that has been very successful in collecting delinquent accounts for hospitals. In that event, knowledge about the hospital market in the new state would be essential.

There are many other variables to be explored in the economic realm, but this is a decision that rests as much on the political and social dimensions as on the economic. Collection practices are regulated by state laws as well as by federal law. Furthermore, society's views concerning collection vary from rural to urban areas, and depend on the nature of the debt, whether, for example, for health care or the purchases of hard goods. These views are reflected in the attitudes of both the debtor and the creditor.

Most other types of knowledge-building work result from the normal operating needs of the business. They include new assignments, new geographical locations, and transfers to different departments. However, a large number of professional employees are not affected by new assignments or are rarely given new assignments. When they leave school they have a background that prepares them for many entry-level jobs and tasks. Upon being hired they find that the job requires them to exercise one part of their knowledge and to utilize only a few of their skills. As time goes on, these skills become more highly perfected but the employee becomes more narrow in his outlook and in his talents. Transfers to new departments do not come often enough to be relied upon as a knowledge builder. Within the framework of the existing job, management must be able to assign knowledge-building work.

Taking a Systems Approach to Knowledge

A system that retains its viability and effectiveness is a system that learns. It is able to assimilate new information about the environment in which it operates, and it is able to assess the effects of its actions. It is a system that is searching for the truth and one that tracks reality. Knowledge is not some absolute quality or asset that a manager seeks to accumulate as he might inventory or cash. Its nature is too dynamic and volatile for that. The systems approach asserts that new knowledge, new ideas, and new inventions find their way into the system because the system is seeking to find them, much as a radar beam is seeking to find aircraft, and once finding the knowledge, disseminates it where it is needed within the system. This approach conceives of knowledge as a constantly flowing stream. Implied in this concept is the realization that:

1. What was thought to be true in the past may have never been true.
2. What was true in the past may not be true now.
3. What was valuable knowledge in the past may not be now, and may be even less so in the future.
4. Ignorance, misconception, and knowledge can exist side by side.

There are hundreds of examples to show that managers have frequently not taken the systems approach to finding truth and new knowledge or disseminated the knowledge to the people in the organization that needed to have it. Henry Ford's insistence on producing black Model T Fords, in contrast with the varied product line of General Motors during the 1920s, is one of the most renowned. The Ford Motor Company operated as a closed system, not assimilating information and not learning.

Of more recent vintage in the automobile industry is the failure to recognize the growing preference that Americans have for cars which economize on gasoline. More than seven years after the oil embargo by OPEC, the major automobile producers have still not made the major shifts in their product lines that must take place eventually.

Regarding human relations, some companies have deluded themselves about the attitudes of their employees, just as government frequently misread the preferences and emotions of the populace. Departments, too, are capable of making decisions based on false or outdated premises and follow procedures which are outmoded. In one company, for example, a maintenance department was inspecting equipment four times as often as was required. Hiring decisions may be based on what a department has done in the past and not what it is going to be faced with in the future. Sometimes a department believes that an internal organization change would be disruptive and produce no significant benefits, only to find when forced into making the change that new initiative and increased creativity is the result. This has been exemplified time and time again when a team organization is carved out of a functional organization.

The question of how to take a systems approach to knowledge requires an answer. Unfortunately, there is no short answer. The various facets of the answer are found in setting goals, making realistic plans, and establishing a flexible, task-oriented organization. Those, of course, are not trivial subjects. Their importance is recognized in subsequent chapters.

Being a Leader in Knowledge

I would like to close this chapter with a few points about building your own knowledge. In spite of counsel to the contrary, your superior may very well not give you knowledge-building work. He may be immensely satisfied with the normal work you are doing, which is causing your T profile to grow in depth but to shrivel at the top. He may not feel any responsibility at all for your lacking the breadth to be promotable. You must take the responsibility yourself for increasing your knowledge. You must take the time to read the books, to attend the classes, to read the journals, to attend the professional meetings, and to seek out other professionals with whom you can exchange ideas and who stimulate your own intellectual inquisitiveness. Within the limits of good judgment, you should volunteer for special assignments and transfer to new opportunities.

How you use your specialized knowledge can be an indicator of your breadth. In meetings you certainly should contribute to the discussion by giving the group the benefit of your specialized knowledge. You need to be emphatic in expressing the facts and the opinions that you hold, making them perfectly clear to the group. On the other hand, you should demonstrate that you have an appreciation for other points of view, and above all, you should not seem to be provincial to the group. If you appear to be the latter, it is a sign that you do not have the breadth of knowledge that is required to fully understand all facets of the discussion or the problem.

Another point: Avoid being laden down with trivia. There are some people who believe they are impressive by seeming to have memorized every part number and every current expense. At meetings they can cite fact after fact, but often the point they are making is obscure. Now certainly, if a particular part is involved in a production problem, or if certain expenses have been identified as being out of line, you should know about these, as a matter of practicing management by exception. But the person whose head is full of numbers often displays a lack of comprehension for concepts and principles. He appears to be deficient in the area of knowledge I call management principles, and he conveys an impression of having little breadth.

Anyone who has ever worked in intelligence knows that information has a time value. What is secret today will become unclassified in the future. There is a time value associated with all knowledge in the world of business and technology. To be a leader in knowledge, you must be up to date. If you know about some technical advance soon after it is available, you are a much more valuable employee than the person who finds out about it years later. The same is true for management techniques.

A final point is to let your mind be an open window to new ideas which may come from any direction. Often knowledge which is not relevant now will be in the future. Although I have never heard them state it explicitly, the successful executives I have known are continually asking, by their actions, "How can I get more exposure to new ideas and new knowledge?"

6

How to create responsibility for accomplishment

To most managers responsibility is a commitment to pursue results through effective work, to persist in seeking the desired outcome. The perseverance that a person employs to get results and the dedication that he or she demonstrates toward the aims are measurements of his or her responsibility. True responsibility goes beyond the limit of rationality.

To further clarify, accountability is a less encompassing obligation or commitment. A person can be held accountable for what he does and for doing those things that are within his power to do. He can be held accountable for an achievable level of quality. For example, the diamond cutter can be held accountable for turning out high-quality gems. The financial officer is most certainly accountable for accurate summarization of the financial transactions he receives. In a sense, the financial officer cannot be held strictly accountable for accurate financial reporting if, for example, operating personnel who are not under his control are careless in reporting their time by account number or in charging materials to requisitions. In the same vein, the salesman cannot be held responsible for making his sales quota. He is strictly accountable for making calls on customers and making proposals and presentations of professional quality, but he has no power to make people buy.

The concept of responsibility is somewhat unjust because it puts a person into a position of being accountable for matters which are beyond the limit of his control. Whereas there seems to be little difference between the diamond cutter's responsibility and accountability for producing high-quality gems, there is a big difference between the two for the salesman and the financial officer. Yet as unjust or irrational as it may be, the practice in business is to hold the salesman responsible for meeting his goal and to hold the financial officer responsible for accurate financial reporting. The old adage that a person's authority should equal his responsibility is rarely true in management positions and frequently not true in other jobs as well. The responsible person feels an obligation for getting results which transcends the limits of his own capacity for direct action. The financial officer who did not feel the emotional commitment to report accurately the financial condition of the firm, no matter what the obstacles, would not be worth his salt.

The examples of the salesman and the financial officer demonstrate three points regarding the nature of responsibility. First, commitment to effectiveness. Second, it is largely an emotional commitment. And finally, a person's authority is rarely great enough to encompass the responsibility that he accepts. Rather, he is dependent on the performance of others for the attainment of his own goals.

Signs of the Committed Employee

Responsible employees are not always the easiest to work with. They may show their emotions in a work-related confrontation, they may be pushy in their perseverance, and they may well challenge you as their superior to make changes and improvements at your level or higher. In other words, having fully committed employees can be a very taxing experience as well as being tremendously productive and stimulating. You can recognize committed employees by six charactersitcs.

1. *They will attain personal satisfaction from achieving results.* There will be a sense of pride in the work they do. Meeting goals of quality, cost, or delivery will be uplifting and a stimulant for further achievement. Sometimes a fully committed employee will devote

himself so completely to a task that his energy and emotions are drained at its conclusion. When this happens, he will need time to recoup before undertaking another arduous task.

This principle, among a few others, was demonstrated in an experience that a company in the aerospace industry had some years ago. It had won a fixed-price contract for electronic equipment by submitting a very low bid. Management decided that the only opportunity for making a profit was in setting up a special group with a very low overhead. The normal production control, inventory control, and production planning procedures, which were highly automated with more sophisticated features than were needed on this project, would be totally bypassed. These functions would be performed manually by one person with some help from the line foremen. The same frugal approach was used for quality control, purchasing, and other functions. Months later, after much hard work, the project was successful in meeting the objectives of cost, delivery date, and quality.

At the project's completion, the superintendent of the manufacturing group called his staff together and outlined a new project that would soon be started. To his surprise, he had a rebellion on his hands. At that point his people were physically and emotionally exhausted. They were not in the mood to hear about another demanding assignment. To make matters worse, they did not feel that they had received any reward for their efforts. In fact, some felt that being cordoned off from the rest of the organization, so to speak, precluded any possibility for promotion.

2. *Fully responsible employees will assess the feasibility of accomplishing the desired results.* They will not become committed unless they believe that the task is possible, and, most significantly, they will tell you if they believe that it will result in failure. This is in contrast to those who are not concerned with being effective and are content to go through the procedure, feeling no responsibility when the desired end is not reached.

John W. Atkinson, a noted psychologist, proposed a theory that is relevant to this characteristic of committed employees. He considered the question of risk taking and motivation. His conclusion is shown diagrammatically in Figure 8. Productive people who are risk takers shy away from the risk that is too great to be accomplished and the task that has virtually no risk at all. They are most motivated by moderate risks that they believe they can overcome. They are success-oriented but do not derive satisfaction from doing the ordinary.

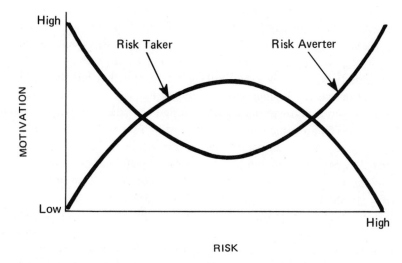

Figure 8. Motivation of risk takers (success-oriented) and risk averters (failure-avoidance-oriented).

The opposite characteristics are displayed by the risk averters. They are attracted to the jobs having no risk. Curiously, they are also willing to proceed with the task that has very high risk. Their thinking in the latter case, where Murphy's Law is inevitable, is that there is no stigma for failure because the task is recognized as being impossible anyway. This person is not success-oriented and not concerned with effectiveness; the prime concern is avoidance of loss of face.

3. *Responsible people provide backup and coverage.* A baseball player will back up a teammate who is fielding a ball. A football player will assist another who is making a tackle to make sure. These are common examples of a kind of action by responsible employees that is probably best illustrated by the story of the Dutch boy who put his finger in the hole in the dike to prevent a major problem.

A corollary of Murphy's Law is, "It is impossible to make anything foolproof because fools are so ingenious." You could substitute irresponsible employees for "fools" without losing this corollary's tongue-in-cheek veracity. But responsible employees are a different story. They know what is supposed to happen and what work must get done. If a co-worker or a supervisor makes an error through action or omission, they are there to help or to fill in the gap.

Not only is it impossible to make foolproof plans, but it is also impossible (or nearly so) to plan so perfectly that the desired goal will be reached by carrying out to the letter the details of the original plan. Instead, interpretations and adjustment must be made along the line. Some responsible person must step in to perform the task that was not identified originally. Responsibility is the mortar that fills the cracks.

4. *Committed employees make appropriate and realistic derivative plans.* Operations planning is a process that cascades down the organization. If you are a manager, your subordinates make derivative plans to carry out what you want done. Suppose that there are three jobs that they can work on and that the frequency and nature of decisions like this make it impractical for you to be consulted. One of the jobs came to them late and is behind schedule. Another is very profitable and its completion would reflect very favorably on the financial statement for the month. The third could be completed under budget, boosting the reputation of the department. Which will be worked on first? If your subordinates are committed to your goals, they can be counted on to consider the underlying purposes and intentions of the broadly outlined plans they receive from you in making the appropriate selection. Then they will go about planning realistically how to get the job done.

5. *Being fully committed, responsible people experience apprehension and anxiety when actual results indicate that objectives will not be met.* They react by diligently taking whatever steps are in their power to correct the situation. Faced with the three choices described above and unable to achieve the desired outcome, they would be forthright in reporting the condition. In these and similar circumstances, they will ask unhesitatingly for assistance from their superiors when they deem it necessary to attain success.

Asking for help, however, is probably the most difficult thing a responsible employee can do, and you must encourage even the most responsible to request assistance when needed. A responsible person may not ask for help when he should because he may want to be completely convinced, as a matter of exercising his responsibility, that outside assistance is really needed before he makes the request. Consequently, help could be too late. Another reason is fear of losing control of the work, or of receiving mandates to do what he believes should not be done. Moreover, asking for help probably goes against his self-image as an achiever. These three reasons combine to create a tendency to hope that somehow all will be well when results indicate otherwise, or that obstacles can be overcome with the resources at hand when this is not realistic. What can offset this tendency?

The answer is a deeply felt responsibility to the task. It has to be great enough to prevail over any personal, and no doubt irrational, fears about asking for help. If people are insecure in their positions, it will be more difficult for them to admit that they need assistance. However, if they do not get it and they need it, the task will suffer and they will experience great anxiety stemming from the conflict between their sense of responsibility to the task and their dread of asking for help.

6. *When Murphy's Law strikes, responsible employees are able to weather the storm and regain momentum.* In spite of good planning and strong underpinning systems, there are times when things *do* go wrong. These are times when everyone must chip in with a solid individual and cooperative performance. Good organizations, which are essentially good systems, have the ability to sustain and absorb shock. The organization, meaning the people in it, learn from the experience and are stronger for it. An organization that is able to display this power of resurgence, has responsible employees.

We have conveyed a concept of responsibility which places demands and challenges on those who accept it and makes outstanding performance possible. We have shown how the responsible employee behaves. Now the big question is: How can you foster this type of responsibility in your subordinates?

There is no single answer to this question. A variety of conditions must prevail and a number of steps must be taken. They may be grouped under five headings: establishing ideals and goals, ideals and responsibility, conflicting responsibilities, the job itself, and the style of management.

Establishing Ideals and Goals

An ideal or an ideal state is something sought after but never fully reached. It is synonymous with perfection. The ideals found in the business world pertain to the ends or purposes of the business as well as its means or ways of doing business. Frequently, the ideal is the basis for a tangible goal or objective, for example, to maximize profits, or to eliminate employee turnover except through death and retirement. These are realistic goals from which to assess performance. Other ideals, such as being an excellent corporate citizen in the community, are not amenable to specificity.

It is important to have ideals that are well known and accepted in the organization because it is to these that you want your subordinates to be responsible. Ultimately, it is not to the job, or to the project, and most certainly not to the supervisor as a person that people have true responsibility, but it is to the ideals that lie behind each of these. The ideal may be producing high-quality work or securing the full satisfaction of customers.

Ideals are vital to organizations in crises or during times of rapid change. At such times rallying around an ideal is almost an automatic reaction by companies, just as countries appeal to patriotism in time of war. People need to know that the old values are still important and will be upheld. Inasmuch as responsible people employ their efforts and talents guided by commitment to an ideal, they need to be assured that their commitment is in harmony with the ideals of the company.

Powerful ideals, created by powerful men, have shaped the destiny of organizations. The early success of the Ford Motor Company was due to Henry Ford's obsession to make automobiles accessible to the common worker of that era. J. F. Lincoln, of Lincoln Electric, holds the ideal that the claims of shareholders come behind those of employees. Although this policy seems to have benefited shareholders greatly too, with dividends and increases in stock value, one outgrowth of this ideal was a formal guarantee of continuous employment for all regular employees.

Who makes ideals? Managers and professionals at every level have a responsibility for establishing ideals. First, they must reinforce the ideals of the organization as a whole and those of the unit of which they are a part. Second, they must establish ideals which are consistent with and perhaps amplify the ideals of the larger organization.

Actions and proclamations. Ideals become ingrained in organizations by repetitive proclamation and by actions which are seen as putting the ideal into practice. Both are vital. Proclamation gives meaning and explanation to the actions. But without actions, the proclamations are soon perceived as insincere.

To a large extent, reinforcing ideals is opportunistic. You cannot identify most of the actions and opportunities for proclaiming the ideals in advance. You have to be alert for circumstances that allow you to take some specific action or to make a decision that reinforces them. If you contend that a high level of professionalism is required, this will have to be supported by personnel development programs and selection processes. Whom you hire and whom you send to a seminar are specific actions that will add to or detract from the ideal.

The informality of any social occasion affords an opportunity for you to reinforce the ideals of your group and your company. For example, at a company dinner the discussion might lead to events and personalities of the past that have contributed to tradition. During business hours, there is rarely the opportunity or the time to relate such anecdotes, real or apocryphal, yet these can hold powerful messages.

No doubt the strongest actions that management can take are those that penalize personnel who do not uphold the ideals of the organization and reward those who do. As the chief executive officer of a corporation recently reminded me, "The incentive might be as limited as merely staying on the payroll." In 1919, Calvin Coolidge, then Governor of Massachusetts, became a national hero by denying striking Boston policemen the right to return to their jobs and proclaiming that there is no right to strike when public safety is involved.

Ideals and Responsibility

The person who thinks of himself as an achiever is demonstrating responsibility. The achiever finds a way to get things done by enlisting the aid of those who can help, and this often requires going beyond the strict limits of authority. This does not mean that the achiever usurps the authority of someone else, but that frequently the willing cooperation of others must be solicited and obtained.

The relationship between responsibility and achievement is reciprocal. Just as a sense of responsibility will produce achievement, so achievement will ultimately produce a sense of responsibility. The implication of this axiom for you as a manager should be obvious. If you can stress achievement, get people to achieve, and recognize achievement, you will ultimately build responsibility.

The ideals a person holds are very much a part of his self-image. A trend that is expected to continue for many years is for professionals to place the ideals of their discipline ahead of those of the organization for which they work. Mobility of the workforce, more specialization required as organizations and their functions become more complex, and more highly educated and trained personnel contribute to this trend.

When working with this type of person, your concern is to do two things. One is to establish the ideals of the organization in the mind of the professional as firmly as possible. (Remember, we didn't say that he has no company ideals, but that these are not predominant.) The second is that where company and professional ideals intersect, use that intersection to your interest. Stress to your subordinates that the two sets of ideals actually do have much in common. Make the point that the true professional uses his skill in ways that are the most beneficial to the organization, that the strength of the profession rests in the long run on its usefulness to organizations and through them to society.

The old story of the three stonecutters illustrates this point. The first stonecutter, asked what he was doing, replied, "I am doing a fair day's work." The second said, "I am cutting the best stones that can be cut." The third stonecutter proclaimed, "I am building a cathedral." The ideals of the first are capable of producing such a limited sense of responsibility that it scarcely merits the use of the term. The third puts the ideals of the organization in the preeminent position, either subordinating his professionals ideals to these or reconciling the two—working at the intersection, so to speak.

The second stonecutter exemplifies the person who has allegiance to professional ideals. You cannot let him spend the time to cut perfect stones for a part of the cathedral which does not require this level of perfection, just as you cannot let the cost accountant create the perfect cost accounting system that goes far beyond the needs of your company. This is the situation that calls for your leadership in upholding company ideals.

Conflicting Responsibilities

What is commonly called responsibility is actually a product of two elements—the ideal which a person is responsible to, and his emotional commitment to that ideal. Society recognizes that ideals have different values. Some are said to be high, even lofty ideals, and others are low, possibly even unacceptable. Moreover, people have varying degrees of emotional commitment to ideals. This leads to a four-way classification, depicted in Figure 9, which is helpful in understanding the nature of responsibility and the qualities required to handle conflicts among ideals.

The person who has low ideals and shows no commitment to even these can be dismissed out of hand as not being suitable for professional work. The person who has high ideals but lacks sufficient commitment is ineffective and is probably a very difficult person to work under. He is like the person who vows on Sunday to make changes in his life, but on Monday morning does what he has always done before. His inconsistency shows a lack of conviction which makes him incapable of inspiring others.

Being consistent. A manager who can be counted on to uphold ideals is seen by his subordinates as consistent. People often express the thought that they at least know where a person stands even if they disagree with him. Without consistency, the manager may be perceived as shallow as well as undependable. With consistency, he is able to build ideals in his group. Actions along with proclamations have to be reinforcing to have a lasting effect.

An unyielding consistency makes it possible for a person to have low or even unacceptable ideals and still manage people. Organized crime is an extreme case. Few of us would agree with its ideals; nearly all of us would agree that its members hold their ideals with forceful tenacity, exacting the penalty of death for breaches.

When ideals conflict. The Henry Fords of this world and outstanding managers at all levels combine high ideals with high commitment. The problem they have to overcome is what to do when their ideals inevitably conflict.

DEGREE OF COMMITMENT

		High	Low
LEVEL OF IDEAL	High	Respected Manager	Inconsistent
	Low	Mafia	Unprofessional

Figure 9. Responsibility: a combination of ideals and commitment.

To illustrate, you have heard professional employees and perhaps managers grumble about being expected both to reduce overtime and to get orders out on schedule. Or perhaps a manager is faced with a new project necessitating an exemplary performance from all his personnel at a time when his most capable subordinate is scheduled to attend a week-long seminar at a prestigious university. Officers of multinational corporations have been put to the severe test of promoting business in foreign countries and dealing with the morality of making payoffs. Managers who shrug off these problems or blame them on their superiors or on society are in effect admitting that they are incapable of producing a solution. Their fitness for management is questionable.

Some courses of action that may seem to solve the problem are counterproductive. Doing nothing about a conflict of ideals will result in a loss of leadership. Decisions that have to be made, generally, will get made—by someone. Taking a course of action that blatantly sacrifices one ideal, in addition to causing guilt for the person who is responsible, will soon cause the ideal to be lost.

A manager can resign. Certainly repeated instances of this will not build a career, but it may be necessary under extreme conditions. Resignation is preferable to being involved in questionable or fraudulent financial dealings, for example.

Many people in management fail to recognize that the conflict calls for intellectual ability and that their inability to resolve it reflects on their capacity for management. The intellectual processes required for a satisfactory resolution are analysis and synthesis.

Using analysis. The analytical process entails finding a course of action that satisfies both the conflicting ideals through an understanding of the nature of the components. Take for example the conflict of the manager who is expected to reduce overtime and yet to meet promised delivery dates to customers. Faced with a situation where it appears that one goal must be sacrificed, he analyzes the reasons and the causes. The reason overtime is required is that the number of man-hours available on regular time is insufficient to accomplish the needed work during the time allowed. However, he might be able to transfer people from another department, or to recall workers who have been with the company in the past, possibly people who have retired and are willing to work part time for an interval.

Another avenue is to determine whether the man-hours for completing the work can be reduced. He could undertake an analysis of the methods in the hope of finding shortcuts that would allow the schedule to be met without overtime.

Using synthesis. The process of synthesis entails finding a higher ideal to which both conflicting ideals can be subordinated. The manager who has scheduled his top aide to attend a week's seminar at a prestigious university and now has a demanding project on his hands may discover by reexamining his ideals that his commitment to management development is really subordinate to having at least one qualified person able to take his place. The project affords an excellent and unique opportunity to give his aide valuable experience. The manager concludes that giving his aide new broad responsibilities on the project team will allow him to adhere to the ideal of having a qualified replacement and still put forth his best team on the new project.

Not rationalization. Does this seem like rationalization? According to the *Random House Dictionary of the English Language*, to rationalize means: "To ascribe (one's acts, opinions, etc.) to causes that *superficially* seem reasonable and valid but that actually are unrelated to the true, possibly unconscious causes" (emphasis added). Certainly it will be seen as the rationalization that it is if the manager seizes any plausible reason to explain his actions. But using reasons founded on an ideal to which he is committed is not superficial and therefore is not rationalization. Incidentally, a way a manager ensures that his reasons are related to his ideals and that he is fully committed to those ideals is through discussions on plans and goals. This is yet another reason for bringing people into the planning process.

When ideals change. There are times when an organization must alter its ideals, for instance, when a company is merged with another, or when the nature of the business or the market is undergoing rapid change. These may be times when the old ideals are no longer appropriate. One way the manager can make the change is simply to abandon the old ideal. He can do this abruptly by making it public that this action is being taken, or for diplomatic and psychological reasons, he can make his abandonment evident over time.

For example, suppose that a company has always prided itself on its field service. The ideal has been to continue to give the best possible service to the customer after he has purchased the product. The policy is changed to reducing customer service and pricing the product lower. This type of change could be made apparent to employees gradually, or they could be informed by one unequivocal communication. The choice depends on the particular situation.

Instead of abandoning the ideal, another approach is to find a new or higher ideal that can be shown to embrace the ideal that is outmoded. This is the process of synthesis described above.

The Job Itself

In order to create a sense of responsibility on the part of the employee, the job or the task must meet certain criteria. The first is that the job must be seen as being effective. That is, the people who are doing the job must understand how the job contributes to the larger purposes of the organization. A job that is mere "busy work" can never foster responsibility.

The second criterion is that it must be feasible. The person with the desire to be effective does not relish failure and will not feel responsible for a task that he believes is doomed to fail. On the other hand, he is not adverse to taking risks: he is not looking for the sure thing. He needs the challenge that comes with obstacles and risk, and, if anything, this adds to his sense of responsibility.

The third point is that the job must be large enough so that real responsibility is possible. This is a matter of delegation. The opportunity for creating responsibility will be lost if delegation consists of merely assigning a series of short-run tasks. That is really not delegation at all; it is using a subordinate as a messenger boy. Also, responsibility will not fully develop if the scope of the job is too narrow. For knowledge workers a narrow scope is especially debilitating. It undermines their sense of responsibility, thereby assuring that plans will fail. The concept of responsibility advocated here is one that transcends the actual authority and the actual limits of the person's discretion on the job. It is an emotional commitment to achieving results which usually are not within the complete control of the person feeling the responsibility. This principle will not work if there is too great a discrepancy between the actual authority on the job and area of responsibility. At some point it becomes ridiculous to expect a person to feel responsible for results when he or she has only a miniscule portion of the task under direct control.

A properly designed job is like an iceberg. The one who is delegating sees only the part on the surface. The person who has taken the

responsibility for getting it done has to overcome problems and perform tasks whose details are not explicitly apparent to the delegator.
Although there may be a general procedure to follow, the details of
planning the work lie with the one doing the job.

The Style of Management

There are as many variations and nuances in management style as
there are managers. Moreover, no one can be shown to be the most
successful, and certainly there is no one style that is best for all occasions. But there is general agreement that managers who develop
strong senses of responsibility in subordinates follow a few general
principles.

Rewards. The first of these is that, since accepting responsibility
entails taking a risk, people who take risks should be rewarded. But
what kind of rewards? Money is always acceptable, but it is not always
possible to award it. When it is given, the amounts available are not
usually great enough to change a lifestyle. There is plenty of evidence
that money alone (in the amounts offered) is insufficient to prompt
people into accepting responsibility. But to the person who accepts
responsibility for whatever reasons, a monetary reward carries a message. It is tangible proof that management recognizes his contribution.

Rewards can be in the form of promotions and new assignments.
Again, this cannot always be done. However, letting a person know
that he has won his spurs, so to speak, and is ready for something more
challenging when the opportunity occurs is a stronger form of recognition than a pat on the back.

One of the most important ways of rewarding an employee who
has accepted responsibility lies in the style of management itself.
Since both the employee and the manager understand that the employee is taking responsibility for the results, the manager need be less
concerned with supervising the employee and more concerned with
managing the work. However, I hasten to add that his management of
the work is more a process of keeping surveillance over what is taking
place—that is, he manages from a *distance.* This means, for example,
that if the employee has need to rearrange his hours, and this does not
effect the effectiveness of others, or if the employee wants to take time
off for personal reasons, the manager need not be disquieted. The re-

ward for the employee is that he or she has the autonomy to plan, organize, and control his or her own work together with the flexibility to accommodate personal and job demands.

This style of management is an important reward or incentive because it is not a one-time event and does not occur at the end of the assignment, but regularly reinforces the value of accepting responsibility.

Sharing risk. A second principle is that the manager should share the risk that is being taken by the responsible employee. Often the risk is too great for one person and he will be reluctant to take it alone. A familiar example is the case of the supervisor who believes that his staff can be reduced but is afraid to take the step. His superior solves the problem for him by laying off some people, and the supervisor is forced to make his plan work, but most of the risk was taken by his superior. That is a rather heavy-handed example.

Another, more subtle example is the case of a West Coast aerospace company, which decided in the 1950s to put in a computer system to do its materials requirements planning, at that time a very avant-garde idea. The system would calculate the quantities of parts that had to be purchased and notify the purchasing agent responsible when it was necessary to take action. In fact, the document that was produced by the computer was called an "Action Notice."

Prior to putting in the system, requirements for parts were computed largely by hand. The sweeping change that this would bring was anticipated to call for a reorganization of the personnel and duties in purchasing and to make it possible to reduce personnel in the department. The program was installed; savings through a reduction in force in purchasing were achieved, and, by all standards, the program was a success—even a model for further extensions of material requirements planning.

A project of this type was too much for one man to champion by himself. The industrial engineering department had the responsibility of creating an efficient and effective system, but it could not have been successful had not the purchasing department felt a responsibility for giving the IE department all the support it could. Top management was also involved, and was prepared to share failure as well as success, which probably summarizes the principle of sharing risk: You are being supportive and sharing the risk if you are as ready to assume part of the blame for failure as you are to share the limelight of success.

Avoiding reverse delegation. A third principle of managing so as to create responsibility is to avoid reverse delegation, or the process whereby the superior takes over for the subordinate. It is an easy trap to fall into for the manager who is trying to be supportive and helpful. Suppose you drop into the office of one of your salesmen who is putting together a proposal. You ask how it is going, when it will be ready—just to keep in touch, not because you feel that the salesman lacks the responsibility to carry out the task. He responds that all is well except he is having difficulty getting the figures he wants from accounting. Being helpful, you immediately volunteeer to get them for him. The next day the salesman stops by your office to inquire if you have received the figures yet. Now who is supervising whom? The process of reverse delegation has just been completed.

When to Let Subordinates Make Mistakes

"There is more than one way to skin a cat." That old expression explains much about what we often term mistakes. For in reality, what is going on is not a mistake at all but merely a different set of steps from what we would have chosen. It will get the result we are after with possibly about the same cost and level of quality of performance and within the scheduled completion date. If this really what you are calling a mistake, then it is the kind of "mistake" that you *must* let your subordinates make.

Suppose you have a feeling that the approach being used will cause costs to be higher or delivery to be delayed. Then what? The first point to keep in mind is that you can't be certain that the poor method will actually cause costs to be higher or will delay shipment. You might be certain that the best method is not being followed; you might even be able to prove this using time study. But your subordinate may compensate for the poor method by working harder or by working longer hours. This sort of thing happens when people feel responsibility.

Even if the results will not be what they should be, you have to balance the consequences of the poor result with the value of avoiding any intrusion which might lessen the feeling of responsibility of your subordinate as well as the value of the experience as a learning device. With these thoughts in mind, you will probably come to the conclusion that your organization will be more effective and stronger in every way in the long run if people are permitted to make mistakes which have only slightly detrimental effects or are easily corrected. Once again, responsibility means taking risks and, by definition, a risk taker will not enjoy full success every time.

There are risks that cannot be taken and decisions that cannot be delegated. The risk of such great financial import that it jeopardizes the existence of the organization should never be taken if it can possibly be avoided. The reason is simple. It usually is not necessary to take risks of this magnitude to get desired results. Businesses nearly always adhere to this principle. That is why insurance companies share large risks, why companies often form consortiums, and why governments are sometimes asked to underwrite the risk of doing business.

When substantial financial risks are undertaken, the decision is made by the chief executive officer and no other. The recent acquisition of Pet, Inc., by IC Industries, Inc., added about $400 million of debt to IC's balance sheet. William B. Johnson, the chairman of IC, had to convince the board to move ahead but there is no doubt that the decision and the responsibility for results is his.

Whether you are a head of a corporation or a supervisor, you cannot let your subordinates make mistakes that cost you your reputation. You may elect to take a risky course of action that, if successful, could propel you into the ranks of higher management or, if it fails, could be damaging to your career. Under such circumstances, you must closely supervise the work of subordinates and not allow them to make any errors except those that are very minor. You should be frank with your subordinates from the beginning of a high-risk undertaking in explaining to them the consequences of failure to you and to them. Inform them that you are going to take extra precautions of checking and double checking their work and their progress. Conversely, you may invite them to informally monitor the work of their co-workers and your own. If people thoroughly understand the circumstances, it is very possible and very practical to create a working environment in which an unusual (and counterproductive, in most circumstances) degree of surveillance is fully acceptable. What's more, unless you do create the type of atmosphere where cooperative effort in preventing errors is the norm, you are doomed to failure. If you are correct in assessing the project as high risk, you can expect big mistakes to occur unless you take extra precautions.

The most perplexing issue and perhaps the most common is how much freedom should subordinates have to make mistakes that are neither trivial nor calamitous, but just plain cause trouble. There are rules for this, too, discussed in the next section. They are the same whether you are depending on a subordinate, other people in the organization, or an outside supplier.

How Much Effort to Take in Preventing Mistakes

Three rules govern the effort you should make to curtail Murphy's Law. One of these is that *the more a mistake contributes to the system's learning and the building of responsibility, the less effort you should take to prevent it.* The positive benefits of some mistakes are greater than the negative consequences.

The second rule, implied by the previous discussion of major mistakes, is that *the effort to prevent mistakes should be directly proportional to the seriousness of the consequences.* Mistakes in hiring are among the most costly for any company. They give rise to costs of inefficiency, ineffectiveness, and lost opportunities which can be staggering in spite of not being measurable. The decision to hire for an important post along with other important personnel decisions should be made jointly by the supervisor and the supervisor's supervisor. This is a minimum; boards and other schemes may be useful to get still greater insurance against making a mistake.

The third rule is that *your direct involvement in seeing that things go right should be inversely proportional to the felt responsibility of those performing the work, providing a product, or supplying a service.* The basis for this rule is that the sense of responsibility of the people doing the work tends to depend on their perception of what poor performance will do to *them*—not to *you.*

Among the thousands of situations that could be used to illustrate this principle, computer operations offer a common example. The risk of error is inherent in reprogramming or in making changes in equipment. What may seem to be a small mistake to the programmer, and one that is easily rectified, may be a nightmare for the user. Faulty information could cause inventories to run short or generate erroneous bills sent to customers. Here the user has much more at stake than the provider of the service, who is not formally accountable. Perhaps I have done an injustice to computer programmers in this example by implying that they would not feel responsible for such an error, when certainly responsibility would be felt. My point is that, being at least one step removed, they can never fully comprehend the unpleasant ramifications that result from their errors. That being the case, their deepest emotional commitment is not to avoid errors in making a transition from one type of equipment to another, but to improve the business system by upgrading information-processing and decision-making capabilities. On the other hand, if you are managing accounts receivable, your deepest commitment is getting out correct statements to customers and getting the money back. There is a fundamental difference here.

To continue the example, there is not much you can do to prevent the programmer from making a careless mistake. However, there is a lot you can do to avoid errors in system design and to minimize the consequences of errors made in the transition. You can be exacting in reviewing the details of the new system. Mock-ups of new reports can be tested for relevance and completeness of information and ease of use. How the system will handle various transactions can be simulated over a wide range of circumstances. The capacity of the system and the schedules for input and output can be examined.

To reduce errors in transition, a full-scale simulation might be employed before going into actual use. The new system might run in parallel with the old until the bugs are out. At a crucial point in the cut over to the new system, extra people from other departments, including your own, could be scheduled to work with data processing operations to ensure that nothing is amiss and to fix it, by hand if necessary, when there is a flaw.

Whenever the consequences of poor performance are more serious to you, the user, than to the provider, you are in a dangerous situation. Your only recourse is to use all the power at your command to investigate, to inspect, to monitor, and to take whatever precautions are necessary to avoid mistakes. You would be foolish to trust someone completely who feels less responsibility for the outcome than you do.

Putting Responsibility in Staff Positions

In comparing staff and line jobs, the president of a large conglomerate said, "I think that the toughest jobs to fill are the corporate staff jobs. They have no authority so their effectiveness is occasioned by their own brilliance. They have to influence rather than command." The staff man must get things done. Furthermore you must hold him responsible for getting things done. The difference between the staff man and the line person is that the gap between authority and responsibility is greater for the staff man. But accomplishment is essential for staff and line alike, because without it there is no effectiveness and there can be no true sense of responsibility.

An obstacle to getting results is the persistent danger that staff personnel will adopt an attitude of superiority or grudgingly conceal their condescension. It is not uncommon to find the staff mentality which conveys to line managers that they really don't know how to do their jobs very well. In addition to causing a variety of negative consequences, it is, of course, impossible to create an environment of accomplishment when such attitudes prevail.

The true responsibility of the staff man is supporting the line organization so that it will be more effective and efficient. This responsibility is dominant over all others and especially over what may be a misguided responsibility of trying to impose his own particular remedy to a problem. Invariably the best results come from programs and solutions to problems that are a product of both line and staff thinking. The staff man will also find that results are easier to get if he is not particularly concerned with who gets the credit. His reward, and one that is visible to his superior and other higher-level managers, is that when he was on the assignment improvements were made, problems solved, or needed changes were implemented.

The professional feels a strong responsibility to his discipline, which, if not carried to an extreme, is a great strength for the staff person. It gives him credibility as an expert in his field, and it is in the interest of the company to reinforce this dimension of responsibility. Perhaps it is as simple as saying that a professional ought to act like one.

Responsibility for results requires considering the problem or the focal point for action in the context of a system. The staff professional who fails to take a holistic view may be insisting on changes which correct the problem in his area of expertise but create still greater problems in other parts of the system. A person who fails in this regard has either a problem with attitude or a lack of knowledge. If you have a person in your organization with this shortcoming, it would be helpful to point out that the truly knowledgeable person is deep in his area of specialty but broad at the top—and that is the type of person you want on your staff.

Accomplishment often requires more than a one-time solution to a problem. It can entail implanting new attitudes or convincing line personnel to carry on the new ways of operation. It might even require establishing an organization with new responsibilities. These are merely examples of the responsibility of a staff man to be a builder. In reality, no one, line or staff, can be an effective performer without being a builder.

Ten Commandments for the Staff Person

Getting results in a staff position is not easy and good staff performers are hard to come by. Following the guidelines below will help to overcome the difficulties inherent in staff work.

1. Know your subject thoroughly and completely, keeping up with the latest trends and developments in the field.
2. Use the systemized approach to solve problems and get answers that are the hallmark of your profession, avoiding shortcuts that undermine the authority of your profession and reduce your credibility.
3. Look at situations holistically, understanding their systemic qualities.
4. Learn to ask questions and ferret out required information without arousing antagonism.
5. Be able to establish rapport with others having various backgrounds and much different backgrounds from your own.
6. Communicate your ideas clearly, succinctly, and emphatically in writing and orally.
7. Take responsibility for getting tangible results in all your assignments though the methods employed or the solutions adopted are not necessarily your own creation.
8. Create an appreciation for your point of view and, if needed, build a group to carry on programs, procedures, and sentiments that have been initiated with your influence.
9. Give credit and take care to see that credit is given by others to line personnel who implement changes.
10. Realize that you have much to learn in your own field and accept continued personal growth and improvement as a challenge.

Using the Concept of "Closing the Sale"

An enemy of effectiveness and hence a roadblock to creating responsibility is the difficulty that some people have in bringing things to a conclusion. It is true that functions and work are ongoing and that frequently there are many phases to a task. Nevertheless, there is a conclusion to each phase. The research project will be concluded or at least a phase of it will be concluded. There is a point when the schedule for production is frozen; changes will not be made except for emergencies. There is a point when the plans for the building are completed, given to a contractor, and subsequent modifications become very expensive. Ultimately, closure must be reached.

The salesman whose paycheck proves he is being effective knows that every sale must be closed. Regardless of appearance, demeanor, or tactics, he is hungrily looking for the moment when the customer writes his signature on the dotted line. As one salesmen put it, "I go right for the jugular."

There is something to be learned by all businessmen and professionals in the way a good salesman goes about making a sale. First of all, he has the end result clearly in mind from the beginning. That is, he knows what constitutes success and he can define success as the culmination of a single act—signing the contract or making the sale.

Second, he keeps the goal in mind as he goes through the steps of preparing a proposal and making a presentation. In this regard, he tries to get agreement from the customer on issues or options as he goes along. He does this (1) to get assurance that he has not failed to detect a point of disagreement, and (2) to concentrate and emphasize points of agreement that will prepare his prospect for an affirmative response. The lesson here is that effective performance requires keeping your eye not only on the target but also on making sure that you have not left behind those around you who must be involved.

Third, the salesman looks for closure at any time and *accepts* it when he gets it. He doesn't say to his prospective customer that he is only on step three of his presentation and that he has three more to go before it is time to ask for the order. Instead, he realizes that an opportunity to close is an opportunity to reach the goal. If more explanation is needed about the product or service it can be taken care of later.

So it is with anyone who is results oriented. If the opportunity is found to bring the task to conclusion, it is taken.

The analogy to closing the sales in the business world takes many forms. It can be making a decision, taking an action, or finishing a report. It is a form of building—one brick has been put in place, and work on the next can begin. And the person who feels an emotional commitment to getting the brick in place or to closing the sale is one who is responsible.

7

Goal setting

People work together and accomplish more when they have a goal. As obvious as this precept is, there is apparently a great deal of room for improving its implementation. Results of a survey by the American Management Associations of 1,275 executives cited "lack of well-defined organizational or departmental goals and objectives" as the factor most responsible for unsatisfactory productivity.[*]

Why Goal Setting Is Necessary

I don't think anyone has to make a serious argument for having goals, since their value has been demonstrated time and time again. Here, briefly, are some of the benefits of goal setting as a reminder.

Goals give direction. The goals of subordinate departments should be coordinated with higher-level organizations to ensure that all are working toward a common purpose. The goals themselves are aimed at attaining results which lead to effective work and use of resources. By working toward goals, managers and subordinates are able to plan their own activities to be more productive.

Goals reduce confusion and chance for error. Just as goals can give direction, they can reduce conflicts and misunderstandings which can lead to cross purposes. Clearly defined and distinct goals can keep two organizations with common interests from destructive competition or costly duplication.

[*] Herman S. Jacobs and Katherine Jillson, "Executive Productivity: An AMA Survey Report" (New York: AMACOM, 1974).

When cooperative effort is required, mutually supporting goals can be set. The knowledge of what each entity is going to do helps to keep things from going wrong.

Goals stimulate innovation, creativity, and just plain thinking. We have observed that a goal is a stimulus to creative thinking. The top man in a subsidiary disclosed that the parent organization lays down an objective for profits and that the planning job at the subsidiary level is mostly aimed at how to attain the objectives. This takes a lot of hard work and thought. As he said to me, "It isn't just SOP."

Goal setting affords an opportunity for broader-based decision making. This occurs in two ways. Goals themselves can be the product of group consensus. When goals are established, groups can decide how they are to be reached.

Commitment to goals inspires greater effort. People work hard to reach a specified objective at a particular point in time when they are committed to the goal. Nothing could illustrate this more than the campaign workers trying to get their candidate elected to office.

Goals are the basis for control. The goal becomes a standard by which to measure progress. When work is off the mark, corrective action can be taken.

Evaluation and appraisal can be based on how well goals are attained. This applies to individual appraisal and to appraisals of results of organizations. Bonuses and other rewards are often geared to objectives for performance.

In summary, goal setting is a vital underpinning of the system for planning, execution, and feedback illustrated by Figure 1.

Elements of Successful Goal Setting

There have been about 30 studies of goal setting and its effects in the last ten years. The results are overwhelming. In case after case higher output is attained and greater improvements are made with goals. However, the studies prove that higher performance does not occur automatically when goals are set. There are some conditions that must be met to get the benefits of goal setting.

Curt Carlson, whose company is a privately held holding company for his diversified interests in hotels, trading stamps, jewelry, tobacco and candy wholesaling, restaurants, and catalog showroom retailing, has said, "I'll never delegate goal setting." He believes that it is his job to set higher goals for his executives than they would set for themselves. One executive had set his mind on opening 50 new restaurants over the next year. Carlson kept goading him with the question of, "If you can open 50, why not 100?" The executive finally adopted the higher goal. A few years ago, Carlson announced a target of $1 billion in sales by 1981, double the amount at the time. It turns out that he hit this mark in 1978. Recently, with much fanfare, he established a $2 billion goal for 1982. *The Wall Street Journal* (May 16, 1978) describes the latter episode:

> Mr. Carlson . . . mixes in some ribbing of subordinates with announcements of new goals for them. . . . He reveals a plan to take his executives on a round-the-world trip to reward them for reaching $1 billion in sales. Then he brings out the stick to go with the carrot:
>
> "Of course, some of you may get left at home if you don't meet your targets."
>
> He saves the big moment for near the end. He points to a giant wall chart that lays out company goals by years . . . and begins chalking up a new set of higher figures. As he comes to 1982, a well-rehearsed aide rushes to the front with a big new sign: "Billions—Two in '82." More applause and a big smile from Mr. Carlson.

This narrative illustrates five elements of successful goal setting:

1. Goal setting and working toward goals must be a natural and habitual aspect of management.
2. Goals must be dominant in channeling work toward their accomplishment.
3. Goals must be accepted.
4. Goals must be challenging.
5. Performance in reaching goals must be rewarded.

How to Make Goal Setting Habitual and Natural

When goal setting is a habitual and natural process it leads to higher motivation, because it is seen as a normal part of the job for which one gets compensated. However, if goal setting is viewed as an experiment or as an optional procedure, it may fire the enthusiasm of a few, but others will be inclined to take a "wait and see" attitude. Those who see it as an extra to the job are likely to give it some attention only when they have time or when their boss asks for some written goals.

Moreover, there is a lasting and continuous benefit when goal setting is a natural process. Studies have proved that the motivational effect of goal setting seriously deteriorates after nine months unless action is taken to revive the procedure. But when goal setting becomes a natural process in the organization, it is viewed as not just a regular duty but as a preeminent target to which all actions are directed. It is not merely an additional duty. As an everyday aspect of management, goals and progress on goals become a part of casual business conversation. For example, dialog before goal setting:

JOHN: "Hey Fred! How are we doing on our shipments to Dallas this month?"

FRED: "We've sent them about $250,000 of materials so far this month."

With goal setting, the same question is answered by:

FRED: "We're on target—we've shipped 60 percent of our goal for the month already."

A point that has been stressed by researchers and businessmen alike is that goals must be accepted in order to have motivational value. True enough, but the precursor to goal acceptance is getting the goal-setting process itself accepted.

Now for the question of how you do that. If you are really interested in making a contribution to the organization to which you belong, regardless of your managerial level, you have already established goals for yourself and for your group. They may not be written down and possibly could be defined more precisely. If that is the case, take care of those deficiencies immediately.

Then make a point of letting your subordinates know what your goals for the organization are. Stress that everything that is done in an organization is aimed at an end result. Demonstrate in actions and in words that you have given careful thought to exactly what the desired end result is. Whenever possible, you quantify the end result, which is the goal—for the present. Do not be afraid to change a goal when it obviously needs changing, but strive to show that goals provide a standard for consistent effort and a sense of direction over extended periods of time. Encourage your subordinates to develop their own goals to support those that you have set for the organization. Keep in mind that your first goal is to establish the legitimacy of goal setting as a natural process of management: more participation and perhaps better methods of goal setting can follow.

How to Make Goals Dominant in Guiding Actions

For goal setting to have any practical value whatsoever, the goals must be dominant in the decision-making process and in the ensuing actions. The usual advice on how to put goals into practice is to establish a system of planning and control. The components of such a system are essentially these:

1. Goals are established.
2. Specific plans, often called action plans, are developed to carry out the goals.
3. Progress is reviewed periodically.

Texas Instruments is a company that has had tremendous success in using a system of goal setting to foster innovation in new products and processes. The fact that this company has been at the fore in a dynamic and volatile field is testimony to the success of its management methods, which stress the three points stated above.

In 1949, Texas Instruments was a good, small company with sales of $5.8 million and profits of $253,000. At that time, Patrick Haggerty, the CEO, and staff concluded that they wanted to run a much larger company, one that had sales of $200 million and $10 million in after-tax profits. They set out to accomplish this feat by pursuing several strategies, one of which was to strengthen the research and development capability of the company. It had not done any exploratory research in the semiconductor field, or in any other field.

Haggerty brought the company into structure-of-matter technology by seeking a license from the Bell Labs to produce transistors. He and a few of his top people attended the now famous transistor symposium in 1952 in which the Bell scientists divulged their knowledge of solid state technology. TI's program was boosted tremendously the next year when Gordon Teal, a leading solid state expert, left the Bell Labs to set up a research laboratory at TI.

Two goals, or strategies as Haggerty calls them, were adopted to exploit the technology that changed the destiny of the company. One was to produce semiconductor devices that would withstand the heat requirements and reliability requirements for large-scale applications to military products. The second was to find a major commercial application for the consumer market. The latter program culminated in the Regency pocket radio, first produced in 1954. Haggerty is convinced that the entire cycle of semiconductor device utilization in the United States and the world was speeded up by at least two years because this relatively small company chose the proper strategy and followed through with successful tactics.

A decade later, it was becoming evident that the informal concept of objectives, strategy, and tactics (OST), Haggerty's credo, could not be perpetuated throughout a company closing in on $500 million in annual sales without the system's being institutionalized. The formal OST system began in about 1963 and five years later the reporting system was modified to identify separately expenditures for sustaining the business and those that were for investments in growth. Now the OST system is ingrained in the TI culture. Under the system, managers have a dual responsibility of running their daily operations and being involved in innovative projects. Both are expected as part of the job. An objective is set and approved. The strategy for reaching the objective is carried out by funded projects called TAPs, tactical action programs. The results are monitored, measured, and reported. TI is counting on OST to harness the creative power and the intellect of its many talented employees in its drive to reach the ambitious goals of the future—$10 billion in the late 1980s.

Texas Instruments is certainly not the only company to use goals; all successful enterprises are goal oriented. On the other hand, probably as many goals are ignored as are followed in business organizations. This is particularly true of less grandiose goals that apply to the department level.

Why is goal setting often ineffective in organizations? The reasons range from not having the backing of the chief executive officer to the fact that executives are conditioned to see their work as making the frequent decisions and taking the immediate actions called for by the function they perform. They see goal setting as an extra duty and one that is either irrelevant or of little practical value.

The inescapable conclusion of anyone who has had practical experience in encouraging goal setting is that system alone (for example, OST) will not cause goals to be dominant in managing. The critical condition is that they must be viewed as relevant by the people who are supposed to achieve them. And above all, achieving one goal must not be perceived as detrimental to performance in other areas considered to be more important. A goal that meets these tests is a *valid* goal. Without validity, goals have little chance to dominate decision making.

The issue of validity brings two points to mind. An organization's multiple goals need not conflict as long as the degree of attainment is kept within reasonable bounds. In other words, it is possible to have compatible goals for quality and cost containment as long as an extreme position in either is not taken. The second point is a reminder that an organization is a system and that a goal which is favorable to one segment may be a hindrance for another. This situation should be avoided or kept to a bare minimum through cooperative efforts that integrate the goals and activities of units within an organization.

There are two guidelines for making goals dominant: (1) You do need a system for converting goals into actions and follow-up; and (2) you must ensure that goals are valid, discarding those that lack relevance, conflict with other more important goals, or are trivial.

How to Get Goals Accepted

Although validity is a necessary condition to getting goals accepted, it is not sufficient. Valid goals are not always accepted by those expected to achieve them.

There is an old story about Charles Schwab, who headed steel companies at the turn of the century. He wrote in chalk on the floor of the mill what the production had been for the day shift. When the night shift arrived and were told what the number represented, they made an effort to surpass it, and they did. Their output was then chalked on the floor, to become a target for the next shift. The process resulted in a substantial increase in production.

Over 50 years later, a foreman in an aluminum plant tried a similar technique. He posted the output in pounds for each crew of inspectors and packers of aluminum. The result was a minor uprising. The union officials working in the department demanded to know the purpose of posting the production records. They viewed it as an attempt to "speed up" work or possibly to have records that might be the basis for future personnel actions. It was very clear that the only motivational effect the posting of the record had was negative, and this was confirmed by lower production on the day of the posting. The record was taken down; labor and management resumed the "truce" that typified labor/management relations in the entire plant.

Essentially the same technique works in one instance and fails in another. Why? An exploration of the underlying reasons would require much more space than can be given here and would take us well beyond goal setting. However, for whatever reasons, it is obvious that Schwab's steel workers accepted the production of the previous shift as a goal to be surpassed. In the case of the aluminum workers, there was absolutely no acceptance of the goal of increasing production.

Participation, yes or no. Aside from properly selecting and defining the goal itself, the most fruitful route to gaining acceptance of goals is through participation. However, the evidence in favor of participation as a technique for getting goals accepted is not as convincing as you might think. But we can learn from it. Here is a brief summary of a few studies.°

1. A sample of nonmanagerial female employees showed that the desire to make improvements was related to the degree of participation in goal setting.

2. The conclusion to a study of participation in goal setting by low-level managers was that men who worked best with high opportunity for participation in all aspects of their jobs performed best when working toward self-set goals. Men who usually worked with low participation performed better when goals were set by their bosses.

3. Participation in goal setting resulted in increased effort for managers with high self-assurance but not for managers with low self-assurance.

4. A study of R&D managers showed no relationship between participation in goal setting and motivation.

5. Logging crews that participated in goal setting achieved higher levels of performance and set higher goals than those that worked toward assigned goals.

6. A survey of first-line supervisors found that participation in goal setting resulted in better performance for supervisors with a low need for achievement but not for those with a high need for achievement.

7. A study of 179 skilled technicians and 28 supervisors indicated

° Studies 1–6 in Gary P. Latham, "A Review of Research on the Application of Goal Setting in Organizations," *Academy of Management Journal*, December 1975, pp. 827, 839, 840; study 7 in John M. Ivancevich, "Different Goal Setting Treatments and Their Effects on Performance and Job Satisfaction," *Academy of Management Journal*, September 1977, p. 417.

slight superiority of the assigned goal-setting method over participatory goal setting. The possible explanation offered is that these people were accustomed to working in a work environment with little participation.

The problem with studies is that there are many variables at work in addition to the ones reported. We do not know how the participation was conducted, for example. Nor do we know if the communications took place in an atmosphere of openness and trust. Was the leader of the group a good communicator? Had previous patterns of decision making created attitudes which were contrary to participation? Could feelings of alienation or estrangement have been present that affected both participation in goal setting and subsequent performance? We know that people who have a strong desire to be affiliated with a group and enjoy the association with the group will be motivated to achieve group goals.

Participation and affiliation. We also know that the process works in reverse; being excluded from goal setting reduces affiliation. One day a senior vice-president announced that his two-woman secretarial staff would no longer do any work for others in the office and would not be responsible for phone coverage. He justified this by stating that the work they were doing was too important and that they were too busy to give assistance and cooperation to other secretaries and clerks in the office. There was no factual basis for his assertion: actually having two full-time secretaries had been a recent and somewhat difficult addition to justify. The real reason for this tactic was that he had felt that he was being left out of planning and decision-making discussions of major importance.

Ridiculous and childish behavior you might say? Yes, but it happened, and I am sure that, albeit with different symptoms, lackluster or disruptive behavior will always occur when an executive feels that he has been excluded from participating in decision making, such as goal setting, in which he believes he should have a part.

In the case of the aluminum inspectors and packers, would participation have created a different attitude causing higher production goals to be accepted? The chances are probably no better than 50–50 in the environment that existed. Even these odds assume that supervision would be able to create a more participative climate for dealing with all matters, not just production goals, and this could not have been done overnight. But at least, participation would have given the foreman a better idea of what the group would accept and what it would not, so that he could avoid a humiliating experience.

Though the studies and experiences with participation in goal setting show mixed results, it is clear that participation cannot detract from the commitment people have toward achieving goals. It seems that in some situations, participation increases the acceptability of goals. If a person has had a major part in defining a goal it is hard for him to deny the legitimacy of the goal later on. Instead, he feels a commitment to attain the goal. When participation takes place in an atmosphere of openness and trust, the ability of the group to explore the difficulty in reaching goals can be discussed candidly. This will lead to realistic goals that people can accept fully. People with greater than average desires for achievement, who have probably been goal setting for years privately, especially appreciate the opportunity to participate in setting their goals.

If you put into practice the doctrine that the person holding a job should be the resident expert in that job, it follows that you should involve him in goal setting. You do need to use your influence to counter the tendency of some people to be too conservative and to tone down the goals of the wild optimist.

Participation not required. Must there be participation to make goals acceptable? Certainly not. The example of Curt Carlson, at the beginning of this chapter, is testimony to this point. A goal may be accepted because of its attractiveness to a manager or because of its relevance to his work. Goals are accepted that are seen as achievable. The power, prestige, or authority of the person assigning the goal can make it acceptable to others.

Some of the research cited earlier suggests that people who have not worked under participatory conditions perform better under assigned goals than they do when they participate in goal setting. In general, people will accept what they are used to. When the practice of assigning goals from the top is well established, as it is in Carlson's company, goals are accepted and apparently do not lack power as a motivator.

How to Create Goals with Stretch

Goals that motivate people to do their best, goals that cause them to stretch themselves to attain great accomplishments, must meet three criteria. They must be *specific*, there must be a *time dimension*, and they must be *difficult*, but not unreasonable. Two of these, specificity and the time dimension, are technical in that they have to do with writing "good" goals. The third has to do with the matter of getting people to go on record as striving for an end result and accepting the consequences of failure or success in meeting that result.

Any boss can decree a difficult goal. The problem lies in how you get subordinates to set a tough goal themselves or to accept the boss's. One way is by helping them to remove self-limiting, faulty assumptions.

I have a friend who conducts motivation meetings with salesclerks in apparel specialty stores. The purpose of the meetings is to encourage the salespeople to set goals for themselves in opening new charge accounts. He begins the session by asking the group whether they believe that the limits for human accomplishment are more definite and more unyielding for physical or for mental activities. The answer he gets is the one he is looking for—that humans are more definitely circumscribed in physical endeavors than in mental.

He then proceeds to ask about physical limits, such as how much heat people can withstand. Individuals estimate what they could withstand and these are recorded on a flip chart. The estimates usually range up to 170° F.

Then he asks the group how long they think they could hold their breath under water. Most say about a minute and a half. (He reminds them that pearl divers in the South Seas and off Japan have been able to go for three minutes, of course with great training.) He records the answers of the group and then gives them the actual records for these facts from the *Guinness Book of Records*. Without protective clothing, the record for withstanding heat is 416° F; the record for holding breath under water is 13 minutes and 53 seconds.

Invariably, the group grossly underestimates the limits of physical activity. Here the group is reminded that its members had agreed that such limits were more rigid than those of mental activity, and they are asked to ponder what the true limits of their own mental capabilities might be. The point is that people establish boundaries in their minds that limit their accomplishments, and the limits are nothing more than faulty assumptions.

This introduction to a goal-setting meeting is nearly always successful in getting people to reassess what is possible and to set high goals. Frequently, the atmosphere becomes too supercharged, creating a tendency to set unrealistically high goals. This is a cue for my friend to step in to bring the goals down to what is realistic.

Group meetings. This illustration has shown how some examples of human accomplishment combined with a little showmanship can lift horizons. The method has other ingredients which stem from the group dynamics that are present. The enthusiasm of a few is caught by others. No one wants to display doubts about the goals that are being set because this puts him or her at odds with the group. The more group solidarity there is, the less likely it is that anyone will speak out against a position that is prevalent with the others. We can conclude that, whether or not uplifting stories are told, a group has the potential of establishing higher goals than would be established by the individuals of the group acting alone.

This does not always happen, and in fact, the reverse can be true. A group that has negative feelings about its management, about what has been done in the past, or about its own capability may take the position of setting very low goals or maybe none at all. Suppose that you as a manager have called a meeting and the result is a low goal that you cannot accept. What should be done?

The first principle is that you should never have called the meeting if you had any doubts about the outcome. A good policy before this type of meeting is to discuss the situation and what performance can be expected with a few of the informal leaders of the group in private in a relaxed setting. If their views indicate that unrealistically low goals will be set, don't call the meeting. Instead, operate on a one-to-one basis. If the views of the group's leaders are changed through individual meetings, it will probably be to your advantage to follow up with a group meeting.

If you failed to test the water and you find yourself in a meeting that cannot produce the positive attitude toward accomplishment which is needed to set high goals, terminate the meeting with some explanation such as "The purpose of the meeting is exploratory in nature and more information will be needed before we can continue the discussion of goals."

One-on-one methods. In dealing with people individually, you are faced with getting them to reach for goals that you believe are attainable. You can do this through explanation, learning, bargaining, or fiat.

Explanation is accomplished through analysis. The goal is broken down into subgoals. Some tentative plans are made. Your purpose is to show how the ultimate goal can be reached step by step. You build into your system a capability to compare results with what is intended and to determine what adjustments have to be made. In trying to convince a person that a goal is feasible, you may be able to compare prior situations with the present and demonstrate that success was achieved in the past under similar circumstances. Or, what is better yet, you may be able to point out that current progress toward the goal is indeed satisfactory. However, what organizational learning really means is that the people learn from feedback which is automatically supplied. The people are part of a system with the kind of characteristics shown in Figure 1, in which results are routinely evaluated without your direct intervention.

Bargaining or negotiation is based on the premise that the two parties have needs that are in conflict but that they also have common needs. If there were nothing that they could agree on, there would be no sense in entering into a discussion, and if they agreed completely, there is nothing to bargain over.

The self-image of both parties is on the line when negotiating, and neither person will want to take a position or exhibit behavior which goes against his self-image. If one person feels that he has failed to attain what is minimally acceptable or that he exhibited self-disparaging behavior during negotiation, the seeds of dissent have been sowed for the future. Needs for acceptance and caring affect negotiations. Most people would prefer to avoid an unpleasant confrontation, especially with someone they genuinely like.

Some of the needs that are likely to come out during bargaining, and should come out, are the often conflicting needs of different levels of systems. The organization, as a system comprised of many subsystems, has needs and wants that are continually in conflict. Most of the time, the conflicts are reconciled, but the potential for the conflict to rise to the surface is always present. Suppose a manager and one of his supervisors are discussing the goal of finishing a project in two months. The supervisor is not sure that it can be done, but thinks it probably could with overtime and extra effort from everybody. While the manager is seeking a commitment to the two-month goal, his most important concern, the supervisor is thinking of the morale in his group and his relations with the group. The supervisor will make use of the discussion on goals to press for some benefits for his group—perhaps some that he and his people have been thinking about for a long time.

When a goal is set by fiat or decree, the problem is getting it accepted. And acceptance, as we have seen, is related to the prestige of the person assigning the goal, as well as other factors.

Rewarding Performance

There are a few rewards that are without cost and generally given as a matter of course to those who attain their goals. One is verbal recognition. Another is more trust, evidenced by more autonomy. In contrast, the subordinate who is not making his goals feels hassled, perhaps as a consequence.

Apart from the gestures of recognition and confidence, the problem for the person giving the reward is to find the reward that will give the most benefit at the least cost. Two principles should be followed.

1. The achievement which is the basis for the reward must be due to the efforts of the person rewarded. The common sense of this statement has frequently been violated through giving bonuses to executives when the high performance of their units has been due to efforts of someone else or attributable to favorable factors beyond their control. In one large corporation the highest bonus was given to the president of a subsidiary who profited from a strike at the plant of his major competitor. The bonus system was changed the following year.

2. Attainment of one goal, which is rewarded, must not come at the expense of other goals to the extent that the comprehensive gain is minimal or negative. There are always tradeoffs between goals, for example, quality vs. cost, short range vs. long range. The point is that performance in one area should not prevent expected levels of performance from being reached in others. The danger is especially acute when a competing goal is not well defined. The goal for long-term growth may not influence a person who expects to be in the position for two or three years and the conditions that must be met for long-term growth may not be articulated as goals. In the absence of some management direction to the contrary, this sets the stage for short-term goals to be dominant to a fault.

Assuming that the linkage between reward and goal attainment meets the two tests above, giving a reward benefits the giver when it produces the following three effects:

The reward conveys the thought that the efforts of the recipient are appreciated.

The recipient feels that his effort has been worthwhile.

The reward serves as an incentive and a promise of future rewards for continued high performance.

Depending on the circumstances, a reward that accomplishes these effects may be nothing more than a dinner or as much as a bonus of thousands of dollars. Some astute choices are required to select the type of reward that completely achieves the three effects at a minimum cost.

Communication in Goal Setting

So much of successful goal setting depends on communication that you cannot hope to get the results you want unless you pay some direct attention to the matter of communicating. It is crucial in getting people to accept goals and the goal-setting process, to assume responsibility for reaching difficult goals, and to use goals to manage. One underpinning of goal setting is the element of mutual trust, which begins with communication. Although trust does not necessarily result from communication, you can be assured that there can be no trust without it.

The example of the aluminum workers and the foreman cited earlier in the chapter illustrates the point. Prior to setting goals, there needed to be some understanding of the purpose of the goal and the desirability of reaching it. Then the workers would have had to *trust* management to use the goals and the records of performance toward those goals for the declared purpose—not for penalizing a shortfall.

I am well aware of the tendency to blame everything that goes wrong on poor communication. No doubt poor communication deserves its share of blame, but to make it responsible for all sorts of problems shows a lack of understanding of two fundamental facets of communication. These are its *process* and its *purpose*.

Process of communication. Allowing for minor deviations, communications experts define the process of communication as consisting of several steps (Figure 10). First, the sender has thoughts he wishes to communicate. He encodes these thoughts into symbols, which we call words. The words or symbols carry no meaning in themselves, they only represent the meaning of the person sending the message. Next is the actual transmission of the symbols or words to the receiver. Transmission is subject to disruptive influences, or noise, a term borrowed from electronics. The words may suffer some damage in transmission as a result of noise. Distraction or preoccupation with other thoughts might cause some of the words not to be heard. Anything that interferes with the reception of the words by the recipient of the message is a form of noise. The next step is for the receiver to decode the words, supplying the meaning to the words from his own memory bank and thus completing the process.

Breaking communication down into several steps allows us to better understand the nature of communication and to be better prepared to deal with its imperfections which cause misunderstanding. The encoding process is a source of error. Even people who are very articulate sometimes have difficulty in finding the right words and phrases to express their thoughts. Obviously noise, in the form of distraction, is another cause of faulty communication. Recognizing this point, you are wise to make sure that a person you want to communicate with has your attention and that there are no distracting sounds to interfere with your message.

If you have accurately formulated your words in thought and transmit the words on a "clear channel," there is still a possibility for misunderstanding because the receiver does not decode the words with the meanings you had anticipated. For example, "urgent," "as

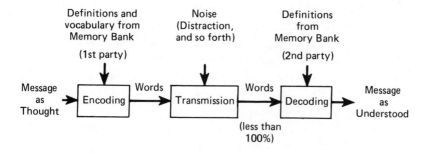

Figure 10. Process of communication.

soon as possible," and "first thing" are terms that may mean one thing to the sender and another to the receiver.

Purpose of communication. The only purpose of communication is to achieve understanding. This is difficult enough. To blame the failure to convince a person to your point of view on communication is placing a burden on the process that it is not capable of carrying. Convincing, selling, or motivating involve much more than communication. For example, a person may understand a projected goal but be unconvinced about the attainability of it because he does not agree with your cause and effect reasoning.

How to avoid misunderstanding. Realizing that there are several pitfalls for faulty communication in its process and that the main purpose of communication is to achieve understanding gives you the basis for improving communication and overcoming Murphy's Law. More important than anything else you can do to improve communication is to actively listen. Active listening, aimed at understanding the thought of the other person, has an effect on every step of the process. When you are actively listening you are trying to go beyond the person's words to his real thoughts.

Active listening works this way. First, you are careful to use meanings which you believe are commonly accepted for the words you hear. Second, assuming that you have eliminated any physical noise from interfering, active listening rules out other types of noise such as distraction. Most important, perhaps, active listening makes you wonder about the process of encoding: Is the sender using words and phrases that convey what he really means?

I once had a student tell me that we were not spending enough time on linear programming in a production management course covering a variety of quantitative and qualitative techniques. I might have responded that the amount of time was about right considering the subject's relative importance, or I might have taken affront at the idea of a student telling me how to structure the course. But these reactions would have missed the student's point and might easily have resulted in hurt or anger. A few questions aimed at achieving understanding revealed what the student was trying to tell me: "If you expect me to learn what you are teaching about linear programming, you will have to spend more time on it in class." Now that is much different from what he actually said: "We don't spend enough time on linear programming in this class."

Active listening involves getting feedback. Feedback confirms that your point has been received as intended. It also is used to confirm that you understand the other person's point of view. You get feedback by asking questions if information is not volunteered.

How to get agreement. Because setting goals and discussing progress toward attaining goals are sensitive subjects, where the likelihood of disagreement and hard feelings is present, good communication skills are very valuable. If you are discussing goals with a subordinate, you must keep in mind that your first objective is to understand what he is telling you. Then you must make sure that he understands your thoughts. A deliberate and thorough attempt to achieve real understanding can accomplish much toward resolving any differences over goals or meeting previously established goals. In fact, once understanding has been achieved, differences may vanish.

On the other hand, despite understanding, agreement may still be beyond your grasp. You have already stated your case and given reasons and evidence to support it. You are certain that your subordinate understands your position. Under these circumstances, your best approach is to get him to reexamine his position. Ask him questions to probe more deeply and to expand the horizon of his thinking. Your purpose here is to have him take a fresh look and not to harden his position by defending it. Here are a few illustrative questions:

What are some other methods we could use?
What would happen if sales were to go up by 25 percent?
What would be the result of doing nothing now?
If we could eliminate that feature, what effect would it have?
How would a change like this affect the purchasing department?
Suppose we could get engineering to give us an up-to-date status
    every month, would it be possible then?

Questions like these have the purposes of testing the limits and the interdependencies of the system. If the failure to agree is due to differences in assumptions about what is possible, getting to the bottom of the problem is a matter of finding out what the true limits and constraints are. Differences may be due to looking at the problem and its proposed solution along a single dimension. In truth, whatever is happening is occurring in a system in which changes in one part have repercussions in other parts. Agreement might be attained through getting a better understanding of how the system works.

Goal Setting down the Organization

Some steps in the planning process may be formulated at low levels to be consolidated and summarized as broader programs at higher levels. However, goal setting is not one of them. Goals must be formulated at the top and be disseminated downward. A manager can never delegate goal setting. To do so would be to abdicate, because the job of a manager in its most fundamental form is to decide what to do and to do it. This does not preclude participation, with its many benefits, nor does it restrict the manager from modifying his goals after receiving new information or counsel from subordinates.

Up to this point I have been deliberately vague about the distinction between goals and objectives. Everything that has been said applies to both. The distinction between the two is the span of time covered. By and large, goals have a time frame of more than a year or two; the time frame for objectives is shorter. Sales of $10 billion for Texas Instruments in the late 1980s is clearly a goal. Some goals are of a continuing nature, such as maintaining leadership in quality. There is nothing sacrosanct about the terminology. Many authors and management experts reverse the meaning of the terms, giving objectives the longer range.

Means/end chain. Inasmuch as goals are of longer duration and hence more encompassing, they come before the more detailed steps in planning and short-run objectives. Yet goal setting is so much a part of planning that it is difficult to identify it as a separate element. Goal setting cascades down the organization in a means/end chain. The chain works like this. The highest level of the organization adopts some goals. In order for these goals to be reached certain other, lower-level goals will have to be attained. These lower-level goals, which are the *means* to achieving the higher-level goals, are in turn broken down into still lower-level goals, which are the means for their completion, and so on. Let me make this crystal clear: The goals or subgoals received from the level above are not the goals for the organizational unit receiving them. They are requirements that must be incorporated into the goals of the organizational unit.

Figure 11 illustrates the downward evolvement of lower-level organizational goals. The dotted lines show that the goals of an organizational level must be compatible with the subgoal of the higher level but the two are not identical.

This process of analysis and identification of supporting goals is the same process that produces the traditional functional organization. Figure 12 is a very simplified and abbreviated organization chart which illustrates that the main purpose of a higher organizational unit is served by its components performing their functions. For example, production is accomplished through each of its subordinate departments doing their jobs.

Input-output of goal setting. Combining the logic of the two diagrams as it pertains to a single organizational unit illustrates the sources of information and influence that a unit receives and the conditions that it must satisfy in defining its own goals (Figure 13). Note that another element has been added to the diagram: the internal

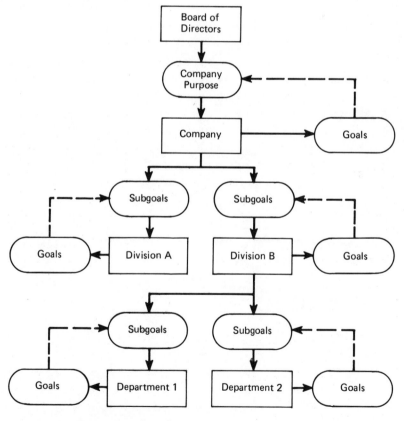

Figure 11. Hierarchy of goals.

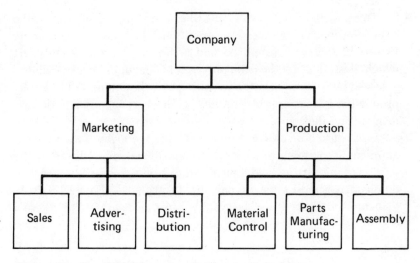

Figure 12. Simplified functional organization chart.

needs. This recognizes that sustaining the viability of the organizational unit is dependent on meeting its own needs.

The organizational unit is not only a component of a larger system but is also a system in itself. Departmental needs will inevitably influence goal formulation even though direct discussion of the needs is suppressed. A better way is to recognize and bring into the goal formulation process the requirement for satisfying (1) unit goals which

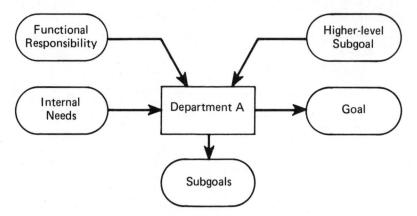

Figure 13. Goal-setting input and output.

are the subgoals of the higher level, (2) the functional responsibility, and (3) the internal needs.

The internal needs are of two types: the needs of the departmental unit itself, and the needs of its subsystems or components. Recruiting and training competent personnel is an example of the former. Keeping requirements for travel within acceptable limits (an example of the second) might meet the need of individuals to be with their families.

It is not necessary for all the needs of subunits to be addressed in formulating goals. Not only would it be impractical, if not impossible, but the lower-level units are far more capable than anyone else in recognizing their needs. Goal setting at that lower level will or should accommodate those needs. The danger to be avoided is establishing goals at one level that make it impossible for the lower levels to set goals, and subsequently courses of action, that simultaneously satisfy the goal handed down by the higher unit (actually one of its subgoals), the functional goal, and the internal demands. An example might be assigning an accounting department a goal which is not compatible with good accounting practice.

The nature of goal setting, as a process integrating goals of higher and lower organizational levels along with integrating functional responsibility, has imposed a somewhat theoretical discussion that I trust has not obfuscated the message. The message is a very real one. If you desire to set goals or you must set goals for your organization, you may envision yourself as being in the middle of the box in Figure 13. How you cope with the forces acting on you, how you identify goals as part of the planning process, and how you prepare strategies and plans are subjects for the next chapter.

8

How to develop a strategy and a plan for your organization

Vou need a strategy and a plan for your organization, whatever level it is on. You cannot afford to let the destiny of your group and your own career be tossed on the waves of fortune. There is far too much at stake. If you don't attend to the critical matter of charting a course of action, you can expect constant surprises and difficulties that could have been avoided. Planning begins with goal setting for *your* organization. Goals must be compatible with the dictated or higher-level subgoals (Figure 11), but they are not the same.

Good goal setting, good strategy, and good action planning produce both *accomplishment* and a *strong organization*. But an emphasis on good planning alone, as a process, will not overcome the deficiencies and errors that lead to poor performance. Instead, the emphasis should be on building a strong underlying system. However, the process is circular. Good planning does build strong organizations.

Although the steps of goal setting, strategy development, and action planning are more interrelated and simultaneous than they are sequential in practice, there is a sequential logic to the process. The arrows in Figure 14 show the logical flow of information and steps. However, the flow of information may at times be in reverse, and

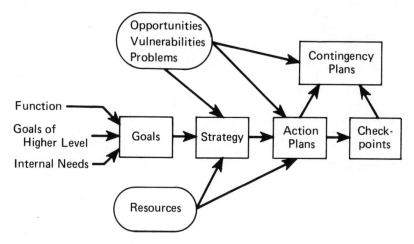

Figure 14. Action-planning process.

there are often loops that go back to prior steps. For example, in the stage of creating plans it may be found that the goals cannot be achieved with the resources available, and that therefore either resources must be increased or goals must be changed. The action-planning process may also uncover the opportunity to achieve results that surpass the goals or achieve favorable results not previously contemplated. A technological breakthrough or an innovative idea could be of such importance that it would trigger a revision of goals on up the ladder. For purposes of explaining how to develop a strategy for your organization, we will follow the left-to-right sequence of Figure 14.

What Should Be Done

There are six steps you can take to answer the question, "What should we do?" A discussion of these steps follows.

1. *Break down the output.* As Figure 14 shows, goals at the department or division level are the first result of the action-planning process. They are the consequence of the goals that are received from or negotiated with the next higher level, the functional responsibility, and the internal needs. Of these three, the key and the starting point for defining your own organizational goals is the functional responsibility.

Understanding the functional responsibility is really a matter of analyzing the *role* that the unit has in the organization. And this begins with an analysis of the output. You should do this using the framework of *product, information,* and *service,* for example:

Product
    Tooling
    Furniture
Information
    Drawings and specifications
    Accounting reports
    Production or performance reports
Service
    Sales
    Purchasing
    Consultation

Product refers to hardware, although the classification lends itself to software as well. As in the case of all the classifications, the output may be intended for use inside or outside the company. These classifications of output should not be confused with classifications of indirect or direct work or with codifying departments into direct work or service. The categories of output as defined here may be performed as either direct or indirect work and by all types of departments.

Many units within an organization have information as their major output. An industrial engineering department could have the responsibility of preparing time standards and generating reports on performance. A production control department, or at least a part of it, would have responsibility for preparing production schedules. Information is data that are available for use, are usually transmitted, and normally do not involve discussion.

Some functions such as sales, purchasing, personnel, and legal services have outputs that are neither a product nor information and are classified as service. Although information is given, it is unlike the output of information—it is not structured information but is given at a time, at a place, and in a form tailored for the situation. Services nearly always require coordination and much personal contact. Consequently, they are the most difficult to manage efficiently and easily balloon into excessive time. However, a service that is performed well is usually worth the extra effort and cost.

Practically all organizational units will have activities that cover two or three categories. Purchasing, for example, performs a service in finding sources of supply but also generates information in the form of purchase orders. It may also be responsible for preparing reports which disseminate information internally. The industrial engineering department is generally expected to perform many services, in addition to generating information. Engineers might be working with line personnel in developing better methods. They are expected to suggest how efficiency might be improved.

To analyze output, arrange the activities of a department into the three categories with an estimate of the time required or the percentage of total time. Table 1 shows such an arrangement of outputs for a credit department of a department store. (An illustration of how the credit department applies the planning steps appears later in this chapter.) As another example, consider an engineering department that designs air conditioning equipment. The key task of the department is to create engineering drawings and other supporting documentation that define the product. This key task would be broken down into major components and the time estimated for each. The department may also have some responsibility for coordination with production. Perhaps there are questions that arise on methods of manufacturing that are related to the design. Engineering may establish a liaison function with manufacturing to make improvements in the produceability of the design. All these cooperative efforts fall into the category of service.

For an outside salesman, the time that he is engaged in selling is time in a service function for his company. On the other hand, he may also perform a service function for the customer in showing him how to use the product or in working with him to ensure that the new equipment he has just bought is operating properly. This is service performed for the benefit of the client or customer and should be distinguished from service to the internal organization.

The purpose of all this is to get a better understanding of the function that your department performs. It helps to define the role and the character of the department. It will raise questions about how much of the time should be spent in the relatively inefficient service activities compared with the more efficient product or information-producing activities. Observe that the output classified as information in Table 1 can be handled routinely. You may compare the distribution of activities with your concept of the purpose of your group. The time

Table 1. Analysis of Output.

Output	Percent of Time	Received by	Use by Recipient
Product (none)			
Information			
Application approval	4	Data processing	Establish account and account number
Credit limit assigned to application	1	Data processing	Enter in account record
Adjustments to customer balance	3	Data processing	Enter in account balance
Applications and payment record of collection accounts	4	Collection agencies	Getting payments
		Legal staff	Sue for balance owed
		Data processing	Remove record from active file
Statistical reports on new accounts opened	2	Merchandise mgr./Controller	Sales projections
Report of accounts written off—bad debt	2	Controller	Entries in accounting records
Credit verification required by sales personnel	25	Floor salespeople	Permission to make charge sale
	41% 41		
Service			
Telephone calls to delinquent customers	9	Delinquent customers	Reassessment of credit situation
Answer inquiries from customers	10	Customers	Clarify status of balance due, etc.
Assist customers in completing charge account application	8	Customers	Filling out form
Correspondence other than routine, with customers	3	Customers	Usually to answer question or confirm telephone conversation
Analysis of write-offs and accounts receivable balances	2	Controller	Basis for "Reserve for doubtful accounts" and bad debt loss
Explanation and review of credit policy	2	Controller and other top mgmt.	Various
Specification for data processing	4	Data processing	Change or add programs
Surveillance over collection agencies and collection work	4	Collection agencies	Maintain recovery percentage that is acceptable to store
Coordination with legal counsel	1	Legal counsel	Sue for balance owed
	43% 43		
Internal Activities	16% 16		
	100%		

spent on an activity and its relative importance are not necessarily proportional. An important function may account for only 5 percent of the time. The conclusion to be reached is whether 5 percent is the right amount.

2. *Identify the users.* The next step in analyzing the output is to identify your customers. These are the people to whom the output is directed. Since most companies have relatively few organizational subdivisions that transact business with external organizations, most of the customers of a unit are people within the organization. This step is merely an answer to the question, "Who gets what?"

3. *Learn the uses.* This step determines how the recipient of the output uses it. How important is it to him? What would he do if he didn't receive it?

The significance of an output cannot be fully understood, hence properly evaluated, unless its use is followed one step beyond the immediate customer. This is true of every type of output and for every industry. It is also true on a very broad scale even for consumer products. For example, the manufacturer of toys should understand the desires of the retailer as well as those of the ultimate consumer, the child.

To find out how the customer really uses your output requires a great deal of understanding and knowledge of his operation, especially when the output is information. There is a temptation to go no farther than the obvious. A production control department that sends production schedules to a line department may think that there is really nothing to investigate further. The line department receives the schedule and produces accordingly, doesn't it? If you have been in production, you know that frequently this is not the case. Sometimes the line department will have to make modifications in the schedule to account for information that only the line has or for circumstances that were unforeseen by the production control department. Possibly the line department takes the information from the production schedule to record on one of its own forms. If the production control department had a greater understanding of the needs of its customer and the way the customer uses its output, it might be able to take more variables into consideration and provide schedules that are not so likely to be changed. It might also provide the information in a format that the line department can use without recopying information.

Often the most important value that can be obtained from understanding how the output is used comes from the use that is not being made. Again, this is particularly true of information as an output. A management information system may give executives pages of statistics for which they have no use and not provide the data they really need.

Understanding the use of the output also has a bearing on the amount of service that one department should give another. The output, either hardware or information, might require technical expertise in the user's organization that is only marginally present. Without some guidance the user may not be able to benefit fully from the output that he has received from you. If this is the case, you should place more emphasis on service.

4. *Compare handed-down subgoals and functional responsibility.* The subgoals that are handed down from or negotiated with the next higher organization should be explicit. If you haven't received specific goals from your boss, you can still move ahead by writing out the goals that you think or know your superior expects you to attain. Some of these might be common standards of performance, such as not having shortages of inventory.

You can now compare these handed-down subgoals with your functional responsibility, looking for compatabilities or incongruities.

When there are incongruities between the handed-down subgoals and the functions your organization is performing, you must make some changes. These changes will be reflected in the goals that you ultimately set for your unit, your strategy, and your action plans. And the bottom line is, of course, that there will be some changes in the activities you perform, which, in turn, will alter your function.

But before changing activities, take care to see that the changes do not have unintended and detrimental effects. This is not so likely to happen if a good analysis has been made of the outputs, who uses the outputs, and how they are used. When this is not done thoroughly there is a chance for serious error, as in the situation of the supervisor who, endeavoring to meet new goals, reduces resources allocated to the functions performed in the past. His customers no longer receive the output to which they are accustomed. And if this output has made a significant contribution to the output from the customer, a chain reaction will have started. Probably somewhere in the chain after the turmoil has subsided someone will take extra steps to compensate for the change—steps that may be neither effective nor efficient.

This is what happened when the "wire list" was discontinued in one company. The wire list was a bill of material for wire going into a military electronic product. It gave the lengths, types, and colors of wire, and had been originated to facilitate assembly operations. Under the burden of other pressures, the department responsible for the wire list discontinued producing it. Although it might not have been essential, there were other groups that made some use of it. After the discontinuance, they were left with the option of either creating their own wire list or somehow working around the gap. Probably more time was spent making up for the lack of a wire list than was spent in creating it.

5. *Define the needs of your organization.* These are the needs of the people in your organization, the needs of the group as a team, and the needs of the subsystems (lower-level groups) that are under your organization. Regarding the needs of lower-level groups, you should be aware of the roles, responsibilities, and abilities of the lower-level groups in assigning them subgoals. To the extent that the subgoals are not compatible with the qualities of the units, changes will have to be introduced.

6. *Write the goals.* Goals are intended to be a guide for strategy and actions over the long term, probably two or more years. Of course, this does not mean they cannot be revised. They can and should be revised as conditions change. Some goals will reflect a standard of performance. (A bank in California displays its goals for customer service for all to see. They are actually standards of performance, stating such maxims as being courteous to customers and answering the telephone by the third ring.) Other goals will specify improvements that are to be made, such as reducing the cost of the operation on a per transaction basis. Still others will relate to improving the professional capability of the organization.

To reflect briefly on these six steps, the intellectual process has been, first, to come to an understanding of how your organization fits into the larger system of which it is a part. You accomplish this partially by breaking down the output into product, information, and service categories. You determine who uses the output and how they use it. Next, you compare the goals that were received from the higher-level organizational unit with the existing capability and capacity of your department. You define the needs of your own personnel and the units below you in arriving at your organizational goals, and, finally, you write your goals.

Taking Stock of Resources

Beyond what you can accomplish as an individual, the performance of your unit is limited by the resources at its disposal. Probably your most important resource and your most expensive one is your staff. In a highly mechanized operation it might be your equipment. Money and materials are two others that may be under your direct control. I am thinking of money as budgeted funds that you may use to purchase outside services or materials. In addition, there are the outputs of other organizational units that you receive, such as semifinished parts, or information, or services. These are certainly resources though not usually categorized as such. Information that is accurate, timely, pertinent to your operation, and presented in the format you prefer can save you man-hours in your department.

Sometimes reaching for a goal means initiating a new activity or making a qualitative leap in an old one. It may appear that the resources are inadequate for this. Perhaps the quantity of output will strain the existing capacity, or perhaps the degree of precision or depth of information demanded is greater than what can be provided. However, at this point, you may not be confident that the existing resources are inadequate or be able to delineate exactly what is required. What is needed depends on the strategy that is used.

Making an Opportunity/Vulnerability Analysis

The analysis of functions, internal needs, and resources up to this point has been based primarily on a static environment. That is, there were no deliberate steps taken to explore the dynamic qualities of the business environment, which should be done by searching out the opportunities and vulnerabilities to the department. A checklist such as the following may be used to stimulate thinking.

1. Will the main functions performed by the department be needed in the future?

2. Are the needs and wants of the people being served by the department being met?
3. Will they in the future?
4. What new services will be wanted, and what additional groups will want to be served by the department?
5. Are the resources adequate for future needs?
6. How is the cost/benefit equation of the department viewed by its users and higher management?
7. How vulnerable is the department to cost-cutting programs?
8. What is the cost of the operation relative to outside service?
9. Are there technological changes that could make the department obsolete?
10. Is there new technology that could improve the operation of the department?
11. Could the functions performed by the department be performed by other organizational units?
12. Could the department be decentralized into smaller organizationally or geographically dispersed units?
13. Are there social or political forces that could change the department's way of doing business?
14. How vulnerable are the organizational units served by the department to changes which would alter their requirements for output?
15. How vulnerable are the organizational units which provide inputs to the department to changes that would alter these inputs?

Coping with Problems

You cannot take wise corrective action to deal with a problem until the true problem is exposed, and this often takes a great deal of probing and questioning. Even then, the sources of the problem might not be completely clear, and frequently there are different viewpoints. Concerted action is often required on several fronts to solve a problem.

This is illustrated by one plant that was plagued by an end-of-the-month rush to get out as much production as possible. The result of this effort was tremendous inefficiency and lower quality. Work in process was pushed through the last operations by personnel temporarily transferred from other parts of the plant. Final inspection was slipshod and some of it was performed by the men transferred from other departments. The aftermath of the rush found that the pipeline of work in process was drained. Until the normal flow could be restored, there was too little work in process for efficient utilization of labor.

The solution to a problem as widespread as this involves some strategic planning at the plant level and coordinated efforts by all the departments. The most fundamental and difficult change required was a change in thinking. Recognition for work well done could no longer be rooted in how much was shipped during the month. Instead, performance goals for efficiency and meeting customer due dates needed to be firmly implanted in the management philosophy. The changed philosophy had to be supported by pervasive changes in scheduling systems and manpower planning.

The Strategy for Your Organization

The strategy you adopt should give the answer to how you are to meet the goals, how you are to use your resources, what you will do to take advantage of the opportunities you have, and how you will cope with your vulnerabilities and major problems. Some general approaches to developing a departmental strategy are discussed below.

Continuation. This is a strategy of doing business as usual. It means that there are to be no major changes. It is a strategy that might apply to some functions or some suborganizational units within a department, but would probably not be a prudent strategy for all aspects of an operation in an environment that is destined to change.

Performance improvement. If the functions that are currently being performed by a department constitute the best answer to the question of "What should be done?" then the appropriate strategy might be performance improvement. All improvements in performance fall into the categories of cost, quality, and elapsed time. This is true for any business, from building guided missiles to shining shoes. Cost is the cost per transaction, however a transaction is defined. It could be writing a requisition, performing a machining operation on a part, or calling a patient to remind him of his doctor's appointment. A cost-improvement strategy is one that is aimed at reducing the cost of labor, machinery, energy, information from other organizations, and the like, for a unit of output.

The quality of a product or a service is a measure of how much value it has for the customer at the price offered. It has both objective and subjective components. The esthetic features of the product may influence the customer to ascribe a level of quality to the product that from an objective point of view is not there. From an objective point of view quality of a product covers a number of attributes such as reliability, consistency, accuracy, precision, dependability, and product life. For a service, accuracy, dependability, and thoroughness are components of quality. Quality is achieved through both the design of the product or service and the implementation of the design.

If the cost and quality features of a service or a product are held constant, the customer is almost always attracted by a reduction in the time that he has to wait for the product or service. Timeliness has been the key to the business strategies of fast food outlets and "instant" printing establishments.

Since the dimensions of cost, quality, and elapsed time or timeliness are rarely independent, strategies may be adopted that favorably improve one at the expense of another. For example, higher cost may be incurred to improve quality, or costs may be reduced by having a backlog of work to provide an even flow as a tradeoff for prompt delivery.

Internal development. This is a strategy aimed at improving the internal organization. It is an investment that will pay future dividends. No organization can ignore this strategy for long.

The ability to have things "go right" depends on the underlying strengths of the organization. Internal development strategies should have well-defined targets. These might include the acquisition of specific knowledge or improving the cohesiveness of the group. The nine areas for building mentioned in Chapter 4 are areas that could be designated for improvement.

New technology or equipment. The amazing advance of technology in the last 30 years has presented some opportunities for radical innovations. Computers are probably the most evident example of technology being used to eliminate many man-hours of detailed work. A departmental strategy based on introducing new technology can have many ramifications. It might cause the outputs to be modified to make them suitable for automated methods. Certainly, people have to be trained to use the new technology. Steps must be taken to provide continued reliable operations during transition from the old to the new technology.

Expansion of same functions. When the department must grow, perhaps to keep up with the growth of the company, the main strategy may be to increase the size of the department without detracting from performance. This can be a strategy demanding a great deal of executive ability when the growth is rapid. The strategy may involve adding space, relocating to new quarters, or establishing satellite operations at different locations.

New functions. Analysis of the functional responsibility, the opportunities, and the goals may show that new functions must be introduced. And new functions will require resources. Unless more resources are available, some functions will have to be discontinued or a parallel strategy of improving performance in existing functions will have to be employed.

Organizational change. The ability to reach goals may be limited by the structure of the organization. Organization is not permanent but changes in response to new conditions. A shift in functions and the introduction of new technology are two of many changes that may render the old organization obsolete.

Organizational change can also be caused by organizational changes in other departments or in the company as a whole. For example, a department doing market research might be organized internally along the lines of function or professional specialty. Now if the company reorganizes to put product lines into semi-autonomous divisions, the market research department might operate more effectively if its staff is organized to serve a particular division.

Retrenchment or displacement. This is a strategy to be employed when your department is reducing the scope of its operations, when its operations are being discontinued, or when its function will be displaced by some other function done elsewhere. The idea of cutting back or going out of business is not a cheery thought. Among other things, it usually means finding other positions for subordinates or laying them off. However, when the strategy is called for, you can approach it in a positive way. The planning and actions needed to carry out this strategy require a high level of managerial skill. If retrenchment or displacement is done smoothly, you enhance your reputation as a professional manager.

How to Prepare Action Plans

You have determined in broad terms what you are going to do by establishing goals and making decisions on the strategies to be employed. It is now time to map out the actions and programs that will carry out the strategy. This is done through programs which are a set of interrelated tasks designed to achieve a result that in turn either meets a goal or is a step toward it. The action plan outlines the tasks of a program, the person responsible, the completion date, and the planned costs and resources to be utilized. It is formulated through the mental process of analysis.

Suppose that your strategy calls for a drastic change in secretarial and clerical functions to implement the concepts referred to variously as the office of the future, or word processing. This is an office system which links together the functions of dictating, typing (capturing information), editing, processing, printing, and information storage and retrieval. Dictation between an executive and his secretary is replaced by dictation equipment and a typing pool. Text-editing typewriters, sometimes equipped with cathode-ray tubes to display written material, allow for revisions to be made efficiently. Information can be processed using computers and printers such as the new IBM 6670 laser printer which can be tied to several computers and print on plain paper using up to four different type faces.

Taking full advantage of the technology means reorganizing the duties of clerical personnel. The traditional secretarial job is to be abolished. The functions are to be divided between correspondence secretaries in a "word-processing center" and a much reduced staff of administrative assistants, each one serving more than one executive.

Making changes such as described above in a traditional office is anything but an easy job. Depending on the circumstances, a breakdown of the major tasks might be as follows:

Determining the scope of the new system—what areas are to be included.

Obtaining new equipment.

Making physical rearrangements in office layout.

Writing new procedures.

Preparing software or data processing programs.

Conducting orientation meetings for executives.

Establishing new organizational structure.

Writing new or revised job descriptions.

Installing new equipment, probably in phases.

Training clerical and secretarial personnel.

Each one of these tasks is, of course, subject to further breakdown; each could be an action plan in itself. It is more likely that the department would not have as many as ten different action plans for making this change. In fact, it could be considered to be just one major plan. Another alternative would be to place all the tasks that pertain to the equipment and technical part of the installation in one plan, and put the people-related tasks in another.

The action plan itself may be organized according to an outline:

1. *The title of the plan.*

2. *A statement of expected results.* The output of the plan should be stated explicitly. It could be a report, a decision producing a purchase order, or employees putting a new procedure into practice.

3. *The person given primary responsibility for the plan.* The action plan should certainly identify the person who is responsible for its implementation. In addition, it is often desirable to name other persons who have important responsibilities and those who are responsible for related plans. For example, a person who is responsible for a phase of the plan such as writing new procedures might be cited.

4. *A specific statement of work describing how the action plan is to be carried out.* This statement should be sufficiently detailed to identify the major tasks that have to be performed. Some of these may be tasks related to obtaining information, getting approval, and defining concepts—tasks that are relatively conceptual or intangible in nature. These tasks, as well as the tangible tasks such as getting machinery in place, should be identified as discrete steps.

5. *A schedule for each phase.* Prior to making the schedule, the relationships between the major tasks have to be established. Some tasks cannot begin until others are completed. In other cases, it may be desirable, though not necessary, to coordinate the timing of completion

dates. For example, it may be desirable to (1) conduct orientation meetings for executives, (2) establish the new organizational structure, and (3) write new and revised job descriptions, before beginning the training of secretarial and clerical personnel. Although the training of personnel could proceed when equipment, software, and related decisions have been made, it would probably be politically prudent to delay its start until the new organizational structure and an overview of the system have been thoroughly explained to executives.

The completed schedule should show a start and completion date for each phase or task. It can be in the form of a Gantt chart or a network chart such as PERT.

6. *The budget or resources required.* Any capital expenditures required by the plan should be noted. The labor and material expenses of the plan which are over and above those for current operations should also be estimated and recorded. At the department level, estimating labor in man-hours may be adequate.

7. *Assumptions and dependencies.* In cases where the success of the action plan rests squarely on the work of another group or on an assumption that certain steps will be taken, the plan should record these facts to bring them into view.

The completed action plan should answer the questions of who, what, when, where, why, and how. Some other points to use in evaluating an action plan are shown in the list below.

1. Time:	Has enough time been allocated to implement the plan?
2. Capabilities:	Are the responsible people really capable of carrying out the tasks required of them within the action plan?
3. Logic:	Are the relationships between tasks logically arranged and sequenced?
4. Legal:	Does the plan comply with government regulations and laws?
5. Consistencey with strategy:	Does the action plan support the strategy? Is the program supportive of other programs that carry out the strategy?
6. Assumptions:	How realistic are the assumptions underlying the action plan?

7. Realism:	Do the costs and benefits appear to be realistic or are they overly optimistic?
8. Risk:	What risks are associated with implementing this action plan?
9. Problems:	What problems could this plan cause? To what extent can the problems be anticipated?
10. Alternatives:	Have other alternatives been evaluated?
11. Redundancy:	Are there backup resources that may be employed to overcome unexpected difficulty?
12. Contingency plans:	Are there plans that can be put into use when the original plan cannot be followed? (See section on Planning for Contingencies in this chapter.)

Establishing check points. The action plan specifies schedule dates which are key points for comparing the plan and actual progress. These may be adequate if they trigger corrective action with a promptness that is in keeping with the seriousness of the deviation from the plan. If this is not the case, additional checkpoints or milestones will have to be set. The principle to keep in mind is that there is a cost involved in every checkpoint. The cost is both an expenditure of resources—managerial time, for instance—and an intrusion into the autonomy of the people entrusted with the responsibility for the task. Good people value a degree of independence.

Getting the Most out of Bottoms-up Planning

The procedures outlined for setting strategy and a plan for your organization are formats for orderly and innovative thinking. Analyzing the functions of your department and taking the other steps leading to strategies and plans ensures that your part of the organization will make a significant contribution toward the achievement of the goals of the larger organization and that in the process you will be developing the long-range strength of your own unit.

Throughout the process there is ample opportunity for your subordinates to participate. In fact, they should. Inasmuch as the goals of your organization are not merely the goals assigned by your boss but those that you select for the betterment of your group and the larger organization, you should tap the minds of your subordinates. This does not imply that the establishment of goals should be done by majority vote. Defining goals is the responsibility of the manager and one that he cannot delegate. But participation could be handled informally by discussing the issues with subordinates; or, on a more formal basis, a meeting could be held to review the strategies and action plans.

Annually or biannually it is desirable to explore thoroughly the business environment and to delve deeply into the entire range of possible actions. Many companies engage in this sort of thing by having the top executives cloistered at a resort for a few days of introspection and contemplation as well as for some hardheaded sessions on business planning. At the midmanagement level or department level, the funds for such culturally and professionally enriching experiences are generally severely limited or nonexistent, which makes it difficult for the department head to play host, but it is possible, nevertheless, to hold meetings on strategy during the normal workday.

If you want to get widespread participation and depth in thinking you need a structure to stimulate the flow of ideas and to codify the ideas that arise. The structure outlined below is a bottoms-up approach to planning designed for a group of 15 to 50 people meeting from one to three days. After an orientation advising everyone of the purpose of the meeting and the ground rules, the agenda should begin with an assessment of how well the department is performing its current functions.

1. The functions or outputs of the department are listed on a flip chart along with the outside group receiving the output (see Table 1). The output should be identified as being either a service, a product, or information. The group should then be asked to evaluate how well the output meets the needs of the recipients. This can be done by every person assigning a numerical score to the output and averaging the scores of the group. It is very likely that the discussion will identify some unmet needs of recipients and reveal a consensus about the relative merits of what the department produces.

During this and the following discussions participants are encouraged to make notes about problems, opportunities, and vulnerabilities that they think of.

2. Next, the performance of the department in terms of cost, quality, and elapsed time is discussed. This is a look at the internal workings of the department. Numerical ratings may be used here also to identify strengths and weaknesses.

3. The relations with other parts of the organization is the next topic for discussion. Within organizations there are natural areas of disagreement between groups that arise from the functions they perform, as in the case of sales and production. Sometimes the level of disagreement can reach proportions that hinder the effectiveness of the entire company. Problems along these lines should be brought out into the open.

4. Resources and management are the final topics of the discussion of how well the group is operating currently. In the open meeting some evaluation of the technical expertise, the esprit de corps, and the cooperation within the department can be expected. However, a full open discussion of sensitive topics like this will probably not take place unless the group has had a lot of experience with very frank, open communication.

5. Having given consideration to the current status of the department, the group should now turn its attention to the future to try to recognize trends that will have a bearing on the operation of the department. A checklist such as the 15 questions used to make an opportunity/vulnerability analysis will help the group zero in on trends. The main points in the discussion are recorded on flip charts.

After identifying the trends, it is revealing to present their impact graphically: Draw a matrix, with the trends on one axis and the outputs of the department on the other. In the squares, indicate how the trend will affect the output. Numerical ratings from 2 to −2 can be used to indicate that the trend will greatly increase the importance of the output (2), will moderately increase its importance (1), will effect no change (0), will moderately decrease importance (−1), or will greatly decrease importance (−2).

6. At this point the walls of the room are probably covered with pages of flip charts. The participants, either individually or in groups of two or three, are then asked to write *planning items*. These are statements in a few sentences of areas that should be addressed in preparing plans of action. Many of these will have been expressed in the open meeting even though the main direction of the discussions has been the state of the department rather than what to do about it.

The lists on the flip charts are used as reminders. The participants should be encouraged to classify their planning items as a problem, a potential problem or a vulnerability, or an opportunity. This classification scheme causes thinking to be a little sharper and also prods people to think about opportunities and not just problems, which is the natural tendency.

7. This process ought to produce from 25 to 100 planning items, each written on a separate piece of paper. These are collected and sorted according to the subject into four classifications: *outputs, internal performance, relations with other groups,* and *resources and management.* The items in each classification should be read to the participants. In view of the current operations of the department and the challenges of the future the question posed is, "Do these planning items cover the issues that the department is facing as it contends with its present role and is preparing to meet the demands of the future?" If the group agrees that the planning items are complete, the meeting is over and there is no further need for widespread participation. The next steps can be undertaken by the manager of the group himself or a few of his subordinates.

8. The planning items in each of the four classifications are reviewed with the idea of developing an action plan that resolves each of them. Because of the similarity of many of the issues and the cause and effect relationships between issues, one action plan would undoubtedly resolve several of them. This step is completed when action plans, tentative at this point, have been prepared addressing all the planning items.

9. The tentative action plans are reviewed for their feasibility, cost, and benefits. Some will probably be discarded. The remaining ones are given priorities. Those with high priorities are more closely examined for the resources that they will require and the probable results. If they pass the criteria for acceptance, they are approved and implemented.

10. Through conceptual thinking at a higher level of abstraction, this process can be carried up to the point of developing strategies and goals. The approved programs represent the strategy of the department. A summary of them is in reality the strategy or strategies of the department, and could be categorized under the eight types of strategy cited earlier in the chapter. Taking a further step, goals for the department could be derived from the strategy and the programs.

Bottoms-up planning summarized. Organizations that have relied extensively and regularly on bottoms-up planning have been disappointed with the results. There is a tendency for the process to be too problem oriented, distracting attention from opportunities. It has also been criticized for producing a plan which is nothing more than the composite thinking of the employees, putting higher management in the position of virtually abdicating from its responsibilities.

On the other hand, my experiences and the experiences of others indicate that the process carried to a point can be a very positive adjunct to the normal participative, top-down planning processes. It certainly gives subordinates an opportunity to voice their opinions, as well as a better understanding of the what, why, and how of the department. But more than that, the real advantage is getting ideas that you as the manager may overlook. Sometimes the maverick in the group has something to say that can make everyone reevaluate his or her position. I think that the advantages of this system warrant its use annually or biannually as an adjunct to top-down planning with informal participation.

Although other approaches and additional steps may produce a different structure from what was presented here, it is vital that a formal structure be used. The early parts of the meeting should always focus on understanding the current state and the changes that might occur, prior to identifying specific problems or actions. Unless the participants have the big picture first, you can expect an overemphasis on dealing with the immediate and the petty.

Planning for Contingencies

On a departmental level, contingencies are of two types—those that arise from a change in the environment in which your department operates, and those which occur unexpectedly in the course of operations, sometimes triggered by the actions of your group. There is a contingency of the first type when the company loses a bid on a contract, forcing a major reduction in staff. At the department level, there is no value in having a contingency plan for something like this other than to find a scheme for keeping your best employees. A change in organization that drastically alters the functions of your group is another contingency. This is the type of event that you should have considered in making the vulnerability/opportunity analysis. If you favor the change, you should have adopted strategies and programs that work toward it. If you don't favor the change, your strategies and plans should have been aimed at getting a demonstrated performance which proves that the present organization is preferred. However, if you find that your efforts were to no avail, and the organizational change is dictated, your only choice is to comply. Again, there is really not much use in having a contingency plan.

Changes that occur in the course of operations are a different matter, for example, not getting a shipment of materials by the promised delivery date. For situations like these, you may want to have a plan ready.

Planning for contingencies has two benefits. One is that it forces you to explore the possible consequences if things do not go as planned. If you must change your plans, you have acceptable alternative plans and you take little risk. Without good alternatives, you take a great risk.

The other benefit is that a contingency plan permits you to change your course without delay. Judging from all the information available to the public, there was no contingency plan in readiness when the USS Pueblo was seized by North Korean warships in 1968. The captain of the ship seemed confused over how much he should resist and our Navy didn't know what actions would be acceptable politically. It is inconceivable to me that with the danger of attack there was no plan that could have been executed immediately.

A company that is hit by a wildcat strike but continues to do business by having its nonunion employees fill in demonstrates that it has a contingency plan. Contingency plans cannot be prepared for every emergency, but if the probability is reasonably high that a planned event will not be reached or that a disrupting event will occur, and there are rewards for immediate action, a contingency plan should be prepared.

Information on how to create contingency plans is found in Chapter 11.

The Essence of Successful Planning

The principles of planning that underlie the step-by-step procedure are more important than the steps themselves. One of the most basic of these principles is that planning begins with an understanding of how the organizational unit for which the plan is being prepared fits into the larger system. This understanding is accomplished at the department level by first identifying the outputs of the department, the recipients of the output and the use they make of it, and the goals that must be achieved to make the expected contribution to the larger system. Second, the needs of the organizational unit are considered from two standpoints: what inputs from others and from cooperative efforts it requires to do the job, and what conditions must be met internally for viability and effectiveness.

Recognizing present and potential opportunities and vulnerabilities not only calls for an understanding of how the organizational unit relates to the larger system, but also depends on a perception of the changes that the larger system is undergoing. Like a forward observer scanning the horizon, the manager should periodically assess the kaleidoscope of forces that impinge on his department. This kind of assessment requires information, most of it gained informally from colleagues. Among the by-products of the cooperative efforts between groups are informal alliances in matters of common interest. These alliances are sources of information, sometimes rumors, that may be of great importance.

An understanding of the environment that a department operates in and an evaluation of its resources are basic to developing a strategy for the department. Strategy is the most vital link in the conceptual chain illustrated in Figure 13. Developing a strategy forces the manager to step back from the day-to-day tasks to grapple with the question of what he is really trying to accomplish in a larger sense. Having a strategy ensures that the programs being undertaken are consistent and coherent. What's more, a strategy that embodies challenging goals imparts to the routine operation an added meaning that is sure not to be lost on the people in the department.

Illustration: The Credit Department

This illustration is a sketch of how a credit department in a large department store can develop goals, strategies, and plans. If you will overlook the many superficialities, necessitated by treating a complex subject as briefly as possible, I believe you will find the illustration helpful in clarifying the concepts presented in the chapter. Other examples might be more ideally suited to the material than this one, but a credit department is a known entity to readers and has the additional advantage of demonstrating that the procedure can be applied to what most consider to be a routine operation.

The credit department in this illustration handles 110,000 accounts representing $17,000,000 in annual charge business. Total annual sales are $40,000,000 currently. Monthly statements and notices of delinquency, duns, are sent out automatically through the data processing system. However, the credit department is responsible for making sure that each customer's account is handled properly by the computer. The breakdown of the output is given in Table 1. Completing this analysis fulfills steps 1, 2, and 3 of the action-planning process.

The credit department has been given four negotiated or dictated goals that serve other departments and the company as a whole:

1. Open 1,800 new charge accounts per month.
2. Keep bad debt losses to 1.5 percent or less of charge sales.
3. Give verification of credit status to sales personnel within two minutes.
4. Keep costs within budget.

The goal of opening 1,800 new charge accounts per month is, in a sense, a merchandising subgoal. If it is achieved, it will have a positive effect on sales. Of course, the credit department does not have full control over making this goal. It depends on the sales personnel on the floor and the advertising department to encourage customers to apply for a charge account. Together these four goals represent the purpose of the credit department: to make it easy for people to buy on credit and to keep the bad debt loss and the cost of operating the department within bounds.

Step 4 in the action-planning process is to compare the goals and the functional responsibility, which has been broken down in Table 1. For example, is the goal of opening 1,800 new charge accounts per month compatible with the activities of the department as they are now being performed? Some of the outputs and activities have a direct bearing on opening new accounts, such as the criteria for approving an application, and the assistance that a customer is given in filling out the form. But suppose that the department is not getting enough credit-worthy applicants, what can it do? It might consider a new output: conducting training meetings for sales personnel on how to encourage people to open a charge account.

The goal of providing prompt credit verification to sales personnel is a part of a larger, unstated goal of encouraging customers to use their credit cards and as a consequence probably buy more. Some other outputs of the credit department that relate to this sales goal are answers to inquiries from credit customers, special correspondence, and the wording on statements when payments are overdue.

Bad debts can be limited at the front end by stringent credit-granting criteria or by aggressive collection at the other end. There are many activities that have a bearing on this goal. Just where the emphasis should be is a strategic decision for the credit department.

Inasmuch as the real purpose of the department is to increase *profitable* credit sales, it might question the limit of 1.5 percent bad debt. Perhaps it should be higher, or much lower. Suppose that the credit limits for customers were reduced, what would be the effect on sales and on bad debt? It might be beneficial for the department to sponsor some research into these questions. These are matters that the department should keep in mind when it develops its own goals, strategy, and plans.

Internal needs. Defining the department's needs is step 5 in action planning. One of the internal needs of the department is increased efficiency. Forty-one percent of the time is used to generate or communicate information, and verifying credit takes 25 percent of the total time. Computer and communications systems could be installed to reduce verification time drastically.

Another need is to improve the capability of the department to control bad debt losses by setting appropriate credit limits for customers. More would have to be known about the effect credit limits have on reducing sales on the one hand and reducing bad debt on the other. Getting the information to analyze the relationship between purchases on charge accounts and bad debts would require the cooperation of data processing. New programs and new reports would have to be prepared. The credit department could take responsibility for specifying how the information is to be summarized and categorized for its analysis. However, this raises the question of whether or not anyone in the department is qualified to do this. In other words, is the present state of knowledge adequate for the task? If not, there is need to upgrade the professionalism in the department.

There is a never-ending need to train the personnel who serve the public at the counter, since this is a job with high turnover. The job requires a person who thoroughly understands how the information on the application is used to establish a customer's credit, who can help a customer who is confused in filling out the form, and who is courteous. Experience indicates that people who do this job well are moved into better jobs, and the others leave the company, producing a perennial problem of training new personnel.

Goals of the credit department. For the credit department there are many answers to the question, "What should be done?" Should it find out how the messages on statements sent to delinquent accounts affect the customers? Do they motivate the customer to pay? Do they antagonize him or her so that the store loses a customer in the future? How far should the credit department go with a delinquent customer before turning over the account to a collection agency? Should the department expend effort in trying to reduce its cost of operation? The credit department's priorities are represented in the following list of goals, which take into consideration the functional responsibility, the four goals that are really subgoals of higher-level organizations, and the internal needs. Writing the goals is step 6 in the action-planning process.

1. Open an average of 1,800 new charge accounts per month or 21,600 per year.
2. Analyze the bad debt losses to determine what the target for losses should be and the best methods for controlling bad debt.
3. Keep bad debt losses to 1.5 percent of credit sales as an interim goal.
4. Obtain 10 percent net recovery on accounts sent to collection agencies.
5. Give verification of credit status to sales personnel within two minutes.
6. Reduce the time spent on credit verification by 50 percent in three years.
7. Upgrade the level of professional knowledge in the department.
8. Increase charge account sales to 50 percent of total sales in two years.

Resources. There are some inadequacies in the resources available that will have to be corrected in order to meet the goals. New technology will have to be introduced to achieve the goal of reducing the time spent on credit verification. The information currently supplied to the department from data processing is sufficient to support the type of analysis needed to improve credit policy and answer such questions as what affect a change on the 1.5 percent limitation on bad debt would have on sales. There is a perpetual need for more training among lower-level personnel in the department, and the professionalism of the senior people should be improved.

Vulnerabilities, opportunities, and problems. The biggest threat to the credit department is the possibility that the management of the department store might discontinue charge accounts, leaving the store's customers the option of paying cash or using a national credit card. Of course, management would not take this step as long as it was believed that the cost of offering charge accounts, including the bad debt loss, was more than offset through increased sales and finance charge income.

Since the passage of the Federal Truth in Lending Act of 1969, several bills and amendments have been passed which establish guidelines for granting credit and collecting delinquent accounts. It may be that with the passage of these bills, the pressure by consumer groups for change has been satisfied and that no new major changes will be forthcoming. However, credit and collection are subjects of popular concern and very much subject to political forces. If new laws or regulations are put into effect, it can be expected that they, like those in the past, will add to the cost of credit.

There are opportunities for the credit department to work closer with merchandising and sales in efforts to promote business. Knowing more about the customers and class of customers who are the big spenders opens the door to special direct mail advertising for that group.

The most visible problem, if not the most important one, is being able to serve the public with courtesy and professionalism. Qualified personnel are needed to assist customers in filling out the charge account application and to answer inquiries from customers about the status of their accounts. The low salaries paid to the clerical personnel who do this type of work make it difficult to retain the most capable people, causing a continual need for on-the-job training.

Strategy of the credit department. After taking a look at the opportunities and vulnerabilities, the credit department came to the conclusion that it could make a big contribution to the company by becoming more involved in marketing functions. Goal 8, increasing credit sales to 50 percent of the total, was then adopted as a stimulus for this effort but with the understanding that it could not be achieved by the independent efforts of the credit department; help from sales and advertising was needed.

The department adopted two major strategies. One, which combines new functions with internal development, is a strategy of elevating and improving the contribution of the credit department to the department store by linking the department more closely to the merchandising department and the controller. It will require some minor changes in the data processing system to highlight statistics that can be used for analysis. If successful, this strategy will make consumer credit more of a marketing tool. And if this can be done, reaching the goal of 21,600 accounts for the year should be relatively easy. Also, the greater emphasis on analysis of bad debt losses may result in new criteria for setting credit limits that would increase sales to customers who have a low risk of default and keep credit to high-risk customers under close control. The ability to do this would of course have a bearing on the 1.5 percent bad debt goal, if indeed 1.5 percent is the correct number. This strategy would also provide a better basis for establishing a norm for bad debt write-offs.

Setting the department on this new course would of itself upgrade the department, enriching the knowledge of the key people in the department as a by-product. However, learning through osmosis will probably be inadequate. It will probably be necessary to create a new position or two to be staffed by individuals with greater analytical skill and a broader business background than those presently on board.

The other major strategy is to improve performance in two areas. The first is in the function of credit verification. The present cost, 25 percent of the total time of the department, is too high and can be reduced. Equipment can be installed at the cash registers on the floor that will communicate directly with the computer to automatically give credit approval in most cases. Only the exceptions would require contact with the credit department. The resulting reduction in personnel would allow for increasing the analytical functions of the department without adding to the total staff.

The second area marked for improved performance is the service to people who come to the counter to apply for a charge account. The goal is to give them prompt service at all times, possibly simplifying the application. One approach may be to have more than one application. For a person who has established good credit elsewhere and in an upper income bracket, recording home addresses for the last five years may be an unnecessary inconvenience.

The thrust of these strategies is to improve the efficiency and the ease of performing the routine functions of the department so that more of its resources are available for analytical work and there is an improved level of service to both internal organizations and the public. Its net effect will be to reduce the percentage of time used for producing the output of information and to increase the time and the substance of the output classified as service.

Action plans. Five action plans have been formulated to implement the strategy, and together they will achieve all the goals of the department except the goal of obtaining 10 percent net recovery on accounts sent to collection agencies. This goal is handled by assigning it to a group within the department. It is a standard of performance. If the group can meet it in the normal course of operation, no plans or particular strategies will be needed. If otherwise, then the group responsible will have to determine the strategy and the plans it will need to attain the goal. The first four action plans are summarized briefly below, and the fifth is represented in the recommended format.

1. *Simplified credit application.* The plan will result in two or more applications being in use. Abbreviated forms would eliminate superfluous information for the more credit-worthy customer.

2. *Training program for clerical personnel in credit department.* This action plan would be aimed at giving new people in the department a better understanding of the role of the department as it is related to the overall operation of the store. This would give more significance to the specific job training which will also be included in the training program.

3. *Training given to sales personnel on opening and using charge accounts.* This plan would be a cooperative effort between the salesforce and the credit department. Its purpose would be to increase credit sales and thereby increase total sales.

4. *Analysis of credit limits, buying habits, and bad debt.* This is

aimed at getting a better grasp of the relationships between bad debt and policies for granting credit. The purpose of the project would be to determine more reliable procedures for controlling bad debt to a predetermined percentage of credit sales and to establish criteria for determining what the target amount of bad debt should be.

5. *Improved system of verifying credit standing.*

A. Title: Automated credit verification.

B. Expected results: The system will reduce the amount of manhours used by personnel in the credit department to verify the credit standing of customers to less than half of the present amount. In addition, it will consistently give verification to floor sales personnel within 30 seconds unless there is a problem with the account. In nearly all cases, problem accounts can be reviewed manually within two minutes.

C. Responsibility: The manager of the credit department. Assistance will be provided by the systems and procedures group and by the data processing groups under the jurisdiction of the controller's department.

D. Statement of work: Credit verification terminals will be installed at cash registers. Inquiries for credit verification by sales personnel will access computer files electronically. When the account is in good standing, approval for the purchase will be transmitted to the floor station automatically. When the account is in marginal status or approval is denied, it will refer the inquiry to personnel in the credit department. Pertinent data from the account will be displayed so that the credit department can quickly decide whether or not to approve the credit purchase. The major tasks in this action plan are the following:

Statement of the concept and scope of the program, cost justification, and management approval

System specifications—capacity, time requirements, form of output and input, linkage to other systems

System design

Hardware selection

Procedures preparation and programming

Pilot installation

Orientation and training sessions

System is fully installed and operational

E. Schedule:

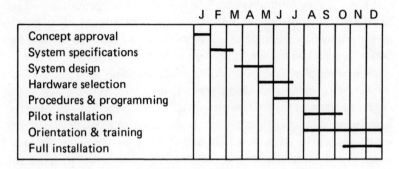

	J	F	M	A	M	J	J	A	S	O	N	D
Concept approval												
System specifications												
System design												
Hardware selection												
Procedures & programming												
Pilot installation												
Orientation & training												
Full installation												

F. Tentative budget: Equipment purchase and installation: $100,-000.

Note: A more accurate and detailed breakdown of costs will be furnished with the statement of the scope of the project for higher management review and approval.

G. Assumptions and dependencies: A technically qualified project manager would be selected to oversee the implementation of the plan. The project manager would either be furnished by the controller's department or be hired. He would work closely with the manager of the credit department.

9

How to organize for achievement

The methods for organizing are governed by the characteristics of the task, the people, and the environment, which to a degree is a product of the first two. All three of these have changed drastically in recent years and will be changing rapidly in the future. However, much of what we see in organizations is a carry-over from the models of the past.

Industrial organizations have until recent times been structured to perform comparatively well-defined tasks with a workforce having predictable qualifications. The structure was based on a breakdown of tasks. Larger and general responsibilities were given to high levels, which in turn divided them into lesser responsibilities and more specific duties as the process of division and specification continued down the organization. Specialization, it was believed, was the route to efficiency. Technical considerations prevailed over human considerations in designing organizations, and little thought was given either to the satisfaction of the individual or to the gulf between the capabilities a person possessed and those that he used on the job.

Synthesis Is the Theme

For a number of reasons, this trend of breaking down work into smaller and smaller segments has been halted and is now in the process of reversal. The change is partly due to the nature of work and the size of corporations. There are three very significant trends:

1. Work is becoming more complex, creating a greater need for specialists. Employing more specialists means that each handles a narrower scope of work but in much more depth.

2. The rate of change in technology continues to advance, which accelerates the need for further specialization.

3. Problem solving under conditions of complexity involves a variety of professional specialties.

These three trends, characteristic of much of today's work, demand more coordination and integration within organizations. Organizing on the basis of specialization alone, which has been the predominant practice in the past, creates functions that become increasingly more narrowly defined at each lower level. This pattern of organization inhibits the communication, rapport, and coordination that are often needed between groups to integrate the efforts of diverse and specialized components of the organization toward common goals in an environment of change.

Today we are seeing the emergence of organizational patterns that are enlarging responsibilities to meet these new challenges. Organizational structure which in the past was based wholly on *analysis* is now being based, at least partly, on *synthesis*. Teams and work groups, often comprising members from different departments, are being combined to create a *whole* that is much more effective than are the individuals dispersed among diverse organizational units.

Automation, both in the factory and in the office, is another trend that is changing the shape of organizations. It has become possible to replace human effort with machines, thus reducing the demand for low-skilled workers.

Data processing improvements in performance and reductions in cost have made data bases a reality. Common data bases make it feasible to put together functions, heretofore quite separate, into innovative combinations. This is an emerging trend that will continue. The company of the future will have the capability of quickly synthesizing disparate components of an organization into a cohesive whole that is tailor made for the task at hand.

Incidentally, it was thought at one time that automation would wipe out middle management, but the added complexity and need for greater coordination ensures that middle management has a vital role to play.

Present Trends

The composition, needs, and attitudes of the workforce are also changing, and this is another reason for the change in organization structure. Consider the following facts and trends:

1. The "baby boom" bulge in the population is crossing from the twenties to the thirties. By 1985, the age mix will have shifted dramatically from what it was in 1975. The population in the 30 to 39 age bracket in 1985 will be larger by 11 million, which is *an increase* of over 40 percent, and there will be 7 million fewer people aged 10 to 19. What is the significance of this for management? People in their late teens and early twenties are willing to accept low-skill and low-paying jobs if they can expect to work up to something better. A large number of people who are at least tolerant of low positions fit the pyramidal structure of a traditional organization—many at the bottom, fewer in the middle, and very few at the top. This model of human utilization has never been a particularly good match with human capabilities, but it becomes a complete mismatch when the bulge of the working population is in its thirties. At that point people will become increasingly frustrated and even surly if they remain in low-level jobs with aspirations unfulfilled.

2. Exacerbating the problem of unfulfilled expectations is the fact that over 40 percent of this group are expected to attend college by the time they are 30, making them the best educated in the country's history.

3. Slow growth in productivity and high inflation make it impossible to reward the low-level worker with a higher real wage, which might take some of the sting out of his frustrations. In fact, if the future holds to the results of 1978, there will be a reduction in the real wage. On April 2, 1979 *Business Week* reported that wages increased by 7.3 per employee, but inflation was 7.6 percent, reducing the real wage by 0.3 percent.

4. Increases in productivity, a reduction in real costs per unit of output, in other words, will require more ingenuity and industriousness than ever before to overcome the high, and rising, cost of energy.

As energy costs escalate, it becomes less economical to trade machine for manual work, thus making it more difficult to automate dull jobs out of existence.

5. A University of Michigan 1977 Quality of Employment Survey, compared with a survey taken in 1973, shows that the trend toward dissatisfaction is under way:

> 53 percent believe work to be interesting, compared with 61 percent in 1973.
>
> 27 percent say that the pay is good, down from 41 percent in 1973.
>
> 32 percent believe they have an opportunity to develop their own special skills, compared with 43 percent in 1973.

What Conditions Must Be Met?

The changes in the workforce, the complexity of tasks, and the use of automation are trends that are modifying the structure of organizations today. Jobholders at the bottom of the hierarchy are being replaced by specialists, middle managers, staff personnel, and skilled operators. The supply and demand curves for knowledge continue to intersect at higher and higher levels.

The question is how to organize to get results. The answer is the formula:

$$\text{Responsibility} + \text{Authority} + \text{Knowledge} + \text{Motivation} = \text{Achievement}$$

The productive organization is one that (1) fosters a deep sense of responsibility, (2) gives people the necessary authority to make decisions, (3) brings the requisite knowledge to bear on the issue, and (4) stimulates people. When these four elements are combined, it becomes possible to plan and execute. Some of the conditions that must be met to enable an organization to be a vehicle for achievement are described below.

Orientation to tasks. The primary purpose of an organization is to perform a function or a task. Through the planning process, discussed in Chapter 8, a department establishes strategies, goals, and goal-facilitating projects. The focus of the organization must be on those ends that largely benefit others. Some of the resources of an organization must be devoted to improving the strength of the organization for continued long-term performance. However, when internal strength is the primary goal, bureaucracy is the product. With bureaucracy comes hindrances to productive work, as if molasses were poured into an engine of progress.

Task matched with ability (knowledge). Getting good people is more than a staffing problem, because organization structures can *prevent* the person who is best qualified to act from even influencing the decision. This happens when an organization is too compartmentalized, isolating those who should be involved. Workers in production may be struggling to assemble parts that don't fit together properly. For some reason communication of the problem doesn't reach the engineering department. However, if you bring the responsible engineer right down to the assembly line where he can see the problem for himself, it will be resolved quickly.

Flexibility. Since situations rarely remain the same, getting the right person in the right place at the right time requires flexibility. As work on a project progresses, there is a need for a shift in leadership, whether it be formal or informal. The person who was the expert in taking the project through the design stage may now be unqualified for leadership as it moves into production. The organizational structure should enable the people who are best qualified for the current situation to exercise leadership.

Flow of information. The relevance of good information to good decisions is obvious. Organizational structure can have a tremendous effect on the kind, quality, and timeliness of information that is available. Much of the rationale behind the newer forms of organization is that they increase access to information.

Controllability. You want to have flexibility and to give people the degree of autonomy that will allow them to put their talents to use, but you must also be able to maintain control. One of the reasons for the failure of the so-called free-form organization is that responsibility for results is hard to pin down.

Stability. A lack of control and too much flexibility will undermine the minimum requirements for stability. Too much stability, of course, results in hardening of the arteries, but too little is a source of anxiety and a barrier to accumulating specialized knowledge. Experience has shown that managers at all levels, not just the workers, need a degree of structure and consistency to be productive. Organizational structures that group together people with the same specialties and maintain these groupings over long periods of time create a condition where this specialized knowledge can flourish.

Unity. A unit of an organization must have a unifying credo. The value system of people who work closely in groups should be approximately the same. When this is the case, the group develops cohesion that makes it effective and productive. Such unity not only supports the special skills in the group, but it also attracts qualified people.

SCM Corporation has recently recognized the importance of this principle in reorganizing its Glidden-Durkee Division. Until a few years ago this division had a corporate staff of 300 people, compared to 280 at the headquarters of the parent company. Because of the large staff, budgeting, planning, and requests for capital expenditures were bogged down in bureaucratic red tape. Moreover, SCM recognized that the people who are best suited for a high growth through dynamic marketing and R&D are not necessarily the ones you want in an organization that must grow through a disciplined, deliberate, and slower process of making capital investments. The solution was to split Glidden-Durkee into four divisions, each of which has the opportunity to pursue its own strategy and develop its own unifying credo.

Avoiding redundancy. A situation that is sure to produce destructive competition develops if more than one group has, or thinks it has, responsibility for the same thing. A group in accounting, for example, that believes it has responsibility for writing procedures is certain to conflict with a group in industrial engineering with the same belief.

Some people feel that having some overlap in responsibility is a precaution against inadvertently having a void. But a void in responsibility should be prevented by coordination, not by a redundancy in organization. For example, the responsibility for scheduling work may be given to two groups, one at the plant level and another at the department level. Ensuring that all aspects of scheduling were covered by having overlapping responsibility would cause chaos. It is mandatory that one group be responsible for scheduling within boundaries and that the boundaries be clearly defined. But what about the special cases, for which unique schedules must be contrived? Does that change or stretch the boundaries of responsibility? It shouldn't. What is required is coordination. In fact, even for the normal scheduling task to proceed there is a need for coordination between levels.

There is a point at which coordination can be carried to the extreme. When people begin to feel that they are spending most of their time in coordinating their efforts with the work of others, you should have some doubt about the design of the organization. This is a symptom of improper division of responsibility.

How to Get the Right Combination

How do you get flexibility and at the same time get stability in an organization? How do you avoid too much time-consuming coordination and seemingly endless committee meetings and still take care of the necessary communication? These are a few of the dilemmas in trying to design an organization.

Some may see the problem as being represented by a continuum of possibilities along a broad scale. At one end are formality, structure, and control. At the other are informality, free form, and creativity. The challenge is to pick a point on the scale that achieves the right balance for the organization and its tasks. Unfortunately, looking at the problem this way never seems to produce the right compromise. Companies that choose a point at either end of the spectrum become either stifling or chaotic places to work, and the middle ground yields mediocre performance.

Fortunately, the range of possibilities in designing an organization is not limited to points on a linear scale. It is almost possible to have your cake and eat it too. One approach is to have systems of organizations within organizations—generally some type of team organization. In all cases the organizing theme is to *synthesize* that which would otherwise operate independently and separately. Although the combinations are limitless, I shall identify four types as benchmarks.

A *work group*, as I am using the term, has a degree of autonomy that goes beyond what is normal for the people working under one supervisor. Typically it is a group of workers who have a great deal of discretion in planning their own work and setting their own work rules. They are guided by goals that they either set or negotiate with their supervisor, who acts more like a facilitator than a traditional boss. Informal leadership within the group is very influential, and the mantle of informal leadership may descend on different people, depending on the situation.

Normally, work groups are long standing, and membership in them is full time, although a work group may be created in a department to solve a particular problem. It is disbanded when the problem is solved. In this regard it differs from a task team only in that its members come from one department.

A *task team* is a group of people generally assembled from different parts of the organization who work together for a considerable period of time, usually, but not necessarily, on a full-time basis to achieve a planned result. During the course of the task, the membership may vary depending on the functional representation required or the phase of the task. In other words, some functions may be excluded in the early stages of the task and others may no longer be needed as the task approaches completion. Although the people on task teams are expected to give foremost attention to the task, they retain very strong ties to their home organization. When the task is completed or their part of it is done, they know they will return to the duties they left in their functional organization or be assigned to another task team. Often task teams are used to launch a new product.

A *matrix organization* is the superimposition of a project or product line organization over a functional organization. For example, Product A would have a project manager responsible for its engineering and production (possibly its marketing as well) and personnel on the product team from functional organizations such as accounting and production control. People on the team have two bosses—the project leader and the functional manager. A project organization differs from a task team in that it is more permanent. The higher degree of permanence creates a higher degree of formality. Channels of communication between project personnel and functional groups become better defined and more routine. The composition of membership in the product line or project organization is less likely to change than that of a task team organization.

A *project organization* is an organization carved out of the functional organization to achieve a specific purpose and retains only a very loose connection to the functional organization. It has very little obligation to coordinate its activities with the parent organization as it pursues its own goals. Larger projects assume the characteristics of independent businesses. Personnel are usually not guaranteed continued employment at the completion of a project although every effort is made to reassign them. Some companies, such as construction companies, are organized almost exclusively on a project basis.

The options of what type of team organization is best suited for you are somewhat limited by the scope of your responsibilities. Unless you have general management responsibilities, it would be very unusual circumstances that would allow you to create a project organization as I have used the term. The matrix organization commonly cuts across a wide range of functions, making it an option only for higher management as a general rule. However, there are plenty of opportunities for exceptions. A marketing department, for example, may have functional departments, but cutting across these functions, teams may be organized by product line. In this manner, a person with an advertising assignment is responsible both to the advertising function and for the advertising of his product line.

Since task team and work group structures are less formal and more flexible than matrix and project organization, they can be adapted to a variety of situations at many levels of the organization. Table 2 highlights some of the characteristics of the four types of team organizations that I have identified somewhat arbitrarily. Differences among them have been cited to aid in understanding and to illustrate the range of possibilities. However, with the exception of the project organization, the various types of team organizations are more similar than different. In general, the principles and pitfalls are the same.

How to Pick a Team

People are put on teams because of their authority, knowledge, and, to a degree, their motivation. The fourth ingredient in the formula for achievement, responsibility, is, largely, a frame of mind capable of being created with leadership, as was discussed in Chapter 6. Motivation, an extremely important quality in any assignment, is not a discriminating factor in selecting a team member except as it pertains to willingness to join a team. There are a good many highly motivated and productive people who are not inclined or equipped to function well in a team environment. Their contribution must be as individuals. The adaptability to team work is apparently not related to individual ability. Highly capable, even great people have shown a disparate adaptability to team work. So it is also with people on the lower levels of organizations. A mistaken belief of behavioralists, now being rectified, is the notion that everyone prefers a job that requires interaction with others and along with this more autonomy. It is simply not true that everyone will welcome the interaction of a group. The

Table 2. Characteristics of team organizations.

	Work Group	Task Team	Matrix Organization	Project Organization
Type of task *Investigative*	Often created for problem solving. Effective as a review and investigative body. Can formulate problems.	Could be used for problem that has been defined.	Part of normal operation within charter.	Part of normal operation within charter.
Implement change	Effectiveness depends on authority given.	Often created to implement change.	Its creation causes change. Effective in implementing change within charter.	Effective in implementing change within charter.
Ongoing operation	Effective when workers are organized in a work group on a full-time basis.	Loses effectiveness as tasks become routine.	Very effective for operations within charter.	Very effective for operations within charter.
Authority	Usually very limited.	De facto authority but must coordinate decisions with outsiders.	Usually high authority—limited by requirements of functional organization.	High authority within boundaries of project.
Responsibility	Total responsibility for comparatively narrow scope of work.	Responsibility among team members and parent organization.	Product or project organization has primary responsibility.	Total responsibility is with project organizations for broad scope of work.
Scope of operations	Usually a narrow scope but varies depending on level of group.	Broad or narrow depending on task and level of task team.	Usually has broad scope from design to production.	Includes all or nearly all functions required for project.

Degree of work definition	Varies from vague to defined.	Can function with ambiguity—will improve work definition.	Well specified.	Highly defined.
Degree of commitment	High commitment to group when group is permanent. Otherwise, commitment is to supervisor.	High commitment to team and parent organization.	High commitment to team and parent organization.	Commitment is mostly to project organization.
Formality/flexibility	Very informal, highly adaptable to changing conditions.	Informal—composition of team may be easily changed.	Formal—members of product/project organization may work informally but structure is well established.	Formal—project structure is as formal as in functional organization but more easily changed to meet changing conditions.
Leadership	Formal leader acts as "coach." Strong informal leadership which may be rotated.	Designated leader but de facto leadership may depend on task.	Designated leader but de facto leadership may depend on task.	Formal leadership follows organization chart as in functional organization.
Coordination and communication with other groups	Very adaptable to coordination and even participation with outsiders.	Fair communication with other task teams. High need to coordinate with functional groups.	Matrix establishes channels for coordination and communication. Communication/coordination outside channels is more difficult.	Separation of project organization makes communication/coordination difficult with outsiders.
Budgetary control	Usually not covered by separate budget.	Budget more defined and controls become tighter as task becomes more well defined.	Well covered by budgets.	Budget well defined and adherence to budget is very important.
Knowledge	Job knowledge is predominant. Knowledge of group members is similar.	Combination of job knowledge and professional knowledge. Members have varied backgrounds.	Combination of job knowledge and professional knowledge. Members have varied backgrounds covering wide spectrum of knowledge.	Wide spectrum of professional and practical knowledge.

record shows that there are always people who show initial interest in being part of a group but later drop out. Some, of course, are not interested in group interaction at the outset. At the General Motors Tarrytown plant 95 percent of the hourly employees have volunteered to participate in training sessions on group involvement, but that still leaves 5 percent who would prefer to go it alone. Inclusion in group processes should be voluntary for hourly employees.

Apart from willingness to join a team, it is evident that the crucial qualifications for membership are knowledge and authority. The first and foremost requirement is that the member bring knowledge of his discipline. If he represents manufacturing engineering, he must know manufacturing processes. Second, he must know the product or the project. In fact, the imperative of thoroughly learning about the product or project as a team member is one of the reasons for its existence. In a flexible team arrangement, such as team tasks or work groups, it is often desirable to include an expert for just a phase of the project. Perhaps a statistician is needed to set up a survey and assist in interpreting results, or engineers with experience in designing test equipment are needed for a one-time task. It is advantageous to the project to make such a person part of the team rather than merely consulting with him or her as an expert or dealing with him or her as a member of a separate function group. As a team member the person becomes more knowledgeable about the project and more committed to it.

Each member of a team should have or be given authority to make decisions that are consistent with the authority of other team members and with the purpose of the team. For example the operations of a team would be hampered if the engineering member and the production member were able to make decisions about their respective functions but a quality assurance member was unable to commit to anything before checking with higher-ups in his department. The quality control person in this situation cannot contribute effectively even if he has the required knowledge. And if he really is knowledgeable, his competence in using his knowledge is apparently not trusted by his own department. Regardless of the reason, the result is an unworkable situation. The quality control representative will either have to be replaced with someone who can make decisions or his department will have to change its policies to give the team member more authority.

The principles discussed above for making up a team may be summarized as follows:

1. Members should have the motivation to work with others in a team environment.
2. Members must bring to the team the specialized knowledge needed for the team to do its function.
3. Team members must have the degree of authority required to make decisions.
4. The actual membership of a team may be and should be changed as the situation or phase of work changes.

How Teams and Groups Operate

Planning and responsibility. These are the keys to successful teamwork. Team and group organizations should be given general assignments for which they must develop derivative plans and assume responsibility for carrying them out. Noting how this process works at the Fisher Body Plant No. 2 of General Motors, where five business teams have been created, the superintendent in charge of one of the teams said,

> The business team concept actually creates a smaller business, which sets its own *goals* [planning] and whose members are *responsible* to each other for the success of the business. A typical business team consists of various manufacturing personnel: industrial engineers, scheduling personnel, material handling, maintenance, quality control, production and material control people; and even accounting representatives. We are *responsible* for a portion of our business and we accept this *responsibility* together.* [Emphasis added.]

When a person makes a statement like that, it is obvious that he fully understands that responsibility is an emotional commitment that exceeds his ability to control the outcome and probably his authority to make decisions. A team organization attempts to have *every member* feel this way about his work. And if it can be accomplished, the team is sure to be a winner.

Litton Industries' use of task teams in its Microwave Cooking Products Division is a classic example of how teams are organized to develop new products and introduce product improvements. In this

---

* *Recent Initiatives in Labor-Management Cooperation,* Vol. II, National Center for Productivity and Quality of Working Life (Washington, D.C.: U.S. Government Printing Office, Spring 1978), p. 15.

field of rapidly changing technology, the key to success is getting innovations into the product quickly and making the product available to the customer in a short span of time. Once an engineering project has approval, a task team is formed consisting of a project manager, a design engineer, a stylist, various technicians, draftspeople, quality and manufacturing engineers, a marketing manager, purchasing representatives, and a home economist. Other personnel are added, such as a cost accountant and an industrial engineer, as the project unfolds.

The task team prepares an annual marketing plan. The planning process begins with a two-day seminar during which team members explore marketing and other project issues, with the participation of personnel from the functional organization such as the sales vice-president and advertising personnel. The team follows up this session by preparing derivative plans. According to William W. George, division president, the process ensures a high probability of success for the plans, barring unforeseen changes in market conditions. The achievement of planning goals builds a feeling of self-confidence and a strong success orientation among task team members.*

How production committees work. Production committees are used to solve problems and make improvements in operations. Generally they have been used in manufacturing settings, although there is no reason why the concept should not be extended to service operations as well. Examples of production committees are those that are organized under a Scanlon plan. Scanlon plans are management-labor agreements to share the benefits of increased productivity. One of the salient features of such a plan is the production committees that work out and approve innovations and improvements.

Under a Scanlon plan the production committees are generally composed of elected representatives from the production area, sometimes including the supervisor of the area and an industrial engineer. However, the leadership of the committee is in the hands of the hourly workers. Not only do the committees work on problems and improvements as a team, but they are also the focal point for receiving suggestions from all employees. They are given authority to spend a small amount of money, without higher approval, to implement suggestions. At Dana Corporation's Edgerton plant the amount is $200. At the Athens, Tennessee, plant of Midland-Ross the amount is $150.

---

* William W. George, "Task Teams for Rapid Growth," *Harvard Business Review*, March–April 1977.

Suggestions costing larger sums to implement are reviewed by a screening committee, which also has large representation from the hourly ranks. At Dana's plant, the screening committee consists of seven elected hourly employees and five management representatives.

Quality circles, an idea imported from Japan, are a type of production committee. The name originates from the fact that quality has been the main emphasis in production in Japan for several decades. Following World War II, Japan was well aware of its reputation for cheap and inferior products, many of which were children's toys. Their automobiles and electronic products have certainly reversed this impression. And their success in their effort to gain recognition for quality products has brought the Japanese methods to the attention of the world. Some companies are emulating their methods on an experimental basis. Northrop Corp. is one of these.

Today, the term quality circle is a bit of a misnomer in the United States and perhaps in Japan as well, because the range of the circle activities is broader than just quality. A better name would be productivity group. The groups are intent on solving problems, discovering ways of turning out a better product, and improving the production process. The installation of quality circles at Northrop is based on a philosophy expressed by the following eight points:

1. People (workers) *want* to participate.
2. People basically *want* to do a good job.
3. Workers are individuals with brains that should be used (and often are not).
4. Each worker has unlimited, untapped capacity.
5. Every worker knows best what is keeping him from doing a better job.
6. Each worker is an expert on *his* job and this expertise should be recognized and deferred to.
7. The company (management and labor) needs each person's help and respects each person's judgment.
8. We (management and labor) as a team can make this a better place to work.

Northrop's quality circles are usually composed of 10 to 12 people from the same work area with a homogeneity of skills who meet voluntarily to solve problems in their areas. After formation the group goes through eight one-hour training sessions which cover the steps in problem solving. The emphasis in these sessions is getting the facts upon which to make a logical analysis of the problem, leading to a well-thought-out solution. Cost-saving innovations are processed through the regular suggestion system but the monetary reward is credited to an account for the entire quality circle. Within broad guidelines, the circle may spend the money in a variety of ways, such as underwriting a social affair.

Special (ad hoc) problem-solving teams. Sometimes a knotty problem yields best to the deliberations of a special team of interested parties, particularly when there are political ramifications. Often efforts to work out a solution of this type of problem through normal channels creates or exacerbates a win-lose attitude making cooperation impossible. But when representatives are working in concert with other affected persons, frequently a more open attitude prevails, enabling everyone to have a greater respect for the other person's point of view. The solution may require that each area do something that it would prefer to avoid but is nevertheless necessary to solve the problem and is in its long-run interest.

In one company, the amount of time that was taken to get a purchase order to a vendor was considered to be excessive. A task force was created representing production control, purchasing, and other departments served by these two. The team was able to make changes in procedure that reduced the time.

Setting up a task team with members from the affected departments is a good way to handle a project like this. The members are given assignments to get information and to make some evaluation of this information. Then they convene to share information and to make decisions. Major decisions are referred to the home departments but the recommendations of the team members carry a lot of weight. Following a group meeting the members again disperse to take individual actions such as implementing a decision that was made or obtaining more information.

The process of converging for group work and dispersing for individual work is repeated many times in the life of a project. The success of the team is highly correlated to its ability to manage this process. The principle is simple: Group meetings should be used for group work, and individual work should be accomplished by individuals. If this simple principle is not practiced, groups will find that they are unable to reach decisions because the information that should be provided by individual members is lacking. Or if assignments of members have not been completed, the planned deliberation of the group on the next phase of the project gets sidetracked. On the other hand, groups can be extremely ineffective when they try to do work that is best done by individuals. For instance, putting together a report at a group meeting is guaranteed to produce a jerrybuilt document that satisfies no one. On the other hand, a group can be very effective in reviewing a previously prepared document.

When a group is operating well, in addition to its many advantages in getting people to use more of their ability, there is experimental evidence that group decisions are better. I have used an exercise in management workshops which illustrates this point. The attendees are put into three groups. Each group is faced with the same problem, the "moon walk" problem. The situation is that their spaceship was forced to land on the moon about 200 miles from the mother ship and that they now must traverse 200 miles on land to the other party. The task of each group is to decide what to take with them on the 200-mile trek by ranking 15 items in the order of their value to the group. (An approved ranking comes with this exercise.) In one group no group decision making is permitted. The individual rankings are averaged into a combined ranking to arrive at the ranking for the group. In the second group, a leader is chosen. He must solicit information from group members by asking questions. No member is allowed to volunteer any information or opinions without first being asked a direct question. The third group operates in a democratic style with no ground rules. The exchange of information is freely given. Invariably, the free-form group scores the highest, the structured decision-making group is next, and the composite of the individual rankings is the poorest.

The example above should not be construed to mean that a team works well when there is no discipline. The unstructured group in the exercise does practice discipline. It has to because there is a time limit for making decisions. And so it is in the real world; unless teams are managed, too much time will be spent unproductively. The work of teams has to be planned and controlled just as it does in any other system. Forms such as those shown in Figures 15 and 16 may be used to keep teams on the right track.

Semi-autonomous work groups. Workers in semi-autonomous work groups are given the responsibility for planning and controlling their

Figure 15. Problem detection report.

PROBLEM DETECTION REPORT

I.D. Number _____ Priority _____
(To Be Assigned By Taskforce Only)

To:

From:　　　　　　　Department: _____

　　　　　　　　　　Section: _____

　　　　　　　　　　Individual: _____

Task/Function Being Performed: _____

_____

_____

_____

Problem Description: _____

_____

_____

_____

_____

_____

_____

_____

_____

Suggestion: _____

_____

_____

_____

(Use Reverse Side if Necessary)

Taskforce Assignment: _____

Resolution Date:_____ /_____ /_____ Resolution: _____

_____

_____

Figure 16. Project control sheet.

Project Plan Task Listing
Responsibility _____
Task Team _____
_____
_____

Project Number _____
Project _____
Output/Result _____
_____
_____

Task Number	Description	Depends on	Duration	Responsibility	Completed

own work. They can change methods, break down the tasks as they please, and rotate assignments. Some companies that have used this system report that production problems have been reduced. Where bottlenecks existed in the past, now workers redistribute the work so that it flows more evenly. Rotation of workers has allowed them to become familiar with more than one task, enabling them to pitch in where needed. The impetus to establish work groups at Broen Armatur, a Danish company, came from the administration of its incentive system. There were enormous differences between pay in a system that included individual piecework, joint piecework, and time pay. In addition to the problem of friction among the workers, the system encouraged incentive workers to relegate the more tedious and routine work to the hourly workers. After establishing an autonomous work group, compensation for all personnel was based on a fixed amount plus a department bonus that was shared equally.

Matrix management. Matrix organizations, predominant originally in large aerospace companies, are now being used in many other organizations. Shell Oil Company is the first major oil company to employ a matrix organization and probably the largest company to use a matrix-style management throughout. At Dow Corning Corp., a matrix organization has enabled decisions to be made quickly at a low level where people have the relevant information. The normal procedure is to have operating decisions made within the project slice of the matrix. If the matrix manager cannot find a plan that satisfies all the functional departments, he may call a meeting of department heads to get a decision.

Pitfalls in Participative Structures

Don't assume that results will be immediate. Research demonstrates that there is a time lag of 7 to 18 months between a change in leadership behavior and improved performance in subordinates. In addition, it takes 6 to 12 months for top management to be able to effect a change in leadership behavior on down the ladder. The message is that a year or more will be required to establish many of the types of organization discussed previously other than on a pilot basis.

Don't ignore the attitude problem. Authoritarian management is given as one of the major reasons for failing Scanlon plans. Management has to appreciate the worker and believe that he has something to offer. According to George Sherman, vice-president of industrial relations of Midland-Ross, those who cannot adjust to the fact that in the last 20 years people have changed a lot more than either management styles or jobs should be reeducated, relocated, or removed.

Not all the burden should fall on management. If the workers are unionized, the union must be convinced that the change in management style and worker responsibility is in its best interest. There are many reasons why a union might be hostile or apathetic to a plan giving workers more autonomy. The union may see it as a loss of its power over workers. If the employees perceive that management is receptive to their ideas, it might make them question the value of union representation.

The only solution to the union problem is to get it involved. It may take the threat of lost jobs to do this. This was the experience of General Motors in its Tarrytown plant. After a truck line representing 800 jobs was transferred to another plant, management-union cooperation eventually led to a quality of working life program at Tarrytown.

At the Harmon International plant in Bolivar, Tennessee, management and labor jointly started a work humanization program which involved work groups and various committees. You can see from this summary of the agreement worked out between labor and management that labor is very much involved in the program and has not sacrificed any of its traditional rights.

Summary of Labor–Management Agreement

The work humanization program was launched with the cooperation of E. T. Michael, the UAW director of the region, along with Ray Casteel, the UAW local representative in Bolivar. The program was jointly sponsored by the company and the UAW, and Dr. Michael Maccoby, director of the Harvard Project on Technology, Work, and Character, was asked to organize aspects of the program.

Agreement was reached on the following:

- The purpose of the program was to make work better and more satisfying for all employees, salaried and hourly, while maintaining the necessary productivity for job security.
- The purpose was not to increase productivity. If an increase in productivity resulted from the program, appropriate rewards to employees would become legitimate matters for inclusion in the program.

- A review committee would meet monthly to review the work improvement program. The committee would consist of members of the local union bargaining committee and three people designated by management.
- A working committee would plan and coordinate the day-to-day work inprovement program. Membership of the committee would consist of the president of the union local, four members of the union local selected by the president of the local, subject to review by the review committee, and five people designated by management. One member of the bargaining committee would attend each working committee meeting.
- No worker would lose his job, pay, or seniority as a result of a work improvement experiment conducted in the plant, regardless of whether he participated in the experiment.
- Participation in an experiment in the work improvement program would be voluntary. No one would be forced to participate.
- Since new ideas require extra flexibility on everyone's part, the union and the company would agree to cooperate in trying new ideas in experimental groups.
- Neither party would relinquish its contractual rights, with termination by either party on 30 days' notice.°

Whether or not there is a union, the groundwork for organizational change must extend to the worker level, if negative attitudes of skepticism and distrust are to be avoided. The worker is going to ask, "What's in this for me?" If he thinks that it is a ploy to extract more work from him for the same pay, you can be sure that the program will fail. The solution is to make the program voluntary and to assure workers that the new system will not eliminate their jobs. Having done that, get them involved in training programs.

Don't put in a team concept unless you are prepared to change. Consultants are unanimous in their belief that one of the greatest pitfalls in establishing teams of any type (matrix, task team, etc.) is that there is a lack of facilitating change in management style and practice. Generally, the difficulty is that managers are uncomfortable with relinquishing what they believe to be their decision-making prerogatives to subordinates. With teams they not only have to do this but they must share information with others to an extent probably not done before. The established manager may see all of this as degrading to his or her own self-image—a vision of being a decisive executive

° *Recent Initiatives in Labor-Management Cooperation*, Vol II, National Center for Productivity and Quality of Working Life (Washington, D.C.: U.S. Government Printing Office, Spring 1978), pp. 24–25.

with a store of business sense gained from years of fighting in the trenches.

At a pet-food company, work teams were, for a time, highly involved in traditional management functions. For instance, they were allowed to interview and hire applicants and to recommend pay increases for fellow members. The early success of this program diminished when some of the management and staff personnel were unable to cope with the workforce's infringing on prerogatives that they believed to be theirs. Engineers resisted efforts by the teams to get involved in engineering problems. Lawyers justified their opposition to a work team's determining pay raises by citing possible infractions of labor laws.

It is obvious that unless managers and professionals alter their perception of how they can make a contribution, destructive infighting can be the result. In truth, a shift in their philosophy to accommodate active involvement by nonprofessionals is very practical. Any professional or manager who does not have more to do than he can possibly get done has not been thinking about his or her job very much. By taking a look at the many opportunities for making a contribution that are not being pursued, the manager and professional should quickly realize that he can use all the help he can get. Furthermore, once he brings himself to the point of sharing the credit for accomplishment, he will be surprised how much more gets done. This theme is simple and logical, but sometimes difficult to put across.

Don't rely fully on internal professional strength. Many case histories show that outside help has been instrumental in inaugurating new systems of organization, whether it be task teams, matrix concepts, autonomous work groups, or Scanlon plans. The Microwave Cooking Products Division of Litton Industries started its program of task teams by holding off-site team-building sessions for management conducted by a consultant. From this beginning, years later the task team concept fully blossomed to the point where it is a dynamic force for getting most of the work done.

In addition to the behavioral aspects of a Scanlon plan, the technical chore of establishing the formula for distributing savings to the workforce calls for a professional. Among the issues that must be covered in the formula is the share of savings attributed to capital investment as distinct from improvements in work methods. There is no standard formula: it must be worked out for each installation.

Don't select the wrong leader. The right leader is one who has knowledge that will enable him to fulfill the role of leadership and has some ability to operate in group processes. Knowledge, as I have stressed before, is a vital ingredient in successful management. A study of 21 small research groups showed that innovation is highly correlated with the technical skill of the supervisor. Regardless of the management style, supervisors who were high in technical knowledge had innovative subordinates.

Knowledge and other attributes, such as self-confidence, enable the leader to be the decision maker he must be as the leader of a task team or a project team in a matrix organization. Frequently, he will be operating without definite guidelines, and must ascertain on his own whether the decision to be made must be referred to higher authority, or whether it can be reported after the fact.

The leader of a group should recognize that group processes are essentially of two types, decision making and idea generating. Regardless of his depth of knowledge, he needs the ideas of others and the dynamics of group interaction to generate ideas. During idea-generating periods, he has the responsibility of seeing that issues are defined and that boundaries and constraints are known. He should encourage probing the boundaries to determine, in fact, if they are real. The leader, more than any other member of the group, must determine whether or not sufficient information is at hand. He knows that complete information is impossible. A key to the leader's success is his ability to balance the idea-generating mode of operation with cloture and decision making. If he strives for conclusions too early, he runs the risk of shutting off ideas. If decisions are delayed, he runs the risk of causing confusion and inaction and, ultimately, failure.

Don't sacrifice a logical structure for a behavioral theory. The radical approaches to organization that were implemented by Non Linear Systems, a San Diego electronics firm, were grounded in behavioral theory. (Some say that the application was a distortion of theory.) The intention was to cause individuals to achieve higher levels of satisfaction from work by putting them into semi-autonomous teams and eliminating rules and structure, such as time clocks. For several years, all the innovations seemed to be a great success. Then cracks began to appear. Andrew Kay, the president, returning to traditional approaches to organization and management in 1970, made big reductions in costs and employment to save the company.

During the experiment, the upward lines of communication were vague. Teams were supposed to get guidance from managers with responsibilities for such things as "productivity," "physical and financial resources," "human resources," "public responsibility" and "innovation." One of the first and most serious problems to appear was the inability of the managers in those jobs to define their methods of operation, and perhaps their roles, in ways that would be effective. Failing to do so, they experienced a great deal of anxiety in coming to grips with ill-defined responsibilities and channels of communication.

Don't allow teams to become independent. It is impossible for a group of people to serve the best interests of the organization if they are isolated from it. Let's get back to some basic principles to understand this caveat. The defense against Murphy's Law is planning, and to get good planning you must concern yourself not merely with the planning process but with the underlying system that carries out the planning process. The system of planning diagrammed in Figure 1 is a system which does strengthen the planning and execution capability. Principally, this is accomplished through the feedback mechanism. The system learns and adjusts from its experiences.

Moreover, an organization should be thought of as (1) being part of a larger organization, (2) having subsystems of its own, and (3) interacting with other systems on its own level. The job of managing an organization can then be thought of as meeting the wants and needs of its own system and those with which it is linked. It is through the interfaces that most of the feedback will come—the kind of feedback that leads to stronger and more effective performance.

Creating a team organization, such as semi-autonomous work groups, does not reduce the need for communication linkages. Communication must be both vertical between teams, higher management, and functional management, and horizontal between teams on the same level. For example, if one team in a manufacturing facility is making radar sets for the Air Force and another is making a different model for the Navy, these two teams should be talking to each other. Each can learn from the other's experiences and there will no doubt be times when cooperative effort is required to make the best use of limited resources.

Of course, unproductive and disruptive competitive practices between teams should never be allowed. Management should see to this. However, there is a tendency for such practices to proliferate when the individual project teams operate in a way that is too isolated from the business as a whole.

Don't let new systems become new rigidities. Just about the time that you think you have the organization perfectly aligned for the tasks at hand is probably about the time that you should begin to think about changes that will have to be made in organizational structure. This is because the tasks and projects change. The mix of work changes as one project increases in importance and another becomes less important. The phases of work change as the project moves through the stages of design, development, prototype or limited production, and full production. The product life cycle of introduction, rapid growth, maturity, and decline may occur over a few years, causing shifts in the type of work that is to be done.

When work changes, the choice is either to divide and restructure the work so that it can be done by the existing organization or to change the organization to address changed work requirements. Although the latter policy is the better rule, its application must be tempered with good sense. Too many changes in organization are disruptive and cause inefficiency.

However, the greater danger is in not making adaptations in the organization to meet changed circumstances. Team arrangements provide the vehicle for changing organizations to meet new needs without causing confusion because the functional organization provides stability by not changing. But this means that when the work has changed, and especially when work is over, the team is either changed or disbanded. *You should not look for new work for a team to do, no matter how marvelously the team has performed in the past.* If this philosophy is not clearly understood, there will be a tendency for project teams and task teams to try to perpetuate themselves. If they are successful in so doing, what once were creative, innovative approaches to organization will have become old-fashioned rigidities.

Don't assume that training is a one-shot affair. The experiences of many companies show that changes in organization which radically alter the responsibilities of employees must be accompanied by a training program. The potential mistake is to assume that after spending thousands of dollars and thousands of hours on training, it doesn't have to be repeated. Training must continue for at least two reasons. First, with the passage of time and with the influx of new people, there will be an erosion of skills and knowledge if there is not continued training. Second, as personnel gain experience with new forms of organization, they are better prepared to learn more about management and organization behavior. Experience coupled with training will give them deeper insights into the dynamic forces at work in organizations and increase their effectiveness in dealing with people at all levels. Litton's Microwave Cooking Products Division, after a thoroughgoing initial training program, still holds off-site team-building sessions about twice a year for its top management group.

Don't assume that teams don't have to be managed. Team organizations have many virtues. They serve to focus work on results. They enlarge the scope of work for individuals. The concept of responsibility is enlarged. And I could go on. But there is a pitfall in assuming that a team organization will prevail over all difficulties without traditional practices. This is far from the truth. The most important step in getting good performance from team organizations is to define their charter. This must be done at the onset and updated as time goes on to meet new circumstances and to improve the charter as more is learned. Defining the charter includes defining the work that the group is responsible for. Next, the scope of decision making should be established, including the amount of dollars that the group can spend. In other words, the team must know what it is expected to accomplish and what the ground rules are.

Having established the boundaries, the team is able to plan its own work. Depending on the type of team, the plan might be a detailed program plan, showing milestones or costs, or it might be an agenda of problem areas that are to be investigated.

In Chapter 8, it was shown how developing a plan for a department will most likely entail identifying specific programs. The responsibility for carrying out one of these programs might be given to a work group or a task team. The general plan and objective has already been set as a part of developing the strategy for the department. The work group would create a more detailed plan to guide it through the project.

A lack of management over team activities is the source of a frequent problem on project work. This is the problem of being unduly optimistic about costs and schedules. The familiar symptoms are:

Actual costs exceed budget, often not becoming evident until the final stages of the project.

Schedule dates are slipped, sometimes "tag end" work continuing after the official completion date for a phase.

There is periodic rescheduling.

There are many causes for problems like these. Sometimes the source is an unrealistic commitment made by management, probably for competitive reasons, that puts the project team in an untenable position from the beginning. There is little the team can do about that other than to do the best it can. However, many times the project team makes its own schedule problem by being too optimistic.

The remedy for this is for higher management to review the budgets and schedules of the project teams, using data from comparable projects in the past. Management must also be sure that the scope of work is fully defined and be especially alert for any changes in the definition of work as the project progresses which are not reflected in changes in cost or schedule changes. Changes which are introduced as trivial can very insidiously be the factors which cause the project to go awry. What's more, it may take months to recognize how the change adversely affected performance. Be careful of changes in the scope of work; they can easily be disguised, and they can put Murphy's Law in motion.

Don't think that controls are unnecessary. One of the reasons for problems of cost overruns and schedule slippages is a faulty control system. Typical accounting systems operate on the basis of accumulating costs by time period. However, for project work, time periods are a secondary consideration. The important measure is the cost compared with the status of work on the project. Although costs are within budget for time periods, this seemingly favorable report may actually be unfavorable if the work is behind schedule.

Don't underestimate people. Organizations should be structured to give people an enlarged sense of responsibility and the opportunity to fulfill the responsibility. Team and group organizations largely accomplish this. At the Midland-Ross plant in Athens, Tennessee, productivity increased by 16 percent and absenteeism was down to 2.8 percent from 5.6 percent after the introduction of a Scanlon plan. The efficacy of the Japanese approach to employee involvement is demonstrated by the transformation of a United States Motorola television plant after being purchased by a Japanese concern. This plant had been a money loser for Motorola. Production was increased from

1,000 to 2,000 sets per day with the same workforce, and the indirect labor was slashed to one-half. This was all accomplished by American workers and supervision.

Don't overestimate people. One of the time-honored principles of management was that each employee should have only one boss. Although this rule is logical and certainly simplifies establishing accountability, it has proved to be too inflexible for the types of complex and interdependent tasks that face many organizations today. Correcting this problem with matrix organizations and multiple "dotted line" reporting schemes calls for more sophistication and maturity from personnel. Indeed, the person who has to keep several bosses happy while carrying out responsibilities that span several functions is almost acting as an independent businessman. People in the group or on the task team also have enlarged responsibilities for performance and communication. They must coordinate with members of the team and usually maintain liaison with others outside of the team, for example, the accountant on the team receiving guidance from the accounting department. Some people are not able to cope with multiple responsibilities for reporting. They become very distressed over ambiguities that these reporting arrangements are certain to produce. If this shortcoming cannot be overcome with training, the only recourse is not to use this type of person on a team.

Blake and Moulton, the originators of the managerial grid, have concluded that many people lack the competence to plan their work and require a high degree of planning, controlling, and directing by others. A small minority of workers have declined to participate in the quality circle program at Northrop. At the Tarrytown plant of General Motors, 95 percent of the hourly employees have volunteered for training in techniques of participation, a very commendable measure of support, but that still leaves 5 percent who are saying, in effect, that more participation and more responsibility are not for them.

There are a very few people who have deep-seated feelings of hostility. Unable to derive any satisfaction from productive work in an organization, they view the supportive leader as weak or manipulative. They resist all attempts to give them more autonomy and responsibility, believing that it is an attempt by management to take advantage of them. As a young foreman, I once had such a person on my shift. He rebuffed any overtures to get him more involved with his job, and showed his hostility by requesting to be moved to a "lower" classification (still in my department). At the lower position his duties were more routine and, of course, the rate of pay was less, a fact which didn't seem to bother him.

A recent study of 30 companies shows that productivity is improved with employee ownership. But this is not always a bed of roses. In 1975 the employees of a GAF asbestos mine in Vermont bought the mine from GAF to preserve their jobs after it was announced that the mine would close. The cost of installing federally dictated antipollution equipment had caused GAF to conclude that it was uneconomical to operate a mine that might have only about six years of asbestos left. However, the new owners, the miners, were able to negotiate a one-year extension on the installation of the pollution-control equipment, and after the purchase of the plant, the worldwide demand for asbestos soared. The stock in the new company, Vermont Asbestos Group, Inc., jumped in price during the next three years from $50 per share to a book value of $2,185. While the mine became profitable, at the same time there was a great deal of discord between the stockholders and the labor-management board over plans for expansion. Finally, an outsider was able to gain control of 60 percent of the company from miners who, tired of the infighting, sold their stock at $1,340 per share. Richard Hamilton, an outside board member and an industrial representative of Vermont's Economic Development Department, called the outcome "a disaster. It's the end of employee ownership. They had it and they gave it away."[*]

From the evidence you can conclude that people have great talents which are often barely tapped in many organizations. Semi-autonomous groups, task teams, project organizations, matrix organizations—all make it possible for people to accomplish more by making better use of their abilities and by reducing barriers to communication and achievement. You can also see that innovative patterns of organization call for a high degree of enlightened and supportive leadership. Merely putting people in new groups without training and without leadership will guarantee failure.

---

[*] David Gumpert, "Employee Owners of Asbestos Mine Oust Directors Who Opposed Sale of Concern," *The Wall Street Journal*, April 10, 1978.

10

How to improve productivity

The dismal rate of productivity improvement in the United States in recent years has become a national problem. During the 1950s productivity typically improved at an annual rate of 3.4 percent. In 1978 productivity improvement was a niggardly 0.4 percent. The decline has been blamed on a variety of factors including a younger and less well-trained labor force, government regulation, large investments needed to protect the environment, a tax structure which discourages capital investment, government policies which encourage demand and consumption but not capital formation, a decline in the work ethic, a decline in government-funded research and development, less investment in basic research and development, the increase in the cost of energy, an increase in service jobs, and a decline in innovation by companies and individuals. As this list of probable causes suggests, improving productivity is not a simple problem.

Regardless of the policies of the government and the national economy, productivity improvement must stem from the actions and decisions of managers across the country. In your organization it is up to you, and your job is not made any easier by some of these trends. For example, a higher cost of energy and higher costs of capital make automation a less attractive option. It is more difficult to improve productivity in services than in direct factory jobs where the work is more structured. For these reasons and many others, the challenge of increasing productivity demands more creativity and more direct attention than ever before.

Productivity improvement begins with an analysis and understanding of the work. Analysis provides the necessary breakdown of the total job into elements that can be evaluated, and understanding supplies the reasons for the work being done. To help you in this task, you need a classification scheme or schemes. Two such schemes are by degree of structure and by sources.

How to Classify Work

In setting out to improve productivity, classifying work or elements of work according to degree of structure helps to point the steps and approaches that may be used. If we think of work as a continuum that ranges from the highly structured to practically no structure at all, jobs with the most structure are those that have a definite pattern or set of motions which is repeated without deviation. Assembly line work is a familiar example. Some clerical operations approach this level of structure.

Next come jobs in which the components are highly structured but the sequence may vary. In this type of job, people are performing familiar operations but are using judgment to determine the sequence of the operations. Some jobs of this type can require great skill as, for example, putting a filling in a tooth or landing an airplane. At lower levels of skill, work consisting of highly structured components is found in many jobs in inventory control and warehousing. The jobs of a bank teller and an airline ticket clerk also come under this category.

Moving to work of still less structure, you will find jobs requiring new patterns of work which for the most part are a new synthesis of past patterns. Past patterns are not suitable because each situation is different. A surgeon performing an operation that is not routine is performing this type of work. So is the project manager who is planning to introduce a new product. On a grand scale, planning the invasion of Normandy in World War II is an example. The components—men, weapons, ships, and aircraft—were known entities, but new patterns of employment and coordination had to be devised.

Finally, there is the type of work for which familiar elements to be synthesized are not immediately apparent or may not exist. This is highly creative work and work that requires a great deal of thought before any actions can be taken. Creative writing and advanced mathematics are in this category. The work of an entrepreneur who trans-

Table 3.   Classifying jobs by degree of structure.

Type	Mental Process	Work Patterns	Benchmark Work
Structured	Little thought or judgment	Cycle of repetitive patterns	Assembly line work Cashier at theater
Semistructured	Judgment required for making choices	Familiar patterns occurring in varying sequences	Airline ticket clerk Routine dental filling Loading an airplane Many clerical jobs
Mostly unstructured	Analytic and synthetic thought processes Outcomes uncertain	New patterns largely synthesized from elements of old patterns	Planning introduction of new product Surgeon performing nonroutine operation
No visible structure	Original thought. High ratio of mental effort to any kind of physical effort, such as communicating or writing	Original—old patterns not relevant	Creative writing Converting a new idea into a business

forms an idea into a new business is another example. Table 3 illustrates the concept of classifying jobs by degree of structure.

The Systems Approach to Productivity

One necessary condition for productivity improvement is that jobholders have the knowledge required for their jobs. At the highly structured end of the spectrum, very little breadth of knowledge is required. Moving toward the unstructured end of the continuum, more breadth and depth of knowledge is required. For structured jobs, people must be trained; for unstructured jobs they must be educated.

Job knowledge is the foundation for productivity improvement. Without it, nothing can be built. In the first place, knowledge has a direct bearing on how well and how quickly a person performs. Secondly, it is the main resource that a person brings to a project aimed at improving his or her job. Others—managers, industrial engineers, quality control experts—have valuable professional strengths, but none of them should have as much knowledge about the job as the jobholder himself. Group processes aimed at improving productivity rely on the hands-on knowledge of the people in the group.

Beyond knowledge, there are four components of the system for productivity improvement, required in every case. The four M's of productivity are measurement, methods improvement, motivation, and management and control of the system. It is easier to apply the four elements of this system to structured jobs than to unstructured. With structured jobs, the key to productivity is efficiency rather than effectiveness. At the far unstructured end of the spectrum, the concepts still apply but they cannot be put into practice through a systematic approach. To illustrate the point, Jan Erteszek started the Olga Company, a major West Coast manufacturer of women's undergarments, in his home with one sewing machine. Paul Galvin, the founder of Motorola, had the notion that people wanted to listen to radios as they drove their cars and began with a few hand-made sets. Hewlett-Packard was started in a garage. Now, how would you measure the productivity of these people? How would you systematically try to improve their methods? As you can see, these questions are irrelevant.

The problem facing most supervisors today is how to improve productivity in work that is not highly structured but contains familiar patterns of work. There are more jobs like this than there are highly structured jobs. Furthermore, improving productivity in structured work is a topic found in countless books. It has been the prime target of industrial engineers since the days of Fredrick Taylor. Having been plowed many times, it is a field I shall not plow again. Rather, as I discuss the four elements of the productivity system, I shall concentrate on the type of jobs found in the middle of the structured-unstructured spectrum.

Measurement

No one really disagrees with the importance of measurement. Without it how can you evaluate performance or improvement? The problem lies in what to measure and how to do it. The first mistake to be avoided is thinking that only costs or man-hours need to be measured. This dimension is important, sometimes the most important, but there are two others: the quality of the product or the work, and timeliness.

What is needed is a yardstick that compares all these dimensions for a unit of work. In most cases the problem is quite manageable because most work, even unstructured work, is composed of frequently repeated patterns of work. Now let's get down to practical steps. How do you pick a unit of measurement for gauging productivity improvement?

1. Analyze the work to determine the degree of structure.

2. If the work is highly structured, the total time on the job can be related to *one* unit of output. This is the typical situation for production work.

3. If the work is structured but contains familiar patterns of work, identify all the units of output.

> Look for one or a few dominant outputs. See if the other outputs are proportional to the dominant outputs. This may be done by keeping a record of all the inputs, with assistance of the people in the area during the period of analysis.
>
> Use as few outputs as possible as the yardstick for measurement by allowing time for the other outputs on a proportional basis.
>
> Try to select units of output that can be readily and verifiably counted.

4. For work that is unstructured to the extent that new work patterns are the rule and there is great variation in the work content of the units of output, the only practical recourse is to use the task itself as the unit of measurement. The time and cost for the task is estimated and actual data are compared with the estimate.

Some examples of units of output are standard hour of work (assumes a work measurement system); physical unit, part, or assembly; engineering drawing; person served; inquiry answered; and proposal written.

An amusing example of a poor unit of measurement comes from the Soviet Union. Because Soviet plate-glass factories are rated by the total square meters of glass produced, they make glass thinner so that their output will be greater in terms of the unit of measure. The result is that 30 to 40 percent of the glass quickly breaks.[*]

---

[*] Robert Keatly, "Let's Make a Deal," *The Wall Street Journal*, May 18, 1972, p. 1.

How to get a measure of performance. After selecting the units of measurement, which are the outputs, the next step is to get measurements for performance in the three dimensions of cost, quality, and timeliness.

Cost is a measure of the resources used to produce a unit of output. It indicates the efficiency of the conversion of labor, capital, energy, and materials into product or service. While this comprehensive concept of cost is theoretically correct, at the departmental level a simplified and more pragmatic approach to measuring input may be employed.

For most supervisors the largest controllable cost is labor. The cost of labor in turn is composed of the amount of labor and the rate. Rate can be broken down into straight time rate, overtime rate, and fringe benefits. If all these costs are controllable by you as the supervisor, you should include all of them in the cost standard. Frequently, rate is not controllable at the departmental level, which then permits the cost standard to be expressed in man-hours straight time and man-hours overtime, if overtime pay is awarded.

The time in man-hours required to produce outputs may be determined by any of the work measurement techniques and by having the employees record their own time during the period of the study or by historical records. For unstructured work, a combination of these is often used.

Materials and supplies may be a costly resource. In some production processes yield is a critical factor in controlling cost. In this event, it would make little sense to introduce labor-saving methods which produced amounts of scrap which completely offset the saving in labor. For example, a sawyer cutting out sections from sheets of plywood may find methods that improve his time per section but waste plywood.

The cost of outside services should be taken into consideration, especially if outside services can be used to substitute for work normally done by employees.

In a capital-intensive process, machine utilization could be an adequate measure of the efficiency of the process, and machine-hours could be the best measure of input.

Some examples of input measurements for cost are total cost, labor cost, man-hours, pounds of material, and machine hours.

Having a measurement for quality is important in its own right. It becomes more important when you realize that costs can frequently be reduced at the expense of quality. Measuring the quality of a service is more difficult than measuring the quality of a product, but it can be done. Hotel chains use inspectors to evaluate the quality of service, and the flight attendants on airlines are periodically checked. Sometimes an error count for routine clerical work can be maintained. However, the courtesy and understanding that an employee shows to the public may be more important than an occasional error.

Some examples of measures of quality are errors, complaints, rework cost or time, deficiencies or "gigs" from an inspection, scrap, defective items, and defects.

Timeliness, the third dimension of performance, is a major determinant of the ability of a company to compete. Everything else being approximately equal, the organization that can offer prompt reliable service has a truly significant advantage over competitors—one that frequently merits higher prices.

Timeliness is also very important for units within an organization. An organization, as a system, is dependent upon the smooth interaction of the components of the system. If the output of one unit within the organization is late, that lateness will affect other units which depend on the output.

There are three aspects to timeliness. One is the span time, which is the elapsed time (not to be confused with man-hours) required to perform a task from start to finish. The shorter the elapsed time the better. A company which can deliver a product in one week has an advantage over a competitor which requires two. An accounting department that can furnish monthly costs two days after the close of the month has a higher level of productivity, costs and quality being the same, than one that requires five days. By doing so, it makes itself more valuable to the managers who need the data to manage their organizations effectively.

Another aspect of the timeliness dimension is the ability to control the time span to give consistent results. Suppose that an organization is able to complete a unit of work in a comparatively short time on the average but there are great variations. To illustrate, company B in Figure 17 has a shorter average elapsed time for delivering an order than company A. However, the distribution of span times represented by

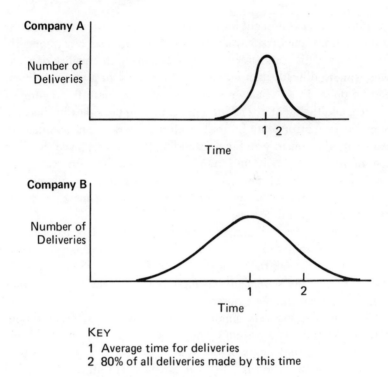

KEY
1 Average time for deliveries
2 80% of all deliveries made by this time

Figure 17. Elapsed time for deliveries.

the bell-shaped curve indicates a wide variation of delivery times for B, showing a lack of control. Company A, on the other hand, takes longer on the average but exercises close control over deliveries. The third aspect of the timeliness issue is what the customer or user of the output is told. Company B, with little control, would have to give itself a considerable cushion in quoting a delivery if it wanted to make 80 percent of its promise dates. Company A, on the other hand, could actually quote less time than company B and still make 80 percent of its deliveries due to its tighter control.

The message for a supervisor of a unit within an organization is that the timeliness of his outputs, which includes reliability in adhering to a schedule along with maintaining the quality of his output, is an aspect of being productive that may be more important than the obvious criterion of cost of man-hours per unit. Some examples of measures of timeliness are average processing time in days or hours, average number of people waiting, average amount of time a transaction is in a queue, and number of promise or schedule dates made.

Cost, quality, and timeliness can be measured relative to a past base period using an index of performance. The formula is:

$$\text{Performance index} = \frac{\text{Measure during base period}}{\text{Measure during current period}} \times 100$$

Examples:

Cost per unit, base period (adjusted for inflation) = $40
Cost per unit, current period = $35
$$\text{Performance index (cost)} = \frac{40}{35} \times 100 = 114$$

Errors per 1,000 transactions, base period = 14
Errors per 1,000 transactions, current period = 11
$$\text{Performance index (quality)} = \frac{14}{11} \times 100 = 127$$

Average processing time, base period = 16 days
Average processing time, current period = 12 days
$$\text{Performance index (timeliness)} = \frac{16}{12} \times 100 = 133$$

The advantage in plotting cost, quality, and timeliness indexes on a single graph is that you can tell at a glance if improvements in one are being attained at the expense of another (Figure 18).

Methods Improvement

Nearly all improvements in productivity are a result of a change in methods. Therefore, the supervisor who is intent on building effectiveness and efficiency in his or her operation must be concerned with methods. Methods improvement cannot be left to some professional group, such as industrial engineering or systems analysis. On the contrary, the manager who is serious about improving the productivity of his unit will make methods improvement everyone's business.

This is the first step in methods improvement: putting across the philosophy that it is everyone's business. It is a matter of making people aware that changes in methods, even small ones, in the aggregate can make a difference. How do you make people aware of the importance of methods improvement? Of course, you talk about it, but that in itself will not accomplish much. Increasing awareness is more often a by-product of training, actual changes, and incentives.

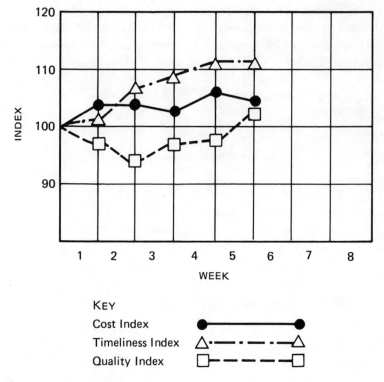

Figure 18. Performance indexes.

Instruction in methods improvement can be structured to follow the five-step approach:

1. Select the job.
2. Break the job down.
3. Analyze the facts.
4. Develop the better method.
5. Install the new method.

1. *Select the job.* Although there is no reason to overlook any job, you should start by selecting work or jobs that have the potential for considerable savings. These are jobs that are performed by a lot of people, or that appear to be disorganized, or that are a bottleneck for other operations.

2. *Break the job down.* There are many tools and charting tech-

niques for breaking a job down into its components or elements. Most of these have been developed for repetitive, structured work. However, one practical tool which is effective for any type of job is work sampling. It is ideal for telling you what is going on in unstructured work and providing clues to methods improvement. It works this way.

After observing the work being done, divide it into 8 to 15 components or elements. Add to these categories two or three reasons for no work being done, such as personal time, running out of work, or waiting for someone else. Each one of these categories should be defined carefully in writing. You may add a miscellaneous category for any work that is not covered by the categories that you have chosen. For example, in a credit department two elements might be talking on the telephone to a delinquent customer and assisting a customer to fill out a charge application. They could be described as follows:

Talking on the telephone to a delinquent customer. This element includes dialing the number, waiting for a person to answer, and talking to a party on the other end of the line. Calls made without an answer or an answer by someone other than the delinquent party are also considered to be in this category. The element ends when the connection to the party's telephone is broken.

Assisting customer in filling out application. This element includes getting up from the desk and walking to the customer at the counter. Answering questions and giving the customer directions on filling out the form are included. Checking over the form in the customer's presence is included. Walking back to the desk to do other work is a part of this element.

The next step in a work sampling study is to make "instantaneous" observations. The times for making observations should be selected randomly. A table of random numbers may be used. I use the term instantaneous to convey the idea that the observation should be like a stop-action snapshot. Whatever the person is doing at the instant is recorded.

The number of observations for each element compared to the total number of observations approaches the proportion of total time spent on that element. The greater the number of observations that are taken, the higher the confidence you can have that the percentage calculated from the study is quite close to the true percentage. You would probably want at least 1,000 observations. With an office force of 25, this could be done by making observations at 40 time intervals. There are some fairly simple statistical procedures for testing the confidence that you can have in the accuracy of your study. These are described in many texts on production management.

After taking the observations, summarize the results. If you have recorded the observations on sheets that identify the time of day and the person being observed, you can do some interesting things with the results:

You can compare the percentage of time for each element or work. You can compare how each group within your department uses its time. You can compare the amount of time spent in activities by different job classifications. You can compare the results by time of day. To do this you would have to summarize the data by time interval, say 8 to 10 A.M., or 10 A.M. to 12 noon.

3. *Analyze the facts.* A work sampling study of the type I have described provides the facts for a diagnostic study of the operations of a department.

Armed with the facts, you next ask many questions: Why is this necessary? Can it be eliminated? Why is it done the way it is? Why is it done this often? Could it be combined with something else? Could the method be changed?

The key to finding better methods is not taking anything for granted.

4. *Develop the better method.* To improve methods in work that is not structured, you have to focus on the patterns of work that are repetitive. Suppose that a person must go to the file frequently to look for some information. You might find a better way of making the information available. It might be stored electronically and be displayed on a cathode-ray tube. A work sampling study of inspectors in an aluminum extrusion plant showed that paperwork took up 12.6 percent of the time of the inspectors. This is a considerable amount of time and it is a pattern of work that is repetitive. It is a signal that methods should be found to reduce this amount of time. Perhaps more information could be preprinted on the form. Maybe the forms could be eliminated entirely by having the inspector record the information at an accessible computer terminal.

Following this principle of looking for repetitive work patterns to simplify can be the key to better methods for executives and managers. For example, an executive in the department of transportation is using the computer and peripheral equipment to handle communications. The system, on an experimental basis now, will eventually be able to recall memos, transmit memos to other offices where they are displayed on a screen, and print them if necessary. There are many innovative ways for the computer to improve the productivity of the executive that are yet to be found. It is an area that promises much for the future.

5. *Install the new method.* There are three basic ways of introducing new methods. One is to show, tell, or sell new methods to the employee. These are all primarily the same. The only difference is in the degree of diplomacy. In all cases, you are trying to get the employee to change his way of doing the job to a way that you have prescribed. While this method is simple and direct, it has one serious flaw. It rarely works. Anyone who has done professional methods work will tell you that it is easier to find better methods than to get them implemented. People prefer their own ways of doing things; they consider themselves to be the experts or professionals on the job and resent anyone telling them how to do their job. This attitude has much to be said in favor of it, as it is the foundation for pride of workmanship and should also be the basis for high productivity. However, if you are intent on installing new methods, it does not yield easily to a frontal attack, regardless of how sugar-coated the technique may be.

Training is another way of introducing change. New employees are trained in the preferred methods and the present workforce may be retrained. Training has a much higher probability of success with experienced employees than the first method, and, of course, should be completely successful with new employees. The reason for its success with experienced personnel is that training is presented as a vehicle for making the employee more professional. If it is done well, it will be seen by the employee as a way for him to upgrade his knowledge and his skills.

Some years ago an electronics company employed a large number of people, mostly women, to wire electronic components to printed circuit boards. A skilled operator used a long-nosed pliers to wrap the wire around a post on the circuit board in two motions, regrasping the pliers in the process. An engineer discovered a method for wrapping the wire in one motion, eliminating the regrasp. Although the time saved was small it was repeated hundreds of thousands of time, making the proposed methods change far from insignificant. It was installed by putting experienced operators through a short training program.

The third and best way to install new methods is with the participation of the workers. This means that they have a say in the development of the method. Participation works because people become *responsible* for improving and installing new methods. They have a special interest in the success of a new method; they are motivated to make it work.

Motivation

Everyone is motivated to do something, unless he is in a coma. So the question is not whether or not you have motivated employees, but what are they motivated to do. Fundamentally, people are motivated to act in ways that serve their own self-interest, in ways that are compatible with their self-image. Because people are different, you may have side by side under virtually identical conditions an employee who does the minimum and one who does the maximum, one whose mind is occupied with what he is accomplishing and one whose thoughts run to break time, lunchtime, and quitting time. And yet, with diverse attitudes and interests among people, some organizations have found ways to create a working climate of cooperation and hard work while others have workforces that are hostile toward the company and discontented. Apparently, there are some general principles that, if followed, will encourage people to give their best efforts.

To address the question of how to get motivated employees, begin by asking what you want your motivated employees to do. Naturally, you want them to be industrious in creating output of high quality on time and with courtesy and cooperation. But, especially in unstructured jobs, you want them to *think*.

You want them to think about what they are doing and why they are doing it so they won't make mistakes. Suppose you have a report that goes to five people every month. Now one of them has taken a new job and his old position is filled by another person. Your secretary knows that, but without thinking sends the report to the person on the distribution list for the previous month, and the new person who should get a copy is left out. Or suppose that a materials control clerk is charging requisitions to an account that with a little thought he would know is the wrong number, for example, charging items to a "cost plus" contract when they should have been charged to another contract on a "fixed fee" basis.

You also want people to think so that they will take the extra step that prevents others from making mistakes. A purchasing agent at one plant might call his counterpart at another to say, "Bob, I heard that you were placing an order with Ajax—did you know that the last time we got parts from Ajax, they were undersized?" Mistakes frequently occur because a person does not have the information that he should have.

You also want people to think so that they can anticipate a problem and work around it. The thinking person always has a contingency plan or two in the back of his or her mind. Take, for example, the problem of coping with a late delivery. In the first place, if the delivery is critical, the thinking person makes some inquiries to find out if it will be on time. If he knows that it is going to be late, he can plan accordingly. If the delivery is unexpectedly late, he still has some alternatives up his sleeve.

Finally, you want employees to be thinking about using the best methods and to be alert to finding improved methods.

If you agree that you want your employees to think for the reasons given above, then you must have incentive systems and an organizational climate that motivates people to do their best with their bodies and their minds. A study of engineers and scientists in a research and development environment identified the following conditions as especially conducive to self-motivation:[*]

> To work for a respected organization in a stimulating environment under competent management.
>
> To have a challenging assignment in their area of professional interest.
>
> To be in a position that contributes directly to the organization's success.
>
> To participate in decisions affecting themselves, their work, and their careers.
>
> To have an equitable system of recognition and reward.

Organizations that stimulate people in any job classification by putting these conditions into effect follow three main principles. The

[*] R. M. Ranftl, *R & D Productivity*, 2nd Edition (Culver City, Calif.: Hughes Aircraft Company: 1978), p. 75.

first is that they make innovation or just plain thinking part of the job. Texas Instruments offers one of the best examples of a company that clearly declares to its personnel that innovation is part of the job. Their OST (objectives, strategy, and tactics) program mandates that executives spend part of their time on new ideas for products. To provide the mechanism for this they have established team arrangements (discussed in Chapter 9), and segregated capital expenditures to identify those that are an investment in the future from those that are needed to maintain existing capability.

Lincoln Electric Co. is another organization that makes thinking a part of the job at all levels. It is well known for giving large bonuses to its employees, enabling them to earn twice as much or more than what is paid to workers in the average company. The size of an individual's bonus is not based directly on the quantity of production but on his "contribution to the success of the company." Each person is rated three times per year by those who have knowledge of his work. The worker is encouraged to be cooperative and helpful in improving his efficiency of production. The employees at Lincoln understand that finding a better way is part of the job.

The second principle followed by companies that stimulate their employees is that they create a team spirit through participation. They practice an organizational philosophy and methodology that gets people in teams, as described in the preceding chapter. A team program was started at a Motorola plant when a problem arose on a new line of complicated receivers. After the experts—supervisors and engineers—had not been able to overcome the problems, the operators on the line were convened to discuss the problems. They made a recommendation of putting a brush on the nozzle of an air hose to remove particles which had been creating short circuits.

Out of this experience, a sense of cohesion developed and regular team meetings were held. Now there are more than 100 teams at Motorola's Communications Group. The company reports that since the start of the program in 1975, there has been a great improvement in production, rejects have been significantly reduced, employee turnover has been reduced, and absenteeism is down to a few percentage points. This is not an isolated case, as the resurgence of the Scanlon plan, mentioned in the preceding chapter, has triggered the formation of many team organizations to improve production methods. Donnelly Mirrors, Inc., is one of many success stories. Since adopting its

Scanlon plan in 1952, productivity per person has almost doubled. Quality levels are up from 92 percent to 98.5 percent. Absenteeism has diminished to 1 percent from 5 percent.*

The final principle followed by successful companies is that they offer incentives for productive work. Of course, there are other incentives besides money, such as recognition, or opportunity for personal growth. By and large, these nonmonetary incentives are not controversial. Furthermore, a company that follows the first two principles advocated here bestows some of these incentives as a by-product.

Monetary incentives, on the other hand, are controversial. Today some people believe that money is not an effective incentive—that it ranks far down the list of what a person wants from his job. Others tout monetary incentives as the carrot that gets work out of people. As in most cases where there are extreme views, the truth lies somewhere in the middle. A monetary reward is an incentive if for no other reason than that it is a signal from management that good work is recognized and rewarded. Even the detractors of financial incentive systems admit its psychological value. In fact, it has been observed that a financial reward may be required to get the worker committed psychologically to his or her work.† A study of the Merrimack Valley Works of the Western Electric Company supports this contention. Among the changes that were made to increase morale and productivity were changes to the group incentive system to make it more responsive to achievement.

One of the reasons for the controversy over incentive systems is that they have frequently been a testimony for Murphy's Law. The universal problem is that the standards become too loose over a period of several years because of many small improvements in method. This may be due to a failure on the part of management to revise the standard when methods change. More often it is attributed to implementing a number of small methods changes, many of which are the creation of the worker. Each change by itself may be of little consequence, but accumulated over time they destroy the accuracy of the standard. Furthermore, since separately they are not material, each improvement is not a basis for changing the standard.

---

* Edward M. Glaser, *Productivity Gains Through Work-Life Improvements* (New York: Harcourt Brace Jovanovich, 1976), pp. 47–51.
† David Sirota, "The Conflict between IE and Behavioral Science," *Industrial Engineering,* June 1972, pp. 34–38.

The experience of many companies has been that when the standards are loose, workers will produce up to some point, say 135 percent of standard, and will curtail output after that, fearing that management will reestablish the standard at a higher level of output. Then the worker would lose out by having to work faster to achieve the same incentive pay.

The best solution to this problem that I have seen is the proposal by Mitchell Fein, which awards the employee with a cash payment when the standard is changed. Fein calls this "buying back" the standard. The amount paid is based on the annual savings. The formula for the amount paid should be developed for each organization.

Management and Control of the System

There must be a good reporting system which compares the actual performance to the standard and perhaps to past levels of performance. Although such stipulation may seem obvious, there are organizations that have standards but do not use them or do not get the most out of them because they do not have a reporting system that makes comparisons that are relevant to the needs of management. A report on productivity in the federal service states:

> Even where engineered measures have been developed (often at great cost and over many years) their utilization by high levels of management is often minor or nonexistent. Much of this lack of use can be attributed to the failure of subordinate levels to report the data in simple, integrated, understandable, and useful formats to higher levels of management.*

The format for a report and the information in the report should be tailored for the organization and for the level of management. A detailed report for the first-line supervisor will probably not be what higher management wants to see.

The second point about managing the system is that the methods of improving productivity should be used selectively and in the combination that gets the greatest benefit. This means hitting the weakest link in the four components of measurement, methods, motivation, and reporting system. An organization can become preoccupied with

---

* Brian L. Usilaner, "Productivity in the Federal Service," Government Activities Working Group, National Commission on Productivity (Washington, D.C.: Government Printing Office, September 21, 1971), p. 7.

work measurement by attempting to reach the ultimate in the accuracy of the standards and at the same time be grossly remiss in making a concentrated effort to improve methods. Certainly there have been plenty of examples of a company having good programs for setting standards and making major efforts to improve methods with technically qualified personnel but completely overlooking the people part of the equation. The recommended approach is to concentrate on the one or two elements that may be lacking instead of an overemphasis on those that are in place.

Applying similar reasoning, you should direct your efforts to improve productivity at the part of the operations system that is the weak link. As pointed out in the discussion on selecting the job for methods improvement, you should direct efforts at the operations that have a big potential for improvement.

Do You Need a Productivity Program?

You do not have to have a productivity program to get improved productivity. Productivity, to a great extent, is the handmaiden to good management practice. If you manage your organization as a builder, if you are setting goals for your organization, if you have a plan and a strategy for carrying out those goals, and if you organize to give people the responsibility and the decision-making capabilities to carry out their responsibilities, you are going to get good productivity. However, you will get still better productivity if you have a program which directly addresses measurement, methods, motivation, and management of the system.

But before you opt for a formal productivity program, give some consideration to the points below. You may not be ready for a program, and, if you aren't, it may backfire, and once again you will be convinced of the inevitability of Murphy's Law.

1. If you have a union, make sure that the union is brought into the planning and accepts the program. A failure to take this step will guarantee that you will be faced with conflict and disruption. If you believe that the union will be a problem, work on this first. There are many good reasons for unions to be ardent supporters of a productivity program. It can lead to greater job security and a more profitable company. However, if it is viewed as an attempt to speed up work, you will gain the opposition of organized labor.

2. Are there fundamental morale problems? If there is a lack of

trust between management and workers, the announcement of a productivity program will add to the distrust.

3. Management must be prepared to share some of the gains with the workers. If management views improved productivity to be for the company's benefit only, you can expect trouble.

4. Management must be ready to listen to workers and share information with them. If a participative style of management or if sharing decision making is threatening to management, workers will soon sense that their contributions are not wanted.

5. Not only must management listen but it must be ready to take action. Nothing will undermine a productivity program more quickly than a failure to implement good ideas. When people are involved, they expect to get implementation of their ideas or prompt answers as to why the ideas cannot be implemented. This type of program gives the workers more responsibility but it also makes management assume great responsibility for being responsive. Before you start a program, make sure that you are ready to carry out your end of the bargain.

If you are weak on any of these points, my recommendation is to postpone any program with the word "productivity" in it. Instead, you need to install some programs which will improve communications, trust, and the sense of responsibility. Your management style must be directed toward "building," not just getting today's job done. You need to get your subordinates more involved in problem solving. You may have to restructure jobs in a way that places more responsibility for workmanship and judgment on the shoulders of the employee, which in turn affords him or her the opportunity for greater recognition.

To state it simply, a productivity program is not a prescription for a sick organization. The organization need not be robust, but it should at least be in moderately good health. A productivity program requires planning and a system for planning. If the underlying system for planning is weak, it will be impossible for the productivity program to be *communicated and understood.* Instead it is guaranteed to be *misunderstood.*

How to Start a Productivity Program

Get the support of top management. A productivity program and the need to improve productivity must be a concern of top management.

Management has to want to improve productivity. It may seem that this point can be taken for granted but unfortunately this is not the case. Management may believe that it is fully competitive without making a special effort to improve productivity. Or it may believe that its success is due to its processes which may be highly automated. But regardless of the degree of automation, the performance of any company ultimately rests on its people and what they do.

Select a productivity administrator. One person is needed to take responsibility for getting the program under way. He or she should be a person who (1) believes in the importance and the urgency of improving productivity, (2) has the ability to lead and motivate others, (3) has the respect and confidence of managers and employees at all levels, and (4) knows the company policies and practices and has a good understanding of the internal operations

Spell out company policy on the productivity program. This policy is required to establish the priority of the program and to answer some rather far-reaching but specific questions. The policy should establish the fact that there will be resources devoted to productivity improvement. This will not entail much cost because essentially the resources required are the efforts of people already on the payroll. However, the program will require a budget for training materials and perhaps a very small staff to support the productivity administrator.

One of the questions that should be answered by company policy is the matter of layoffs. The company must make it clear to all that no one will be laid off as a result of productivity improvement. If displaced people cannot be absorbed by company growth, then the reduction should take place through attrition.

A policy for giving awards should be established. As mentioned before, the benefits of improved productivity must be shared to some extent by the employees that made it possible. The details of the incentive and reward system may be developed later as part of a comprehensive plan for the program, but the administrator should have some guidelines for his detailed planning.

Increase awareness. This is a phase of gathering and disseminating information. The administrator should prepare presentations that show the trend of productivity in the nation, in the industry, and in the company. The presentations should also refer to success stories within the company. It may also be appropriate to cite the experiences of other companies. Above all, the administrator should make it clear that the productivity program is not going to be a "one shot" affair but something that will be a fixture in the company for the long haul.

In addition to making people aware of the problem, the presentations should also create enthusiasm and the belief that "something can be done." The underlying purpose of the presentations is to gain the support of managers throughout the organization.

Optional: Conduct an attitude survey. A survey will uncover problems that not only need correction but could be severe enough to derail a productivity program. Misunderstandings, a lack of trust, a feeling that management doesn't care are some of the negative attitudes that should be addressed directly. If an attitude survey is made, the results should be communicated to the employees. Management should undertake action to correct the problems indicated by the survey and should let the employees know that such steps are being taken. You cannot oversell the corrective action which might lead employees to think that the problems will be quickly overcome. On the other hand, to the more insightful employee, a promised quick solution would be merely an admission that management doesn't understand the problem.

Surveys, followed by thoughtful positive action on the part of management, can demonstrate that management does care.

Prepare a plan for productivity improvement. A productivity plan outlines the major phases of the program, the schedule for those phases, the goals of the program, and its costs. Topics that may be covered in the plan are:

The organization for productivity improvement.
The goals of the program.
Either the measurements that will be used or the criteria for establishing measurements.
The reporting system.
The training program.
The details of the reward or incentive system.
The use of attitude surveys.

Create the organization. The basic organizational scheme is to have the workforce in productivity groups, with coordinating councils at the next level and a steering committee at the highest level. Worker representatives and representatives of first-line management should be included at all levels.

The organization works like this (starting at the bottom). The productivity groups are made up of from 5 to 20 workers and their supervisor. For the workers, participation in these groups is strictly voluntary. They have authority to implement changes that could normally be made by the supervisor over the unit. The groups meet for about one to two hours per week for training and discussion of improvements.

At the next level, corresponding to the department level, are coordinating councils. The department managers preside over these groups, which are composed of his supervisors and elected representatives from the first-line productivity groups. The purpose of these councils is to make decisions for implementing changes and to coordinate changes that affect more than one productivity group. The coordinating councils should also have authority to make awards up to a certain amount which are shared equally by all members of a productivity group.

The coordinating councils are under the surveillance of the productivity administrator. The administrator will audit and monitor all programs, coordinate the activities of the departmental coordinating councils, encourage the councils to set goals and meet goals that in turn will achieve the goals for the entire program.

The productivity administrator is the link between the councils, which are operating units, and the steering committee, which is at the top management level. The steering committee is composed of the department heads, a few selected or elected lower-level supervisors, and elected worker representatives. It is responsible for setting policy, generally overviewing the progress of the program, and providing for coordination between the departmental coordinating councils.

This sketch of a general plan of organization will fit many companies. There can be many deviations and adaptations to suit the needs of an individual company.

Write the procedures required to get the program under way. These should spell out the responsibilities for the various levels of organization, the procedure to be followed in recommending and approving improvements, the requirements for holding meetings, and the like.

Start the program with a pilot productivity group. It is desirable to find a group with a supervisor who is eager to be a part of the program and who has good intragroup communications. After starting one group, the program should be expanded step by step to others.

Arrange for group orientation and training. The people in the group should be instructed in the five-step approach to methods improvement discussed earlier in the chapter. It is especially important to get across the point that problem solving and methods improvement depend on getting facts. People without training are inclined to take positions supported by opinion only.

How fact finding leads to the acceptance of new methods is illustrated by a group in an aerospace company that was having trouble with drill bits that were breaking. Complaints about this to the tooling department which sharpened the drills were dismissed as being nothing more than the usual amount of griping. After the group received training in fact finding and problem solving, it collected information methodically. Drills that had broken were taped to a poster showing the number of holes each had drilled before it broke. The poster demonstrated dramatically the wide discrepancies between drill lives, showing some that lasted only for a few holes and others that had long lives. This factual information was presented to the tooling department. Friction between the two departments was replaced by cooperation. The tooling department changed its methods of sharpening drills, and that alleviated the problem of breaking drills.

Improve productivity, document improved productivity, and publicize improved productivity. When the productivity groups emerge from the training stage to the point where their main emphasis is on improving productivity, there will be savings in cost, elapsed time, and better quality. These improvements are recorded, appropriate awards given, and the success of the group is publicized to all employees.

Continue the program by forming more groups and continuing education. New groups will of course require training but you will also need to conduct refresher sessions with existing productivity groups. New people will have joined groups for one reason or another. Experienced people also learn from review sessions and there is, unquestionably, a motivational component in all good training.

How to Improve Personal Productivity

The general approach to improving personal productivity has already been given. The seven principles of time planning in Chapter 3 really say it all. In this section, I offer a framework for analysis and action that is subordinate to the principle of "knowing where time is spent," and some suggestions for using time more effectively.

In order to improve your personal productivity, you must first know how you spend your time. Then you can address the question of how you should spend your time. One classification scheme that helps you to understand why you allocate work time as you do and also points to the direction for improvement is based on the *source* of work. The five categories of source and what can be done about them are explained in the paragraphs that follow.

From the boss. This applies to assignments, directions that you receive, and suggestions that have the force of an order from your boss. Work in this category must be done. Frequently, it cannot be delegated. And when parts of it can, it still requires some of your time.

You can reduce the time spent in communicating with your boss by being more efficient. In this regard, you could suggest that the meetings between you and him be given a definite time limit. You might be able to reduce the time spent by giving him information before the meeting. For example, a meeting that normally takes one to two hours to review progress on projects might be considerably shortened if you presented him with a set of well-prepared graphs in advance.

From peers. This is work that is requested by people on your level and, for that reason, is optional. A supervisor from another group may request you to compile information for him, as an example. You will generally try to comply with this type of request. You would like to be helpful to others and you might encounter circumstances at a later date when cooperation from the other party is extremely important to you. Furthermore, if you refuse, there is always the chance that the other person might be able to request your assistance from your boss (perhaps by going through his boss) and now the assignment is in the boss-directed category.

Your first line of defense against assignments of this type is to question the effectiveness of the project. This is a perfectly reasonable and rational step. You are merely ascertaining whether or not the results are worth the effort. One very important outgrowth of questioning is determining if the work requested will really provide the results that are wanted. How often it occurs that a person asking for some type of study does not get what he really wants *even though he gets just what he asked for.* By questioning, you can prevent misdirected time and energy.

Having established that the effort is effective, you next consider how to perform the work efficiently. The question to ask yourself is whether this type of request is a one-time occurrence or whether you can expect a number of similar requests in the future. The reason for raising this issue is that the methods for dealing with the request are likely to differ depending on whether or not it becomes a regular occurrence. If you believe that it is a one-time affair, you will probably use the most expedient method. If it is a precursor of many future requests, you should take the time to organize the work so that it can be done most efficiently.

From subordinates. Subordinates request help, want to talk over a problem with you, ask you to review progress, or need a decision from you before proceeding. Although one could argue that all time in this category is elective on your part, your operation would soon come to a halt if you declined all such work. Certainly, the amount of time in this category is controllable by you.

If you think that you are spending too much time with your subordinates, it might be due to a weakness in your organization. It simply might be a matter of having too many people reporting to you. However, the source of the problem is often more subtle than that. Your subordinates may feel accountability for performing tasks instead of feeling responsible for their work. As a result, they do not perform well with general directions. (Or perhaps you are not giving them general directions.)

From the job itself. There is some work that is not top-down-directed in the sense that it is expected to be done without any discussion from your superior. It is just part of the job. Generally speaking, failure to do this type of work is immediately noticeable. If it is not noticeable, it raises the question of whether or not it is necessary.

Often work in this category is similar to work done for peers in that the output of the work is information that is used by another person who is not your boss and not in your organization. The difference between this and peer-requested work is that it is done without a special request and is not optional.

There are two avenues to reducing time spent on this category of work. One is delegation. As in the case of boss-directed work, maybe a part of the task, if not all, can be given to subordinates. The other route is to increase efficiency. Work of this type will often contain repetitive work patterns which, as we have seen, become the target for methods improvement.

Your desk can either be a millstone around your neck or it can be an efficient work center. You should view your desk as an instrument to help you create ideas, make decisions, communicate with others, and handle transactions efficiently. A desk is not a bookshelf or a filing cabinet: it is best not used for permanent storage. It should contain incoming work and outgoing work, as well as work in process. Projects and reports in the formulative stages are in this category. Desktop vertical organizers are useful for holding several folders so that each is accessible without going through a stack. The equipment you need such as a calculator, typewriter, computer terminal, or dictating equipment should be positioned for easy access on a stand or table near your desk. And don't consider a typewriter to be a symbol of lower status and, hence, to be avoided. If you are able to compose on a typewriter, you might find this to be your most efficient method of getting your ideas on paper.

At your own discretion. The line of demarcation between any of these work categories is not always sharp, and this is particularly true of this one. Be reminded that the basis for classification is the *source* of the Work and not the amount of independence that you have in performing it or the amount of creative effort that it requires. Before extolling the benefits of discretionary work it should be recognized that there are opportunities for building activities, such as solving problems generically, in work that stems from any source.

Sometimes work which is initiated from an outside source can become discretionary. This is the case when you enlarge the scope of the work so that it fulfills the purpose sought after by the originating source, and the added discretionary elements achieve results that you desire. For example, your boss might ask you to train one person to operate some new equipment. You might decide to train several. Or you might be asked to investigate the benefits of acquiring a text-editing typewriter. Some preliminary investigation could convince you that you should undertake a thorough review of new office equipment and technology. In other words, the idea or the impetus may not be yours but when you define the scope of the work it becomes, at least in part, discretionary.

Work which begins as being discretionary can become a required part of the job. For example, starting a newsletter is discretionary. Then over a period of time, publishing a newsletter becomes an expected part of the job.

Making the Most of Discretionary Time

The justification for discretionary work, which is also the reason for its value, is that it makes a contribution to the organization which, incidentally, is uniquely yours. People in managerial positions have a great opportunity to make a worthwhile contribution to the organization through discretionary work. The problem is that they frequently find that they have very little time to work on the things that they want to work on and that they believe to be important.

If this describes you, you can get more done if you reduce the amount of time spent in the other four categories and become more productive in using your discretionary time. I have already given some suggestions for reducing time in the other categories. As for being more productive, the biggest mountain to conquer is procrastination. We have a tendency to put off the hardest work that we do by substituting work which is less demanding. The hardest work we do is *thinking* and oh, how we like to avoid it! The hardest part about writing a report is thinking. The hardest part about getting a project plan is thinking. The hardest part about resolving a staffing problem is thinking through the solution.

Instead of hard thinking, we decide that it is about time to check on the production from the new machine. Or we decide that a trip to the purchasing department would be a good idea to see if procurement on the project is going as planned. Or another favorite dodge is that we tell ourselves that we should not be aloof from our subordinates and that it is about time to circulate around the office or the production line. Now all these discretionary activities, if handled well, will make some contribution toward a better performing unit. But you have to ask yourself if you have made the best use of your discretionary time. If you believe that little forays like those mentioned above are in your best interest, ask yourself if you have, perhaps unconsciously, stretched them out to avoid going back to the office where the difficult undone task lies. *Are you engaging in busy work when you should be engaged in knowledge work?*

You can put a halt to procrastination by using a few simple planning and control devices. You can identify the tasks that you have to perform and estimate the time that each should take. Then try to hold to your estimate and compare the actual time with the estimate. If you have blocked out a period of time each week for discretionary time, check to see if you have upheld your schedule and evaluate what you accomplished during the period. You can look at the number of times you have performed a routine activity, asking yourself if all these times are really necessary or if the activity is an *escape*.

There are many opportunities to improve your productivity through making better use of your time. I have accumulated a long list of tips from too many sources to remember and from my own experiences. They have been grouped under the principles of time management discussed in Chapter 3 and are presented for your consideration in the list below.

Visualization and goal setting
1. Discuss your resolutions and your use of time to become more committed.

Knowing where time is spent
2. Try keeping a time log for two weeks.
3. Use a time log for a special project.

Setting priorities
4. Work on the jobs that have a big payoff.
5. Distinguish between urgency and importance.
6. Use the 80/20 rule as a guide in planning activities.
7. Recognize the obsolete parts of your job or the duties that you have delegated to others and eliminate them.
8. Invest time in your own growth.
9. Follow plans based on priorities.
10. Learn to say "No."

Saving and making time
11. Try to spend time in large blocks on important work.
12. Group similar jobs together.
13. Group telephone calls.
14. Concentrate on the job at hand. Use a pad to write down ideas that you want to remember but are distracting at present. Do one thing at a time.
15. Control meetings by being on time, starting on time, and having and following an agenda.
16. Organize desk and files to have room to work and to be able to find what you are looking for.
17. Delegate whenever possible.
18. Avoid being trapped into reverse delegation by subordinates.
19. Try to eliminate system-imposed work.
20. Be careful to communicate clearly and get feedback on your important messages.

21. Use driving time to think, learn, or dictate.
22. Read selectively and rapidly.
23. Avoid shuffling papers. Try to handle a piece of paper once.
24. Write down your own personal time wasters and resolve to do something about them.
25. Reduce your time in conversations by:
    Standing instead of sitting when talking.
    Visiting the other person in his office.
    Letting people know how much time is going to be taken.

Planning, scheduling, and controlling use of time

26. Control conversations that are not job-related. Appear to be busy and you will find that people will respect your time more.
27. Get control over interruptions as much as possible.
28. When time is available, do not let it be filled with routine jobs or work that you have allowed to stretch out.
29. Have a file or a list of things that you want to talk over with a person or your boss.
30. Know your prime time for work that requires concentration and make use of this time for the tough job.
31. Schedule, start on time, and finish on time.
32. Set your own deadlines.
33. Do not procrastinate. Do it now! Or plan a start, make a start, *get started!*
34. Allocate your time with a time budget.

Staying flexible

35. Make use of waiting time. Always have something to read.

Being master of your own time

36. When at work, concentrate on accomplishment, not on putting in time. Think in terms of output and results.
37. Know what you are doing right now and why you are doing it.
38. Think of time management as a team problem. If everyone is aware of making the best use of time, the priorities of others will be respected.
39. Conduct your own time management meeting, possibly renting a film on time management.

Minimal Policies for Productive Managers

After you read many dos and don'ts, your most important ideas sometimes lose their perspective. The most important principles for getting productivity from subordinate managers and knowledge workers are not in this chapter. The real bases for productivity are in the many aspects of being a builder, especially building knowledge, goal setting, and planning. The importance of these concepts is illustrated by the results of a survey of executive productivity undertaken by AMA-COM, a division of the American Management Associations. Replies were received from 745 managers and 530 company presidents. (See Table 4.) You can see that all of these except "financial incentive programs" are related to building and planning.

Productivity and Murphy's Law

In this chapter the importance of improving productivity has been stressed. It has been demonstrated that there are some rational approaches toward productivity improvement. These can only be ac-

Table 4.   Respondents' evaluation of which remedies are most likely to contribute to improvement in managerial performance.

Remedy	All Respondents (Each Respondent Selected 3 Remedies)	Presidents	Managers
More meaningful and challenging managerial work	45%	50%	41%
More effective management control methods and techniques affecting budgets, scheduling, personnel relations, information flow, etc.	42	47	39
Better management education programs to improve managerial competence	39	39	41
"Financial incentives programs" for managers at all levels	37	35	38
Greater dissemination down the line of information pertaining to executive-level decisions and the reasons for them	37	34	38
Increased organizational decentralization wherever possible so as to delegate more responsibility and authority down the line	36	34	37
Better managerial performance appraisal approaches	29	30	29

complished by hard work and dedication but they will pay off. It has been said before, but the caveat is worth stating again, that a "quick and dirty" approach to increasing productivity will lead to disaster. An ill-conceived and ill-planned productivity program will be interpreted as a "management program" for speeding up work. After this negative reaction has permeated through the ranks, it will take a lot of time and work just to get the organization back to where it was.

11

Control, change, and coordination

It has been said that hindsight is 20–20. Every department, every task team can look back on detrimental events that could have been avoided if different decisions were made or different steps were taken. Frequently, the difficulty is not with the original plan, but with a failure to ensure that the plan is being followed or to ascertain that new circumstances have rendered the plan obsolete—a failure of control, in other words.

Deciding what, when, and how to control has been called establishing *strategic control points.* The decision itself is based on the simple idea that the cost of the control must be more than offset by the value gained through control. Applying this principle leads to the selective use of controls. One familiar example is the ABC inventory system, in which A items are closely controlled, C items are hardly controlled at all, and B items are controlled at a level somewhere in between.

In keeping with the concepts of management by exception and strategic controls, here are some checkpoints for designing control systems:

1. Have a definite purpose in mind for a control. Be able to answer the question, "Why is this being controlled?"
2. Make sure that the control is measurable against a standard or a norm so that exceptions can be clearly defined and reported.

3. Keep the degree of control commensurate with the magnitude of the potential adverse results. In other words, don't be lax and don't overkill.
4. Try to design the most economical and simplest control system. A very complex system will invite "controls on the controls."
5. Establish controls that produce timely results. Learning about a problem after it is too late to do anything about it is not much good.

The control system must be closely linked to planning. A good control system supports planning, contingency planning especially, by pointing the way to taking corrective action or altering the plan. When the control system registers a deviation from the plan, it should not leave you wondering what to do. Instead, it should aid in the evaluation of the situation: the system should learn from the deviation, and it should facilitate improvements in planning in the future.

The Natural Control Cycle

Many processes have a natural control cycle attributed to either convention or physical reasons. Sometimes there is a major and a minor cycle. For the chief executive officer, the quarterly report establishes a quarterly cycle but the major cycle is the fiscal year. Production supervisors customarily get a weekly report reflecting efficiency and output. A monthly summary might be the major cycle. For the office manager, a monthly report of expenses compared to budget establishes the month as the minor cycle, and a year is probably the major cycle. Training schedules for military units are sometimes capped by a large maneuver, held once per year. The combat readiness of the unit is largely evaluated on how well it performs during the maneuver.

Inasmuch as these cycles establish points in time for measuring performance, they are also an incentive for performing in a way that produces a favorable measurement of performance at the end of the cycle. This can create a problem of control when the natural cycle does not conform to the correct cycle for planning and control. A farmer, for example, must plan annually for harvests, a practice which is in harmony with markets and growing cycles. However, an agronomist would urge the farmer to extend his planning further than one year to plan for crop rotation and for times when the land is to lie fallow.

The chief executive has a similar problem. He has pressures for quarterly and annual performance but his important and lasting contribution will only be visible over a period of years.

The natural control cycle can be too long as well as too short for proper control. A production facility that has a month-end rush to get out the quota is reacting inefficiently and ineffectively to a monthly reporting system—which may be the natural cycle for the business as a whole. A no-nonsense control of daily or weekly schedules should be imposed.

Since natural cycles are well ingrained and convenient, there is an inclination to use them without reservation. However, the examples above are a warning that the natural cycle cannot be trusted to be a satisfactory checkpoint for control or to put performance in proper perspective with long-range plans. Checkpoints should be established which are commensurate with the scope and duration of the plan.

How to Set Up Contingency Plans

Contingency plans can be formal or informal, that is, written or not written. The choice is yours, but if the stakes are high and if others must lend their coordinated efforts, the plan had better be written.

There are four closely related steps in contingency planning: (1) ask what can happen, (2) estimate the probability of the event's happening, (3) assess the consequences of the event to your operation, and (4) take measures to reduce the probability of the event's occurring and/or prepare for its occurrence. The contingencies that should be planned for vary with each business and organization within it. In uncovering these latent sources of trouble, it helps to have a framework of categories. Six problem categories for contingency planning are listed below.

1. Customer-related
   New competitor
   Shutdown at customer facility due to strike, fire, etc.
   Sudden drop-off in orders submitted
   Bankruptcy of a major customer
   Sudden increase in workload

2. Supplier-related
   Sudden increase in price
   Failure of supplier to deliver (strike, fire, etc.)
   Failure of utility: power, water, communication, etc.
   Very poor quality of materials received
3. Employee-related
   Illness or injury to key employee
   Epidemic
   Fraudulent acts
   Theft
   Destruction of property
   Strikes and sick-outs
   Failure to perform in accordance with plans and procedures
4. Equipment-related
   Failure in major production equipment and processes
   Failure in data processing
   Failure in communications equipment
5. Related to societal environment
   Interruption of public service (police, fire, medical, sanitation, postal, transportation)
   Civil disorder and riots
   Vandalism
   Government expropriation or seizure of facilities*
   Kidnapping and extortion
6. Related to physical environment
   Fire
   Earthquake
   Flood and tidal waves
   Storms
   Airplane crash, if located near airport
   Explosion, release of a dangerous chemical, or fire in neighboring facility

After estimating the probability that an event might occur and then assessing its impact on your organization, you can clarify and evaluate risk by using a grid of probability and seriousness, such as the one shown in Figure 19. Further analysis of the situations that could occur may lead to taking some containment steps which would reduce the probability of the event. Examples are procuring standby equipment, duplicating records and computer files, cross-training person-

---

* Applies in some foreign countries.

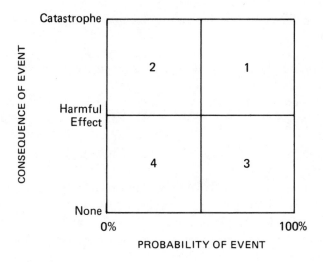

Figure 19. Classification of risk.

nel, and improving the physical security of equipment and confidential information. Some of these steps may eliminate the need for contingency plans by reducing the probability of the event to near zero.

Any event that remains in the first quadrant *must* be covered by a plan. Second-quadrant situations should also be covered with a formal plan unless the probability is very small. It is desirable to have the third quadrant covered with written plans when several groups or individuals are involved in getting the contingency plan into action.

Many, perhaps most, contingency plans are not disaster-oriented. In these plans there should be a predetermined trigger point that sets the plan in motion. The trigger point must be something that is easily measurable or identifiable. It could be a predetermined number of orders received in a time period that is higher or lower than normal; if the number is reached, plans for changing the level of production go into effect immediately. At the department level, contingency plans are useful for handling problems related to the flow of work. A backlog of work beyond a certain level might be the trigger point. Failing to reach a milestone on a project within the scheduled time could be the trigger for putting contingency plans into action.

A written contingency plan may include the topics in the outline below:

Description of event(s) that can trigger contingency plan.

General course of action.

Detailed instructions or procedures for implementing plan.

Reference to other procedures or contingency plans as needed.

Names, addresses, and telephone numbers of people who are to be informed of contingency and who can authorize emergency action.

Names, addresses, and telephone numbers of outside organizations whose assistance might be required. This includes companies specializing in some type of assistance, vendors who provide service to equipment, and public agencies such as police, fire, medical, etc.

Depending on the particular nature of the contingency, the plan may include the following topics:

A group of employees—a task team—to be brought in for the emergency.

Equipment designated as backup and instructions for making a switch.

Electrical power backup.

Backup for computer processing, computer programs, and data files.

Off-site support through a sister organization or another company.

Contingency plans should be tested, if possible. This is the idea behind a fire drill. If the plan is never tested, you can be almost certain that when it is needed it won't work the way you thought it would. Suppose that you have arranged for data processing backup at an outside source. This organization must have the opportunity to go through your procedures on a trial basis. Furthermore, this procedure should be repeated periodically, annually perhaps. In the data processing field, with its continual change in equipment, procedures, and personnel, you would be lost if, after five years without a test, you needed the off-site support for an emergency. Contingency plans are like insurance policies: there is an annual premium to pay.

Observation: Facts and Clues

The three top executives of Datacomp, a 50-man company of computer and programming specialists, were celebrating the new contract they had just negotiated with a national credit card organization.* A $1 million contract for a company that was striving to reach $2 million in revenues wasn't bad. Coincidentally, the contract arrived as the company was preparing for its tenth anniversary. It certainly was an occasion for breaking out the champagne.

Getting the contract had been hard work, with many nights of pushing pencils and grinding out figures. Performing the scope of work would not be easy and the contract was far from fat, but it could be done with a profit for Datacomp. Indeed, it was a victory that could lead to more opportunities in a growing industry.

The plan called for Allen Sims to be the project manager, heading a staff of about ten experienced Datacomp employees initially. Over a period of a few months, the team would build up to 25 to 30 people. Allen and all the people on the project were highly motivated. They dug into their work eagerly.

Six months later the picture was entirely different. Allen had become apprehensive and a bit uneasy about the progress that was being made. Checking into the status of work, he found that he was seriously behind schedule. He reported this to Jeb Felding and Paul Fisher, Datacomp's president and executive vice-president, who investigated further. What Allen had seen proved to be only the tip of the iceberg. The programmers and systems experts had run into many problems. Datacomp was facing a major overrun on this fixed-price contract that would force it into bankruptcy. Jeb arranged a meeting with the customer hoping to renegotiate the contract. After several meetings and more analysis of the situation at Datacomp, it was estimated that $300,000 more would be needed to complete the scope of work. That was an overrun of one third of the original $1 million contract!

What followed was a business and personal tragedy. The customer refused to renegotiate. This triggered a massive layoff. A vice-president who probably had the strongest technical background left the company, breaking off still another part of the business which he was able to take with him in a new venture of his own. The company was

---

* This is a true story with names disguised.

virtually dismantled. The shell of its former self was finally sold to another company. Jeb Felding had nothing to show for ten years of work when he was forced to look for another job.

How can a project get so grossly out of control in such a small company? Did no one watch the store? It is not quite as simple as that—the output was not widgets that can be counted but pieces of paper of varying complexity, length, and quality.

Regardless of the output, there was a failure of *observation*, which caused a failure in control. There were tasks that were unfinished, problems still awaiting solutions. These were *facts*, and somebody, the person with firsthand knowledge, knew these facts. At his level he might not have known the seriousness of the situation. But there were people with more responsibility and with more of an overview who had *clues*, if not facts, that all was not well. Perhaps these clues were dismissed by wishful thinking that the situation would solve itself. I am positive that some of the problem can be accounted for by that frame of mind. I am equally certain that many of the clues went unobserved.

A formal control system is designed to produce facts, generally numerical, which the observer compares with some standards he has in mind, or which are compared for him in the report. Either way, it is up to the observer to conclude whether this fact (the number) is a clue to some underlying problem which he or she should investigate.

Without formal controls the process is basically the same. It begins with observation. It then follows the old adage, "Where there is smoke there is fire." The smoke is a fact, but it is also the clue to another fact, the fire. The manager cannot afford to ignore little puffs of smoke that may signal a potential bonfire. He must investigate to find out if there really is a fire or only a few smoldering embers that will die down.

The Principle of Visual Control

What is visual control? It is an office layout, or a plant layout, or an arrangement of work flow that enables a manager to determine readily by observation how well work is progressing. The principle of visual control mandates that physical layouts be orderly. Backlogs of work at work stations or desks are easy to observe. Work which is behind schedule is very identifiable. Color coding of job tickets or batches of paperwork is a method for getting visual control. When there is visual control, an informed person is able, without recourse to reports, to note operations that are overburdened and probably falling behind schedule.

This is not to say that a formal control system reporting status, backlogs, problems, and exceptions is not valuable. Rather, both are needed. The formal control system is needed to report facts that cannot be seen, such as monthly costs. Formal controls are also valuable in making sure that facts that can be seen, such as delinquent orders, get attention. But visual controls operate in real time. They expedite the process of observing clues and getting facts. If you have not organized the flow of work that you are responsible for to get visual control, you are forgoing a powerful management tool.

Feedback and Fear

In ancient times the messenger who brought bad news to the king was in danger of losing his life. We have progressed quite a bit since then, but we must recognize that fear can still cause feedback to be filtered and distorted. We can cope with this phenomenon by various ploys such as making an automatic mental correction to data given. In other words, on the basis of past experience, we might multiply the severity of the problem, as it is told to us, by two. We can also make our own investigation or have one made by a third person. None of these approaches is a model of good management. The only real solution lies in dealing with fear itself.

Building confidence and trust will dispel the false fears that hinder the performance of many people. People have false fears when they imagine that negative performance will result in such unpleasant consequences as verbal chastisement, subjection to close surveillance in the future, removal of prerogatives, or even a loss of position or employment. Certainly, people who harbor false fears such as these are motivated to do many things which hamper performance.

If your normal reaction to not getting the full facts about a subordinate's mistake is to correct him for the mistake and really take him to task for not leveling with you, you have probably compounded the problem. A better approach would be to ask him why he was reluctant to give you the full information. If he understands that the type of mistake he has made will not result in dire consequences, you will probably get more truthful answers under similar circumstances in the future.

This approach does not apply to legitimate fears. One of the largest conglomerate corporations in the nation had a policy of forgiving a division manager who did not meet his business plan *once*. The second time, unless there were circumstances clearly beyond his control, he was out. In this case, fear of being removed was a real fear. If this causes a person to color the truth, confidence and trust will not be a remedy. How a person acts under these circumstances depends on his character and his self-image.

How Incentives Can Go Wrong

Incentives often produce unintended and undesirable results when they reward one dimension of performance. Much may be accomplished in the dimension that is rewarded, but performance in other dimensions is frequently worse than it would have been without an incentive. Examples range from the person who has an incentive to work just long enough to qualify for unemployment benefits to the executive who relentlessly pushes for short-term profits which yield a fat bonus to the detriment of the strength of the company. In a business setting the typical situation that produces a distortion of effort is an incentive system tied to an important unit of output which is easily measured. For a salesman, it is dollars of sales; for a production worker it is the number of pieces (perhaps the number of *good* pieces). The production worker may then be tempted to abuse the machine to increase output. As a rule, if the machine is out of operation, he will receive pay at his average incentive rate, inasmuch as management assumes that he is stopped for reasons beyond his control.

The salesman on a straight commission is tempted to go for volume instead of trying to sell the most profitable items; he is not motivated to hold down his expenses, and he finds little incentive in training new hires. Furthermore, some type of an economic carrot will have to be hung out for him to take a transfer to a new area that might have high potential for sales but will produce fewer sales for him to begin with.

Incentives are only one aspect of the total reward system. Salary, promotion, status symbols, perquisites, and fringe benefits, together with approval and recognition, combine to motivate people. High-level federal employees who earn more than about $34,000 are rewarded by having executive-type wood office furniture instead of steel. According to Louis J. Brindisi, Jr., national executive compensation specialist for Peat, Marwick, Mitchell & Co., the most ego-satisfying perquisites are access to private dining rooms, superior office space, and memberships in clubs. While fancy desks and club memberships may be rewards that can be doled out by upper management, they are usually not an option at the disposal of a middle- or lower-level supervisor. The person at this level has to rely on his ability to lead and to motivate.

Unfortunately, the reward system, whatever its components, often does not get the desired results. In a company where management complained about the tendency of lower-level people to avoid risk taking and to "polish the apple" with their bosses, a survey showed that about one third of the lower-level people believed that being a yes-man and going along with the majority were attitudes that were rewarded.[*]

Another problem that is likely to be created by reward systems is the tendency to borrow time from one project to be used on another. Suppose project A is due for completion in eight weeks and project B is planned for a twelve-week completion. If there is a problem in getting project A done on time the temptation is to take resources from B to apply to A. This puts B behind schedule, but never mind; resources can be borrowed from project C for B. This kiting practice is devastating not only for the potential of seriously missing a schedule, but also for the lack of honesty, discipline, and control that it generates.

To counter these and similar problems of distorted results from rewards, you should first find out what your employees believe to be the types of behavior that are rewarded. This can be done through discussion or by a confidential survey. The results may call for a restructuring of the formal reward system to include monetary incentives, if that is possible. It is more likely, however, that correction will have to be made through a change in management philosophy and practice— a change that makes the manager a builder, as discussed in Chapter 4. When this is done, the first promotion based on performance and knowledge will be a signal that won't be missed. The apple polisher

---

[*] Steven Kerr, "On the Folly of Rewarding A, While Hoping for B," *Academy of Management Journal*, December 1975.

and the project manager who is always on the verge of running out of control, borrowing time from one project to use on another, will be left standing in the wings.

Monetary Incentives

There is no question that monetary incentives have the biggest potential for distorting performance from what it ought to be. That does not have to be the outcome, but the safeguards that are needed to avoid misdirected effort may not be worth the trouble. If so, don't use monetary incentives.

Loctite Corporation, a leader in anaerobic adhesives (adhesives which harden in the absence of air), is an example of a company with an incentive package that gets the intended results. Loctite's president, E. Russell Eggers, has said that the company salesmen are paid for "growing a business, not for what they did in the past."[*] The system is tilted to reward salesmen for finding new applications for Loctite's products rather than grinding out more volume. For example, some years ago, at the urging of salesmen, the automobile industry began using a method of impregnating powdered metal with Loctite anaerobics to produce parts which are lighter than castings but just as strong. The acceptance of this method has increased the sales of Loctite's products used in powdered metal parts to five times what they were three years ago.

Following are five guidelines that can often be employed in devising incentives which properly motivate and control.

1. A portion of incentive pay can be linked to long-term performance. If the normal pay period is weekly, part of the compensation can be put on an annual basis. For monthly systems, part of the incentive can be related to annual goals or goals over several years.

2. All or a part of the incentive pay should be related to the success of the organization of which the person is a part. A group incentive plan carries out this guideline. Another instance is rewarding a president of a division for the performance of his division and the performance of the next higher organization of which his division is a part (probably group or corporate level).

---

[*] "Loctite: Ready to Fend Off a Flock of New Competitors," *Business Week*, June 19, 1978, p. 118.

3. Incentives should be paid only for *net* gains. Parts that fail inspection should not be counted in determining a production worker's pay. At a less tangible level, the cost of the increased performance must be fully accounted for—for example, high travel and entertainment expense for a salesman—and deducted from the gross gain.

4. Inasmuch as rewarding performance for a single dimension, such as sales, is always risky, consideration should be given to establishing more than one criterion for incentive pay. This may be done by using an incentive formula that has several variables. It can also be done by setting well-specified standards or constraints that guard against shoddy performance in important but ancillary activities to the main purpose of the job. Coaching inexperienced people is an example of the kind of activity that may need safeguarding.

5. Incentives must be reviewed and revised. Organizations, situations, and duties change. Incentives must be kept up to date.*

How to Make Control Everybody's Business

To make control everybody's business, you have to create a culture in your organization which encourages control and makes the concept of control entirely acceptable. If this seems hard to do, then substitute "communication" for "control." After all, when control breaks down, it is due to a failure of communication. Looking at control as a type of communication changes its negative connotation to a positive one. Almost everybody wants to know how well work is progressing and what the problems are. The time you take to pass on current information to your subordinates not only makes them more knowledgeable, hence better prepared to make decisions about their work, but also tells them that you value them as important persons in your organization.

You can put this theme into practice by posting graphs of progress for all to see. Briefing meetings are even better, but take more time. Whatever the methods, the belief that you want to instill is that trust and confidence are totally compatible with control systems. Control systems are dependent on communication, and without trust and confidence there will be gross distortions and filtering of information. On

* These five points are abstracted from an unpublished paper by Wayne Howard, executive vice-president, James Jones Company.

the other hand, the open organization can talk about its progress candidly, even when there are serious problems. The message you should give to the person who resists giving information is that there are degrees of trust and confidence. These are not absolutes. A person builds trust and confidence by communicating regularly, accurately, and fully.

"Economy of direction" is a corollary to control. It means that you give as little direction as possible to get the intended results. The importance of this concept becomes evident by considering the effects of overdirecting. Too much direction conveys an impression of distrust. Moreover, it is costly because it is time consuming and discourages responsibility.

Without a control system, formal or informal, that reports status, there is a greater tendency to give instructions constantly. The more the system is self-correcting, the less top-down direction is required. And the freely flowing information that is the basis for control in business will not be achieved unless everyone believes that he has a responsibility for making control work.

How to Kill Bureaucracy

Bureaucracy may be an unfortunate by-product of control. It is often started as a reaction to a problem which is deemed to be beyond the ken or reach of the existing organization or the people in it. Or it may be that the existing organization is believed not to have the incentive to eliminate the problem. These circumstances call for a new organization or an enhancement of the resources and capabilities of the existing organization. In any case, it involves more cost and people.

Frequently, the added power is greater than what is required to solve the problem. But that is not the main cause of bureaucracy. Bureaucracy emerges after the problem has been brought under some sort of control. Of course, the problem is not likely to be eliminated entirely because the newly strengthened organization must ensure that the problem continues, if only in latent form, to guarantee its own existence.

The maturing of the new group or the added component of an old group is accompanied by a forming of new goals, policies, and procedures that not only address the original problem but also solve or prevent related problems, some of which have not occurred and may never occur. If this tendency is allowed to grow unchecked, the bureaucracy develops a terrain of responsibilities and functions that are further and further removed from the original problem and much more encompassing in scope. At this point, you might say, the bureaucracy has matured.

What is wrong with a little bureaucracy? In the first place it represents a cost for which there is little benefit. More important, it makes organizations inflexible, and organizations must change if they are to survive. A bureaucratic unit asserts its inflexibility in two ways. First, it creates red tape, which needlessly complicates the effective efforts of other units. Second, the bureaucratic organization will foment self-serving decisions which support the status quo and are not in the interest of the customer or of the larger organization of which it is a part. Moreover, there is the threat that important business decisions will be made by people who do not have the requisite knowledge but are thrust into a decision-making position by virtue of their membership in the bureaucracy. From bureaucracy it is but a short step to poor decisions and from there an even shorter step to poor consequences.

There are two fundamental cures for bureaucracy. One is starvation. Zero-base budgeting, traditional budgeting, and good planning nip at its heels but don't get at its heart unless accompanied by scarce resources. The austerity that comes with a depressed economy along with good planning will hold up the bureaucratic organization to scrutiny that it cannot withstand. The budgetary knife will either eliminate it or reduce it to the bare essentials.

Change, the enemy of bureaucracy, is the other cure. Although change can benefit bureaucracies, the odds are against it. The probable outcomes in any changing situation are more unfavorable to it than favorable.

Organizations which are continually changing, as when new groups and task teams are regularly being formed, never give bureaucracy a chance to develop, except in parts of the organization that do not change. When change does not occur naturally, then change should be considered for the sake of change—and what it would do to the vested interests of entrenched groups.

When progress is stymied, you would be wise to make changes that disrupt the organization chart. This advice may seem irrational, or extreme, or crippling, but it is not. You will probably find that your rationale for dividing tasks among individuals and groups is not so immutable as it seems. Work is accomplished through a series of small steps that are integrated into a system. As managers we make decisions to divide the flow of work into segments which are then given to elements of the organization to perform and manage. How we break up the flow of work is logical but also arbitrary in that more than one manageable arrangement often exists.

In a business school departments are usually established along the lines of business disciplines—marketing, management, finance, accounting, business law, business economics, and so on. If these long-established departments become too preoccupied with fighting over and protecting their own turf to the detriment of the welfare of the school, a change to totally new departments might be the correct antidote. The new departments, carved out of segments of the old, might have titles like human behavior; quantitative analysis; financial planning and control; legal, social, and economic analysis; and task management. This change would produce much turmoil but out of it would come new ideas and a release of pent-up energy from the previously frustrated.

How to Achieve Consistency and Flexibility

One of the most radical transformations that the aerospace industry has seen since World War II is the conversion of manufacturing from mass production to the production of small quantities and prototypes. Building airplanes or the electronic systems that go into them is a complicated business no matter what system of manufacturing is used. The number of parts is in the tens of thousands and the requirements for quality are stringent. To cope with mass production of a complex product, aerospace companies had built up elaborate systems and subsystems for controlling inventory and production as well as for handling the physical components and assemblies.

Under conditions of essentially prototype production, the systems created for mass production proved to be too slow to respond to changes in the product configuration and too expensive to administer. Changes were needed and they were resisted. It is difficult for anyone to scrap a very technically sophisticated and advanced system even though the change in the business has rendered the system obsolete.

A new ideal had to replace the old one to make change acceptable.

The old ideal of efficient mass production of a complex product was outmoded. A new ideal of flexibility in manufacturing that can respond to short lead times and quickly incorporate new and changed engineering designs had to be communicated to all levels of management. The changes that were required cut across organizational lines. Cooperation could be obtained only if everyone realized that the concept of the business had changed and there was a new ideal toward which all must strive.

Most changes are not as drastic as the example sketched above, but nevertheless, most require some adjustment in ideals, if not new ideals altogether. There was a time when women who left jobs for maternity could expect that their upward progress had come to an end. When able to return to work, they considered themselves very fortunate to get their old position back. Now this attitude or ideal, if you will, about the role of women in the world of work has changed radically. At Prudential Insurance Co., for example, women on a six-month maternity leave get special writing assignments such as proposals for group insurance that they can complete at home. The ideal at Prudential, and many other companies, is an expectation that qualified women will have long careers with increasing responsibility.

Using ideals rather than reason as a basis for change is a safeguard against inconsistency. New reasons can be found quickly but ideals persist longer. Of course, there are many reasons for change as well as many degrees of change. It would be absurd to insist that every minor change be accompanied with a change in ideals. However, there is a limit to the number of minor changes that will be accepted in a space of time. Too many changes do reveal inconsistency and a lack of planning.

Change is like the game of "crack the whip" played on ice or roller skates. It takes only a short strong motion by one person at the one end of the chain to start a force which increases in magnitude until the last person on the opposite end is propelled for some distance at high speed. In fact, the person who started the whip in motion finishes his movement long before its final effect is carried to the end of the line.

Similarly, a change can be started quickly by one person, but it takes time for it to get to the "end of the line." The more profound the change, the more time must be allowed to instill a new or radically modified ideal in the philosophy of management.

Like the leader in the crack-the-whip game who has started the whip in motion, the business leader cannot immediately change direction. The first "whipping" action will keep a second change in direction from being felt immediately. When changes in opposite directions come in quick succession, the people at the end of the whip are "cracked."

How to Introduce Change

The danger of not making changes when they are needed can be twice as devastating as making a needless change. Entire businesses have been lost because they have not changed to adapt to new circumstances. So change you must, but how? There are three tenets for successfully introducing change, discussed below.

Philosophy. There must be a philosophy of change in the organization. In other words, one of its ideals is that the organization is able to make changes. The ability to implement change is valued for its own worth just as are other abilities such as to innovate, to be efficient, to adhere to high-quality standards. As in the case of other ideals, this one must be directly expressed in certain terms. It might be conveniently expressed in the formal written goals of the organization. In any case, making it explicit is a fundamental part of creating the ideal. When this philosophy of change is ingrained in the organization it helps to create a system which supports and engenders successful planning for change.

Planning. Changes must be planned, and the more comprehensive the change, the more formal and deliberate must be the planning process. The pattern for planning change has been outlined in Chapter 8—especially applicable are the sections about program planning.

Practice. Just as a manager and an organization can err on the side of making too many changes and becoming inconsistent, not making any changes will cause change, when it comes, to be too traumatic. And when the big change comes, almost everything will go wrong. An organization or a unit within an organization cannot hope to learn to manage change if there never are any changes to manage.

To summarize the general approach to getting consistency with flexibility, a change of significance should be tied to a changed or new ideal. The fact that ideals are not easily changed throughout an organization is a reminder that changes which are too many and too frequent will not be accepted. Every organization should put the management of change on its list of objectives, so that change is carefully planned, and proficiency in implementing change is gained through practice.

How to Make Delicate Personnel Changes

Preparation is the key to making personnel changes that may backfire if handled poorly. Here are three examples of changes that have to be handled delicately.

1. A person is removed from his position to be given a lesser assignment. He or she is a capable person but has not done well in the last assignment. Management probably made a mistake in putting him or her in that assignment in the first place. But this is a person that you want to keep in the organization.

2. A person's department is divided, and half of it is given to another manager. This typically occurs when the department has grown to a size and a complexity that is much greater than when the person heading the department was first put in charge. What has happened is that the department has outgrown the competence of its manager. But the person in charge has shown that he or she can capably manage a smaller department.

3. A department opening occurs which would be a promotion for people in the department, but instead it is given to a person new to the department or to an outsider. There are people in the department who believe that they are qualified for the post and should be given a chance.

These three situations have the potential for causing knowledgeable and competent employees to be disgruntled. In the third example this is particularly true because the one or two people who feel they have been slighted are probably the best in the group and have potential for greater responsibility with more seasoning.

The only approach that will work is one that prepares people for the changes. The preparation should take place over some period of time. Sometimes that is not possible, as when a person abruptly leaves a position, and you believe that no one in the group is ready to step into his shoes. In that case, do the best you can to prepare people for being under the supervision of an outsider, but be prepared to have some of your best people polishing up their résumés.

I recall how well the manager of industrial engineering handled a situation that involved me when I was an industrial engineer in the department with a master's degree and only two years of IE experience. He was looking for a senior industrial engineer who would have the qualifications in both technical and human skills to put across a methods program that called for participation at the worker level and on up. When he first announced his plan, I felt slighted in not being considered for the position, and this feeling persisted for some time.

At each of the weekly staff meetings, the IE manager would give us the status of his search for someone to fill the position. Through discussing the qualifications of the applicants that he had interviewed and why they were not hired, he helped the rest of us understand exactly what he was looking for and, indirectly, why I and the others were not being considered for the job. For one thing, he was looking for more maturity than I possessed at the time. Finally, after two or three months, he hired a senior industrial engineer to fill the position. By that time, I was ready to accept the new arrival in the department. I no longer believed that my aspirations for advancement had suffered. Private conversations with the IE manager had convinced me that my strengths were valuable, especially my mathematical strengths which it turned out were much greater than those of the new IE. When he reported, I welcomed him cheerfully, sincerely determined to learn as much as I could from observing how he handled the new project.

How to Gain Coordination and Avoid Conflict

Some of the natural conflicts in organizations, for example between production and sales, are often greatly magnified because of a lack of understanding of the other party's point of view, which is brought on by a lack of communication. It is granted that units with different functions are going to have different views which are often partially in conflict. However, when there is no communication, the differences in views become grossly exaggerated. You may hear a salesperson remark that operations doesn't care about giving good service to the customer, it is only concerned with getting high efficiency. Sales personnel are accused by operations of habitually making needless concessions to customers that are costly.

Two Harvard professors, Paul R. Lawrence and Jay W. Lorsch, concluded from their studies of interdepartmental conflict that companies must pay attention to both differentiation and integration. Differentiation comes from the specialization of functions found in any modern organization, and if it is not balanced with integrative efforts it leads to and exacerbates conflict.*

Some mechanism must operate to counter the parochialism that is the by-product of differentiation or specialization. It can be merely the manager over two groups who assumes the responsibility for breaking down communication barriers. He personally accomplishes integration through his leadership. This classic theory of the responsibility of a manager begins to disintegrate in a dynamic environment of some complexity. Changing conditions impose high requirements for integration—frequently more than one man can supply.

In these circumstances, the organization must be structured to achieve integration. Task teams of the type discussed in Chapter 9 are one method. Committees can also be the vehicle.

Sometimes integration is best handled by an organization created for that purpose. An organization overseeing the approval and implementation of engineering changes is an example. By itself, the organization adds no value to the engineering change nor does it find the best way to implement the change in manufacturing. Instead, it considers the merits of the proposed engineering change in light of its cost or disruptive effects. It understands the exigencies of the situation and the desires of the affected parties. It then approves or disapproves, frequently in the form of a recommendation with the force of a directive. If the change is approved, it ensures that a plan for implementation is established and agreed upon.

If you have conflict between groups in your organization, this may be a symptom that there is not enough attention being paid to integration. It may seem to you that constantly warring factions are to be expected. Or you may view the problem as attributable to aggressiveness in each department—an attitude that is mainly productive. You may feel that looking at every issue as a win-lose situation is a necessary concomitant of aggressive management. Although some of these tendencies may be so deeply rooted in the personalities of your key people that very little change can be expected no matter what is done, you may find, on the other hand, that a concentrated effort to improve communication between groups and to develop an effective integrative mechanism causes much of the prior conflict to evaporate.

* Paul R. Lawrence and Jay W. Lorsch, *Organization and Environment* (Cambridge: Harvard University Press, 1967).

12

Putting it together with MBO

John Barnett (not his real name) was contacted by an executive search firm for the position of manager of industrial engineering in a medium-size electronics firm. He landed the job and was filled with enthusiasm for the opportunity to manage a function for which he had postgraduate education and for which his ten years of experience was excellent background. The challenge of the job was exhilarating. It would be a culmination of years of preparation.

However, in a few months, the exhilaration was being replaced by a dogged and grim determination to get programs for production standards started, to get procedures written, and similar plans. Nothing was going smoothly. The problem was that no matter how he presented his programs to the director of manufacturing, it seemed that he rarely got approval, and then it was only a grudging assent to go ahead but with "misgivings."

Discussions between the two men, which never solved any of the problems, came down to bickering over details. As various versions of this scenario unfolded almost daily, John Barnett's determination turned into frustration. Soon frustration became insecurity and anxiety, and ultimately he was fired from the company.

Some attributed the conflict to a personality clash. Perhaps it is as

Parts of this chapter are taken from William C. Waddell, "The Four Cornerstones of Management by Objectives," *Los Angeles Business and Economics*, Summer 1975, pp. 9–12, 20–21.

good an explanation as any. Nevertheless, for whatever reasons lodged in the personalities or attitudes of the two men, there was a total failure to agree on the goals and methods of operation that would guide the manufacturing arm of this company and the industrial department within it.

Why MBO?

Would a management by objectives (MBO) program have been the catalyst to bring these two men into agreement? Not by itself. MBO is both a procedure and a philosophy. The procedure is simple enough. The subordinate writes his objectives and discusses them with his superior for approval. If needed, modifications are made. During the course of a year, they meet several times to review the progress being made toward the objectives. New and modified objectives may be introduced at the review sessions.

However, this procedure will not produce any dramatic changes in how people go about their business or in the results that they get unless they *understand and practice the philosophy of MBO*. If John Barnett and his boss had been able to internalize the philosophy of MBO along with the procedure, there would have been a striking difference in their relationship and in results.

MBO is an integrating tool of management because it provides a *structure* which reinforces effective management practices and style. And it is exceedingly important to have a structure. A common problem of most management development programs that sweep across the country from time to time is that they lack a lasting effect because there is no reinforcing structure. Executives attend sessions on how they can get their subordinates to be more involved in their jobs and more motivated to perform to high standards. After leaving the session, they are determined to make some changes in their management style, usually to shift from a Theory X to a Theory Y mode. Once back on the job they find that the old environment has not changed: the same old job pressures prevail and old attitudes of subordinates and superiors persist. Their attempts to alter the roles of subordinates (to say nothing about the problem of changing a superior) through exhortation and explanation are not understood well enough to be applied. Topics such as participation in decision making and what responsibility really means (see Chapter 6) never go beyond the discussion stage.

Subordinates are sure to say or think, "All this is well and good but how do we make it work?"

At that point the procedural or structural side of MBO becomes important. MBO is a mechanism for stimulating planning at every level. Under an MBO system, managers, professionals, knowledge workers, and even semi-autonomous groups are responsible for stating what they can and will do. Not only is planning improved but the underlying system for planning is strengthened. The system gives the supervisor an opportunity to ensure that standards of performance are set high. Each of the nine areas for building cited in Chapter 4 can be expressed in one form or another as an objective. The supervisor is also sure to be confronted by his subordinates with problems that he should use his power to resolve, such as a lack of proper resources or equipment to do the job. He will be on the line to support his people with actions that speak louder than words.

How to Start an MBO Program

Whether it be zero-base budgeting, zero defects, quality of working life, or some other, I don't think that there has ever been a management program for which its advocates didn't say, "You must have top management support." I won't argue with that statement in principle. It certainly helps to have the big boss behind you.

On the other hand, there is no reason why MBO can't be practiced within a division or within a department. If you believe that MBO will help you and your group do a better job, there is no reason why you can't implement an MBO system just in your group. I can't imagine that your supervisor would prevent you from making use of this philosophy and tool. However, without higher-level support, you will have to be very determined. You will also need a great deal of knowledge about writing objectives, reviewing objectives, and administering the system, and you will have to get this knowledge through reading and workshops or through the services of an outside consultant.

Another possible problem is that you may not be able to designate a person as the MBO coordinator if you manage a fairly small group of people, which means that you will have to be the coordinator. If it sounds like starting an MBO program is a lot of work, it is, and it is more work without top management support. But even if it is merely within your own group, the time you take to get an MBO program under way will be worth every minute.

Indispensable to starting an MBO program is a resolute, unswerving, and irreversible commitment to making MBO work. That type of attitude is essential at the level adopting MBO. In other words, if the chief executive officer does not have that attitude, MBO will never be successfully implemented throughout the company. If a division manager is influenced to give MBO a try in his division, but is not really thoroughly convinced, MBO will never be successful in the division. But if the person at any level is truly committed, there is no reason why he can't be successful in implementing MBO within his organization.

How much time does it take to get MBO working? Three to five years is often quoted. When Dave Babcock was hired by Stanley Goodman to bring MBO to the May Department Stores Company in 1967, he said that it would take six or seven years. Nine years later, the system was operating very well, but there was still more to be done. (Babcock and Goodman credit MBO with being the key to a turnaround in profitability during the seventies.) The amount of time depends on the existing management philosophy and the number of people who will be involved in the system. A determined department head should be able to get the program operating fairly well in its second year if he has no more than 20 people writing objectives.

After concluding that you want an MBO system in your organization and that you are willing to take the time and effort to assure its success, the next step is to designate an MBO coordinator. (As previously noted, this might be you.) For the coordinator, a theoretical and working knowledge of MBO is an indispensable requisite. Of course, this is why many organizations have used outside consultants to get the program started. The outsider brings both knowledge and credentials that an employee may not have. Additionally, since he is not part of the internal power structure, he can't be viewed as using MBO for his own political gain.

Role of the MBO coordinator. The MBO coordinator is a facilitator and a trainer. Perhaps his role is best understood by first taking a look at what he does *not* do and what he is *not* responsible for.

1. He is not responsible for the quality of written objectives nor does he write objectives for others.
2. He does not conduct reviews nor is he responsible for the quality of reviews.

3. He is not responsible for getting objectives written on time and he is not responsible for the reviews being conducted according to schedule.

4. He takes no responsibility for the achievement of objectives.

These are line functions to be performed by the managers in the operating organization. They cannot be delegated to a coordinator, because to do so would deter them from being ingrained in the system of management.

The coordinator *does* do the following:

1. Prepares procedures that are needed to activate an MBO program.

2. Conducts workshops and discussions on MBO and related management topics.

3. Arranges for speakers to conduct training sessions in the areas that he elects not to cover himself.

4. Acts as an advisor to management at any level with regard to the philosophy, implementation, and performance of the system.

5. Participates in sessions for writing and reviewing objectives at the pleasure of line personnel.

6. Reports the status of the execution and implementation of MBO to management. The MBO coordinator should receive copies of written objectives and reports on review sessions to enable him to perform this duty.

Training sessions. The next major step in getting an MBO program under way is to institute a training program, which has three aspects. The first and most important of these is training in philosophy and style. These sessions are aimed at putting across a philosophical understanding of how and why MBO gets results. There may be substantial lead time between the start of management development sessions and the initial preparation of objectives. A year or more may be required before there is an adequate understanding of how a person should manage to make MBO effective. If a manager does not embrace the philosophy of MBO, the procedural part will become an administrative burden and eventually MBO will be a sham. The tenets of the MBO philosophy are discussed in the following section.

A second type of training informs personnel about the operation of the MBO system and gives them elementary skills in writing and reviewing objectives. These sessions are largely technical in nature, but even in these the coordinator or trainer should never pass up the opportunity to reinforce the philosophy of MBO as he or she discusses the system.

Third, there must be an ongoing program which reinforces both the philosophy and the administration of the MBO program. Without a sustaining effort, the program is very likely to lose its significance in the face of new programs and new operating problems. Furthermore, the addition of new employees makes a continuous training program mandatory.

As for new programs, those as yet unheard of, with acronyms and terminology of their own, we know that they will come. But there is no reason to believe that any of these will replace MBO. MBO does not preclude any of the programs of past or present, so there is no reason to believe that it will not be compatible with those of the future. The reason is that MBO is an integrating approach—a tool for putting it all together.

MBO Philosophy: The Four Cornerstones

The model manager, professional, or knowledge worker in an MBO system is a person who is able to make an individual contribution to the results of the company. He understands the broad goals and objectives of the company, and, perhaps, he has had a part in defining them. He is able to translate his knowledge or overall purpose into specific plans, projects, and actions for his own organizational unit. He is encouraged to innovate, to find new solutions to problems, and to take advantage of opportunities. Because he defines his own work, he finds it natural to take full responsibility for the results.

This type of person may be contrasted to one who operates in a management by drives or crisis atmosphere, a style of management that is characterized by activity without commensurate results, by confusion, by inconsistency, and by a lack of real contribution from lower-level managers. Managers find themselves reacting to orders and programs and trying to implement the whims of their superiors without understanding and adequate explanation. Frequently they focus on procedure—the steps or the method—without concentrating on results, as they substitute form for substance.

The philosophy and structure of an MBO program is aimed at moving management from the latter paradigm to the former. To accomplish this, the management development sessions should stress what I call the four cornerstones of the MBO philosophy. These beliefs are the underpinnings for the system.

Self-control. Are managers capable of controlling themselves and the important aspects of their jobs without close supervision from their supervisor? Douglas McGregor (creator of Theory X and Theory Y) answered this by writing: "The motivation, the potential for development, the capacity for assuming responsibility, the readiness to direct behavior toward organizational goals are all present in people."[*] The whole philosophy and purpose of an MBO program hangs on the veracity of this belief and the acceptance of its veracity by the managers themselves at all levels. In other words, *managers are capable of controlling themselves and the important aspects of their jobs without close supervision from their superiors.*

Of course, this self-control does not come about automatically. Rather, it seems to me that two conditions must be met. First, there must be substantial congruence between organizational goals and personal goals. In a managerial or professional position, most people can experience a high degree of congruence between their own desires and the expectations of the organization. To fully exploit this point, the development sessions should introduce the concept of building. The manager builds capability in subordinates; he establishes a commitment to quality; he improves operating procedures; he introduces improvements in products and in services; he creates goodwill with customers and the community; and he is careful that in making the crucial decisions of hiring and promoting personnel he is building long-term strength in the company. These are activities in which a person can take pride. People in managerial and professional posts by and large want to do these things. Emphasizing in development sessions that this is what management is really all about helps people to see that most of their aspirations for personal growth and competence can be achieved on the job.

Related to the concept of congruence is the "whole man" idea. This is the idea that everything you do contributes to what you are and that attitudes in one sphere of your life carry over into others. A

---

[*] Douglas M. McGregor, "The Human Side of Enterprise," *Management Review*, November 1957.

person who achieves recognition and personal growth on the job is likely to carry over an optimistic and positive attitude to other activities, such as volunteer work for his or her church. The reverse is also true. No doubt, you have seen what appears to be the exception to this rule; for example, the person who seems to get little satisfaction on the job but is energetic in outside activities. However, in those cases, you cannot help wondering how much more effective the person would be if all of his or her activities contributed to growth instead of only some.

The second condition for self-control is that your management must take positive steps to put into effect its belief that you and others have the ability to control yourselves. Not just affirmation, but action is required. You need to be given (and to take) responsibility, not assignments. Surveillance which consists of monitoring inconsequential details, gauging daily performance by inconsistent standards, or failing to recognize departures from plan on a timely basis and then imposing a crash program must be replaced by a sensible control system. Having mutually agreed-upon objectives and reviewing progress are controls in themselves. The objectives and the plan for monitoring progress can be carefully prepared to employ the principles of control discussed in the previous chapter.

The third condition is that people must know how to exercise self-control. A person who is self-controlled confronts issues. Sometimes making no decision is the best decision, but that is never the case if the decision will be made anyway by someone else who is less informed or less qualified. A manager who confronts issues is one who usually finds the root causes to his problems and has the courage to apply appropriate remedies. He is not deterred from facing an unpleasant situation when he knows that it will get worse if left alone.

Discussions of real and hypothetical situations in management development sessions will show managers what is expected of them and how to handle themselves in various situations. Cases, role playing, and films can be used to good advantage.

Self-control and time management are inseparable. Every manager and professional must learn to manage his time if he is to practice self-control. There are many seminars on this topic given by experts in the field and, again, films are available. A training session or sessions could be patterned along the lines of the seven principles of time management found in Chapter 3.

A corollary to the cornerstone of self-control is that a person must have the opportunity to exercise self-control. He must be able to use his discretion in organizing his work and have some control over priorities. In jobs like this, effectiveness is more important than efficiency. Whether or not these conditions exist is a matter of job design and job level. At managerial levels, they should always exist; at lower-level positions and in staff positions, it depends on how the job is designed not only formally, but in practice. The real content of a job may have more to do with the jobholder's relationship with his boss and with his peers than with the formal description.

If the conditions for self-control do not exist in the job, do not include the jobholder in the MBO system. It would be a farce to ask a person who has a structured job to write his or her objectives. (This is not to say that people in structured jobs cannot participate in group goal setting or in establishing performance standards.)

Knowledge. The manager on the job is in the best position to assess the realities of his job. Unless he is new to the job, he should have more knowledge of how to perform in that job than anyone else. If this is not true—a superior, a peer, or a subordinate knows more about the job than he—then that manager is not working up to his capability. Knowledge of the job implies far more than a technical understanding of the function. It means that he understands the subtleties of how his function and his department relate to the others, the nuances of company policies, and the inevitable gap between policy and the way things actually happen.

Of course, the manager discusses his department's goals with his superior along with his plans for achieving those goals, and, of course, he receives guidance from his superior. No one expects the manager to operate in a vacuum. But he is the *resident expert* in that job. Like any other resource, his knowledge must be used to the best advantage. The superior must allow the subordinate to put his knowledge to work, and the subordinate manager must understand that his "value added" is through the application of his unique knowledge.

Discussions of "putting knowledge to work" in management development sessions are the predecessors to writing objectives. Job descriptions may exist but they do not define the contribution that the manager must make in coping with problems and in pressing opportunities. The job description should be helpful as a source of information but it does not relieve the manager of the responsibility of coming to grips with the question, "Why am I here?" And after asking this question, he then should ask, "What activities, projects, and just plain work should I be undertaking so that I can make the greatest contribution in the role that I am being asked to fulfill?"

In answering these questions, the manager analyzes the activities that he performs. He must sort these out into categories of importance and urgency. Any manager who has really taken responsibility for his job in the sense that he is self-controlled finds that there are far many more things that he can do than he has time to do. He would like to work on a new idea; he needs to spend more time with certain employees; the budget needs to be updated; he needs to prepare a proposal for a business contract; time must be spent in reviewing and making decisions on personnel matters, and, unfortunately, time is demanded on occasion to mollify a customer or to correct the work that was done incorrectly the first time. The list is endless. The manager must be selective and plan what he can do.

Management development sessions should stress three points: First, simply that the person in the job knows more about it than anyone else and he should therefore put his knowledge to work. Second, his superiors should respect his knowledge, which does not preclude giving him specific assignments. This is a normal condition of working in an organization. Respecting the knowledge of a subordinate means that the superior expects, even demands, that the subordinate largely define his own contribution. Third, the manager must plan his time and his activities on the basis of goals and objectives. The next step is keeping a record—the third cornerstone of the MBO philosophy.

Record of progress. A system is needed to establish a record of progress and accomplishment. In the absence of such a system, the record merely shows that a person spent so much time in various positions. What he accomplished in the positions he held is unknown. Unanswered are questions aimed at demonstrated results, such as: How did the group that you supervised perform before you came? How did it perform when you left it? What did you do to help prepare employees for increasing responsibility? What was the relationship between units of input, say, man-hours, to units of output before and after your taking charge? What improvements were made in ways of doing business, in products, or in services?

Management by objectives answers these questions because it focuses on results. In this way it gives a person a legitimate record of accomplishment which is far superior to a record showing only the time spent in various positions.

Why is it desirable for a person to have a track record of accomplishment? It is not primarily because it is a means of evaluating performance for salary increases and promotion. In fact, undue emphasis on this use of MBO will surely lead to a compulsion to have the record read well instead of attention to contribution.

The real value of a track record is not as a report card for higher management but as a motivator and a guide. It is a motivator because it highlights achievement. Attaining goals is personally satisfying. Striving for a goal adds a new dimension to a job which gives it more meaning. Recognition received for meeting difficult objectives is known to be genuine.

As a guide, a track record will influence decisions, large and small, in your daily life—on and off the job. Attention to a goal can substitute another call on a customer for an extra long lunch. It can cause you to read the morning paper in ten minutes instead of twenty; it can direct you away from some of the routine chores into tackling the hard work of fact finding and analysis that is required to support a major impending decision.

The motivation, the guidance, and the track record itself depend on your having established written objectives. Monitoring the progress against the objectives may entail keeping additional records. For example, a log book might be used to determine the time taken for forms to be processed through a department. This is extra work, but if it were not important to control the time for processing forms an objective to this effect should not have been written in the first place. Objectives and supporting records should be concerned with areas of performance that count.

Two-way communication. A firm understanding between superior and subordinate regarding what the latter is attempting to accomplish lays a foundation for cooperation, coordination, and good interpersonal relations. Hardly anyone would disagree with the notion that a superior and a subordinate should communicate, or that this communication should be at a level where real understanding takes place. Each should know what the other is planning to do. Certainly the subordinate must know what is expected of him and must have an opportunity to discuss his ideas with his superior.

Yet, judging from what has been written and said on this topic, the blame for many management problems is attributed to faulty communications. In fact the breadth of the problems and the broad interpretation that is often given to "communications" makes you wonder if there are any other underlying causes of problems. Be that as it may, the point is that two-way communication between superior and subordinate is a very important aspect of management and that it is frequently done poorly.

Management by objectives improves communications between levels of management because it places a requirement for communication on the shoulders of both and provides a structure for communication. Originally, objectives are discussed and agreed upon. They then become a covenant between superior and subordinate. Periodically, progress is reviewed and changes and additions are made to objectives.

Some training sessions on communication are very desirable as a basis for the subsequent discussions on the specific subjects of how to review objectives and performance. The topics discussed in Chapter 7—Process of Communication, Purpose of Communication, How to Avoid Misunderstanding, and How to Get Agreement—are appropriate for this purpose. Most important of all in these sessions is to stress the value of communicating. While MBO provides a structure for communication, this does not offer assurance that it will be done properly.

MBO: Are You Ready for This?

A questionnaire that you can use to evaluate your and your group's readiness for an MBO program is shown here. Answer the 19 questions yourself and then have a few of your subordinates answer the same questions. The answers can then be compared and discussed. If you feel uncomfortable in doing this, that in itself is a clear signal that you need to do some work on getting open, two-way communications in your organization.

The 19 questions fall into the categories corresponding to the four cornerstones of MBO. The first seven pertain to self-control and its related concepts, such as confronting issues and managing time. The next four questions address the issue of knowledge. Questions 12 and 13 pertain to having and using information to establish a track record and questions 14 to 19 deal with the very crucial topic of communications.

The questionnaire is most useful in esposing weaknesses that you may have which could be detrimental to MBO. The answers to the

Questionnaire on Philosophy of Management by Objectives—Are You Ready for This?

	1	2	3	4
1. How well do you understand the goals of your company or division?	Not known	Vaguely	Have general understanding	Understand explicitly
2. Are you able to relate your work to the larger goals of the organization?	Never	Rarely	Usually	Nearly always
3. Where is responsibility felt for achieving the organization's goals?	Mostly at top	Top and middle	Fairly general	At all levels
4. What percent of your work satisfies you personally?	20% or less	40%	60%	80% or more
5. Over the last year, what has happened to the relationship between you and the person(s) you least like to work with?	Gotten worse	About the same	Little better	Much better
6. How are you currently handling your most difficult problem?	Procrastinating	Giving it a lot of thought	Working on it as time permits	Have plan and implementing plan
7. How well do you control your time?	Cannot control time	Some control	Able to make time for important work	Use a system for control

8. How well do you understand the responsibilities and goals of your superior?	Not at all	Vaguely	Have general understanding	Understand explicitly
9. How well do you know your job?	Know little	Adequate knowledge	Quite well	Very well
10. Who specifies your work and activities?	My boss	My boss and demands of others	Combination of me and others	I do, most of the time
11. Are your subordinates involved in decisions related to their work?	Not at all	Occasionally consulted	Generally consulted	Fully involved
12. Do you keep records to measure progress?	No	Some, but very informal	Good records for some things	Good records for most important things
13. What are cost, productivity, and other control data used for?	Policing, punishment	Reward and punishment	Reward, some self-guidance	Self-guidance, problem solving
14. How free are you to talk to your superior about work?	Not at all	Not very	Rather free	Fully free
15. Do you seek and use subordinates' ideas?	Seldom	Sometimes	Usually	Nearly always
16. How much communication is aimed at attaining objectives?	Very little	Little	Quite a bit	A great deal
17. How well do your subordinates accept your communication?	With suspicion	Possibly with suspicion	With caution	With an open mind
18. How accurate is upward communication?	Often wrong	Censored for the boss	Limited accuracy	Accurate
19. How well do subordinates know problems faced by subordinates?	Know little	Some knowledge	Quite well	Very well

questions will provoke further analysis and discussion. The questionnaire may be scored by assigning points from one through four to answers, according to the columns. The scores may be interpreted as
follows:

55 plus	You are ready
40–54	Doubtful
Below 40	Much work to do before you are ready

How to Integrate Goals and Objectives

An MBO program is an extension of the goal-setting and planning systems discussed in Chapters 7 and 8. Whereas goals frequently extend
beyond one year, objectives are usually limited to what can be accomplished within a year. Furthermore, goals are more oriented to an
organization, whereas objectives are more individual. The connection
between goals and objectives is usually at the derivative plan level,
the last step in the sequence of goals, strategies, and derivative plans.

In the illustration of the credit department in Chapter 8, goals first
were established which led to certain strategies. One of the strategies
called for a cooperative effort between the credit department and the
salesforce. One of the action plans emanating from this strategy was to
train sales personnel on how to encourage customers to open a charge
account. Getting this training initiated could be the subject of an objective. In fact, several objectives could be written by different individuals who could have responsibility for developing portions of the
training program. In this way MBO is a system whereby objective setting (and planning) cascades down the organization, involving professionals and knowledge workers as well as managers.

You should not interpret this example to mean that all objectives
must be explicitly related to a chain of goals or higher-level objectives.
Just as the functional responsibility is the static basis for the dynamic
goals, strategies, and action plans, so the job description is the static
basis for the dynamic objective. This means that you should look to
your job description to assist you in formulating objectives.

But suppose that you are the department head—does that mean
that after writing goals for the department, you have to start over
again to write your own objectives? Except for personal objectives the
goals of the department can be essentially your objectives. There may

be some value in restating some of the goals to delineate what is to be done during the course of a year when the goal goes beyond a year. You may want to add some items that support the goals of the department but are not mentioned explicitly as goals. If you were the manager of the credit department discussed in Chapter 8, you might state the objective of hiring a person by a certain date to do the analytical work needed to attain some of the ambitious departmental goals.

In addition to extending the concept of goal setting to professionals and staff personnel in nonmanagerial positions, MBO reinforces the concept of goal setting. It contributes to making goal setting a habitual and natural process of management. Of course, reinforcing benefits of MBO will be achieved only if the system is closely linked to goal setting as a part of the planning procedure.

MBO can be linked to goal setting by timing, by the people involved, and by the content. Linking by timing means that goals and objectives are scheduled to be prepared at about the same time. You would not, for instance, have a meeting for group participation in departmental goal setting and then have objectives written six months later. Instead, people should write their objectives soon after goals have been established. Linkage by people means that the people who are involved in writing goals are also involved in writing objectives, although the reverse may not be true. For example, you might meet with a small group of subordinates to map out departmental goals. The people in this group would also prepare individual objectives. Furthermore, they probably would require some of their subordinates to write objectives also. Linkage by content is usually accomplished by tying objectives to action plans which themselves are derived from goals and strategies.

How to Write Objectives

This is a section about content, not style (which is insignificant by comparison). You begin to formulate your objectives by thinking about your effectiveness areas. What is it that you do, are supposed to do, or can do that will make a contribution? Effectiveness areas are identified by the results that you are to achieve in the various spheres of your activities.

Start to define these areas by considering the goals and objectives of the larger organization of which you are a part. Then ask yourself what you can do to support these goals. Also consider your mission or function. This might be called an unwritten job description. It is represented by the expectations that others have about the work you do. These expectations are the result of the experience that others have had in working with you in your current capacity. Even if the job description is current in reflecting all the things that you do, it can never supply the emphasis on certain aspects of your performance that comes about through experience. But, of course, don't ignore the formal job description since it is also a source for defining effectiveness areas.

Writing objectives is a time to review the concept of being a builder. The nine areas for building discussed in Chapter 4 are reminders of effectiveness areas. Particularly important is building knowledge. An organization or unit within an organization cannot hope to perform at even a satisfactory level without an ongoing effort to improve its knowledge.

The performance dimensions of timeliness, cost, and quality are other concepts for jogging a person's ability to identify effectiveness areas. What do you do, for example, to keep costs in line? Timeliness and quality are ways of judging how well work is performed. Examining timeliness, cost, and quality can make you realize that work you thought was routine is potentially an area for increased effectiveness.

Categories of objectives. There is value in using four categories of objectives as a checklist. The first is the *key task*. In this category are objectives related to the fundamental purpose of the position. One of the criticisms of some MBO programs has been that managers and professionals are so encouraged to work on peripheral tasks and projects which may have great value for the future that they neglect their main duties. The *key task* category serves as a reminder that there must be objectives which state what is going to be done in the basic job functions.

This type of objective may be about the same as a performance standard. The credit department discussed in Chapter 8 adopted a goal of getting a 10 percent net recovery on accounts sent to outside collection agencies. This could also be a one-year objective of the credit manager or someone else in the department. As such, it is a moot question whether it is also a performance standard.

The second category of objectives is *innovative*. In this category are objectives that cause you to consider opportunities for improvement. Earlier it was said that what is done and planned to be done may be described in terms of urgency and importance. Urgent work tends to get done whether or not it is important. What many persons fail to do are the important things that are not urgent. Frequently, these are building types of projects.

The other side of the coin is the *problem-solving* category. Whereas the innovative objective is intended to add to the strength of the organization, the problem-solving objective is to remove a weakness. In both cases, the work itself tends to be in the nature of a project. The value of both categories is merely to trigger the thought processes to explore both opportunities and problems. The ultimate treatment of a problem is to use your creativity to turn it into an opportunity.

The fourth category is *personal,* as it pertains to your own personal development. This may apply to new knowledge that you want to acquire or to changes in your attitude or personality. Your ability to lead is dependent on your self-image. You can visualize what you want to be and can take steps to get there.

I believe that everyone should have personal objectives, but I don't believe that all of them or any of them should necessarily be part of the written objectives in an MBO program. If you have confidence in your superior's ability to help you attain these objectives and if you trust him to use the information ethically and wisely, written personal objectives could be very advantageous. Of course, if there is a personal deficiency that is recognized by both you and your boss, and if it is one that you are striving to overcome, there is more reason to address it with an objective. You have gone on record to correct it.

Guidelines for writing objectives. Fourteen guidelines for writing objectives are listed below. These are intended to be self-explanatory, but I would like to touch on the reasoning behind some of them.

1. Categories may be helpful as a checklist but shouldn't be compelling. Categories often used are (1) key task, (2) innovative, (3) problem solving, and (4) personal.
2. Opinions differ widely on the number of objectives that a person should write, ranging from 3 or 4 to 20. For most people 6 to 12 would probably be about right but there is little to be gained from making an issue over the number of objectives.
3. If possible, objectives should be written in terms of output or results rather than in terms of input or effort or activity.
4. The objectives of lower-level units should be meshed with those

of the higher-level units. Once again, this is not a hard and fast
rule for every objective that is written. Also, this guideline still
leaves a lot of room for creativity on the part of subordinate units.

5. An objective should be expressed in terms that are appropriate
for the organizational level at which they are being written. This
means that the degree of detail and specificity in the objective
corresponds to the personal involvement of the writer.

6. It is highly desirable to state objectives quantitatively so that
progress can easily be measured. *But....*

7. If performance in a key area does not lend itself to quantitative
evaluation, it is much better to write the objective than to omit
it.

8. A completion date or a time interval must be specified.

9. A method of appraising progress should be agreed upon by the
subordinate and the superior at the time the objective is approved.

10. Although all objectives may not be quantitative, they should
never be vague generalities.

11. At the time the objective is written there should be some sort of
plan for its accomplishment. The plan can be very general at this
stage.

12. Objectives should be written so that people have to stretch to
make them. Success reinforces a person's ability to succeed, but
only if he knows that success was not certain. If there are no fail-
ures then people are being too cautious.

13. Writing objectives is a good opportunity for group goal setting.
This may result in the objectives of the next higher level being
raised to incorporate the higher expectations of the group.

14. Frequently, an objective cannot be attained by one person and
must become a joint objective. This is often the case when a line
manager and a staff department are working together to solve a
problem.

The question of how to measure is a theme underlying guidelines
3, 6, 7, 8, 9, and 10. Guideline 3 says that the objective should be
written in terms of the results to be achieved, not effort required. Indeed, this is a very important principle. As a manager, you would be
grossly ineffective if you were concerned only with how people did
things, not what they did. On the other hand, there are times when the
true result cannot be measured or is too difficult to be measured. Take
for example the objective of the public relations department to improve the standing of the corporation in the community. I suppose
that this objective could be measured by polling the community, assuming that the process of measuring (polling) did not affect the out-

come. However, without going into detail, there are many reasons for not polling the community and therefore being unable to measure community attitudes toward the corporation. On the other hand, the public relations department could write objectives about press releases and about its role in community activities such as fund raising for charity—all of which are measurable. And although they are not quite the same thing as community standing, they are steps along the way.

Guidelines 6 through 10 in effect say that there must be some way to tell if the objective has been met. Quantitative measures are preferable but you should not let the inability to quantify something stand in the way of writing an objective when it is important for other reasons to do so. An untoward emphasis on quantitative measurement can contribute to the downfall of an MBO system, because people tend to exclude important effectiveness areas from objectives when they find they cannot state objectives quantitatively. When measurement is not possible, you can use descriptive adjectives and adverbs. "Working harmoniously with department A" is commonly understood to be different from a "hostile relationship."

Applying guideline 5 eliminates needless repetition in objectives at different levels. Suppose that a plant manager believes that the procedures governing procurement are hamstringing operations and that he and the manager of purchasing agree that they need to be revised. The job is given to a systems analyst. Although all three levels are vitally concerned with getting revised procedures, the objective should not be written three times. You can see that restating lower-level objectives at higher levels of management, carried to the point of absurdity, would result in hundreds or thousands of objectives for the top executives.

Forms or formless MBO? MBO programs run the gamut of elaborate forms to simple forms to no forms. The use of elaborate forms implies, perhaps demands, that the objective be supported by considerable planning. These forms often require that expenditures related to the attainment of the objective be itemized to be compared with the expected detailed benefits. Frequently a plan for implementing the objective showing milestones for completion of phases of work is recorded in spaces provided on the form. Persons and departments that have a supporting role in achieving the objective may be cited for what they are expected to do.

The primary advantage to fully supporting goals with plans and budgets is that it forces detailed planning which adds to the probability of success. The very process of planning ensures that the objective is realistic. Superiors and others who review and approve objectives, possibly authorizing expenditures, are presented with information in a standardized format upon which to base their decision. Furthermore, the milestones and the planned expenditures supply a basis for reviewing progress.

It is difficult to argue against the logic of thorough planning, but in practice too many people are discouraged by many boxes and spaces on forms calling for detailed information. At the time they are required to write objectives, they may not be ready to do detailed planning and there may be no need for planning at that time. By requiring the objective to be submitted with a plan, you are either causing the writer to do more planning than he or she is prepared to do at the time or tempting him to forget the objective altogether. A person who is deflected from tackling a tough job by premature and overly stringent planning requirements may be tempted to embellish ordinary and probable outcomes into sought-after objectives, beautifully documented with facts and figures. This, of course, reduces the MBO program to an onerous, nonproductive exercise that will soon earn the disdain of all.

The case for using a simple form or a blank sheet of paper to write objectives is that people are more likely to be encouraged to take the risks that are usually present when the payoffs are high. Guidelines 11 and 12 recognize that the planning for a major contribution is difficult and its execution is risky. The person responsible for the objective should have some ideas as to how it will be accomplished, but working out the details can be considered as part of meeting the objective. Plans and budgets can be submitted when it is appropriate to do so.

The acid test for objectives. There is a tendency for any MBO program to drift away from a philosophy and method of managing toward a ritual of administration and paperwork. To counter this, I suggest that after objectives are written you sit back and reflect on them by asking yourself: Do these objectives really cover the important aspect of my job? Will attention to these objectives influence my decision making? Are they ambitious enough? Do they relate to those of the next higher organization and the company as a whole?

How to Conduct Reviews

There are a few guidelines and admonitions regarding the review process, but all of these pale into insignificance beside the most obvious one of all: *The reviews must be conducted.* Why it is that after a superior and subordinate take the time to thoroughly discuss the objectives of the subordinate—objectives which should deal with the essence of performance and achievement on the job—and then fail to take time for periodic reviews remains a mystery in the world of management. They will take time to discuss trivia and the problems of the day but frequently do not find time to review objectives. It is not logical but it happens. Quite naturally, people lose interest in writing objectives and in striving to carry them out when there is no review process.

More than a cog in the MBO system, the review process is fundamental to building a management system and philosophy which underlies the mechanics of MBO, planning, and budgeting. Correctly done, a review is a time for introspection, inspection, and positive reinforcement. It is an opportunity to gain understanding and insight. Without deep understanding, plans will be faulty or inappropriate; execution will often fail to carry out the plan as it is intended to be carried out. Moreover, without understanding, the main thrust of the plan may be carried out, but in a way that is inefficient and causes new problems to arise. If the only value in an MBO program were that it forced superior and subordinate to talk seriously about their work, it would be a program well worth the effort. Review and feedback are excellent defenses against Murphy's Law.

Review of objectives. There are three kinds of reviews in an MBO system, the first being the review of objectives. The purpose of this initial review, in a meeting between superior and subordinate, is to arrive at agreement on the objectives themselves, which have been prepared by the subordinate. It is of foremost importance that both sides have the same understanding of the effectiveness areas of the subordinate—just what, in other words, this job is supposed to accomplish. Without this basic understanding, there could of course be no agreement on objectives. Having come to a mutual understanding about effectiveness areas, the next consideration is priorities—the urgency and importance of work. If there are differences in priorities, they must be ironed out. Surely it is not possible to arrive at a consensus on the written objectives if superior and subordinate differ on priorities.

After reaching agreement on the objectives, the question of measurement and validation of performance should be discussed. This is especially important when it is not possible to measure performance quantitatively. It is important that both sides have a clear and identical mental picture of what constitutes success.

The initial review meeting is also the time to discuss action planning and problems of implementation. The superior may be able to use his influence to overcome a roadblock. Known requirements for support and resources outside of the control of the subordinate should be identified. The amount of detail that it is possible to discuss of course depends on the amount of action planning that has been done at the time the objective is prepared. If very little action planning has been done, the review should establish a milestone for more detailed planning at a later date.

The final topic for the initial review session is to set a date for the first intermediate review of progress on all objectives.

Intermediate review of progress. A good rule to follow is to conduct a progress review of objectives every quarter. If a quarterly review doesn't seem frequent enough, be aware that most organizations have difficulty in holding to that schedule. There has been some research which shows that frequent reviews are beneficial, but, to my knowledge, no research that demonstrates that review can be too frequent. But it is just common sense that there is a point of frequency at which reviews become counterproductive. Regarding the desirability of frequent reviews, two researchers have found that the more frequent the review:

The more positive the feelings toward the MBO program.
The greater the goal success.
The greater the improvement in relations with the boss.
The clearer the goals appear to be.
The more time the boss was thought to be spending on the MBO program.
The more it was perceived that the company had a strong interest in the MBO program.
The greater the satisfaction with the boss.
The more influence the subordinate felt he had on decisions made by his boss.

The more he viewed his boss as being helpful and concerned about him as an individual.[*]

The intermediate review is a time to identify any problems that are a threat to achievement. To this end some supplementary planning might be required. If there are circumstances that were unseen at the time the objective was written, it may be necessary to make an adjustment in the objective. Moreover, there is no rule that says that new objectives cannot be adopted during the year. They may be added as the need arises. At the end of the session, the time for the next review should be put on the calendar.

Final review. To some extent how a final review is handled depends on the nexus between the MBO system and other systems or procedures, such as performance appraisal and merit increases or bonuses. Speaking generally, however, the final review is a time for summing up progress. Performance is evaluated; kudos are given for success. When there is a lack of goal accomplishment, there should be a searching inquiry as to the causes of failure. The problem may go deeper than the objective, its plan for accomplishment, and the execution of the plan. Rather, the real underlying source of failure may be a lack of understanding, knowledge, team orientation, and the like. The fundamentals upon which an MBO system rests may be lacking.

In an MBO system that operates on an annual cycle, the review of past performance is a prelude to formulating new objectives and starting the cycle over again. New objectives may be presented and discussed at the final review session, but it is preferable to allow a breather of a couple of weeks before starting again.

Role of subordinate. The subordinate, as the resident expert, prepares his objectives and takes the lead to explain them in the initial review session. Similarly, he takes the initiative in the intermediate and final reviews. He should explain what he has done and what he has yet to do. He should state what has interfered with his not attaining anticipated results and what he plans to do about it. Recommendations for changes in target dates, new approaches, and new objectives should be brought out by the subordinate. This format reinforces the concept of self-control because he is responsible for presenting the record of his own performance.

[*] Stephen J. Carrol, Jr., and Henry L. Tosi, Jr., *Management by Objectives: Applications and Research* (New York: Macmillan, 1973), p. 98.

When the subordinate can control the review he is in a much stronger position psychologically. In the first place he is more comfortable in preparing for the meeting and will probably do a better job of preparation knowing that the result of his work will show in *his* presentation. He can feel more confident and feel less anxiety knowing that he is in control and having a better idea of what to expect. Moreover, he has an opportunity to stress accomplishment, whereas if the superior takes the initiative he is more likely to dwell only on the shortcomings. In addition, by making his case, the subordinate is able to demonstrate his qualities of leadership.

In the course of describing progress and accomplishment the subordinate should be open to new ideas and suggestions from his superior. He and the boss should be concerned with *what* is right, not *who* is right. There should be a firm understanding and agreement about what future actions will be required to attain each objective.

Role of the superior. During the initial review of objectives, the superior should take the position that the objectives prepared by the subordinate are the subordinate's, but the superior also has a responsibility to make them happen. He certainly doesn't want to saddle his subordinate with requirements that he knows can probably not be achieved. Instead, he wants to be a helper, a believer, and a positive influence.

Although the ideal is that the objectives are completely prepared by the subordinate, in practice the superior may have to suggest or even demand changes or additions, since he himself may have objectives or goals which can only be realized if the subordinate achieves certain results. If he has to depart from his role as a helper to one of being a director who determines objectives for his subordinate, so be it. At least, even in this mode, both parties should come away from the meeting with a clear idea of what is required and, in general, how it is to be done. That's better than going along on a day-to-day basis with surprises, bickering, and fault finding.

Prior to a review of progress, the superior must prepare himself with the facts at his disposal which have a bearing on the progress of each of his subordinate's objectives. Then he is ready to listen. For example, if the subordinate has an objective for a level of quality, he should know about how quality has been running and what some of the problems have been.

If the subordinate is carrying out his responsibility for the review, the main responsibility of the superior is to *listen.* He should listen actively, realizing that there are many opportunities for error in the communication process. He should question when clarification is needed and he should probe when treatment of the subject is superficial. While it is the responsibility of the subordinate to present the status, it is the responsibility of the superior to ensure that the session produces a full discussion of progress. The superior, in other words, cannot shirk his responsibility for ensuring that the review is productive.

The superior should show concern for the person as well as the task. Handled properly, a review session can hold many benefits for the subordinate. The person being reviewed can get recognition for accomplishment, greater insight into the opportunities for growth and achievement in his job and in the company, a deeper understanding of the mission of his organization, an improved interpersonal relationship with his superior, the motivation to seek still higher goals—these benefits and many more.

On the other hand, the review process carries the potential of creating fear, distrust, and the motivation to play it safe in the future. The difference between a meeting with positive overtones and one with negative can spring from only a few words or intonation. Let me illustrate. Suppose the subordinate who is reporting to you on progress says that an important schedule was prepared by Jane, one of his subordinates. Knowing that Jane is a new employee, you remark, "You mean you had Jane prepare the schedule?" Now a question like that will immediately put your subordinate on the defensive.

Any negative tendency in a review session can be completely counteracted if the review concentrates on *understanding* the current state of progress and then goes on to what is to be done in the future. Recriminating over the past is not productive. You should ensure that the discussion on each objective ends with a new plan or confirmation of the old one.

How to Integrate MBO with Other Programs

The boxed checklist is aimed at the philosophy of MBO rather than at its mechanics. If the philosophy of MBO is accepted, a natural outgrowth of this is to integrate MBO into other management systems. Indeed, as an unintegrated system, not part of planning, budgeting, or performance appraisal, it can easily become a burden and receive inadequate attention. In fact, unless integrated, there is a good chance that the requirements of MBO and other systems will be in conflict. As pointed out at the beginning of this chapter, MBO is a mechanism for integrating management systems and it should be used to do so.

Checklist: Four Cornerstones of MBO

1. **Self-Control:** Do managers have adequate self-control and self-motivation?
   - Are they meeting their needs for achievement and growth?
   - Do they let their subordinates exercise self-control?
   - Do they know how to practice self-control through time management?

2. **Knowledge:** Do managers apply their knowledge to their jobs?
   - Do they have adequate knowledge of the "big picture"?
   - Have they asked, "What is the main purpose of my job?"
   - Then have they asked, "What activities, projects, and just plain work should I be undertaking so that I can make the greatest contribution in the role that I am being asked to fulfill?"

3. **Record of Achievement:** Are managers building a track record?
   - Can they answer questions such as:
     How did the group that you supervise perform before you took charge?
     How do they perform now?
     What have you done to prepare subordinates for more responsibility?
     What improvements have you made in ways of doing business?
   - Do objectives stimulate extra effort?
   - Are objectives a guiding hand?
   - Have records been set up to measure accomplishment?

4. **Two-way Communication:** Is there two-way communication between levels of supervision?
   - Are reviews being conducted?
   - Does the subordinate take the lead during a review when discussing his performance?
   - Do the reviews avoid recriminations over the past?
   - When performance has not met objectives, are adjustments made to bring performance and objective together in the future?

Planning and goal setting. It is absolutely essential that planning and goal setting be integrated with the MBO system, or vice versa. Inasmuch as this topic was addressed in earlier chapters, only a few points will be singled out for emphasis.

1. Except for personal objectives, the objectives of a department manager and the goals of the department may be the same. If they are not the same, they must be fully mutually supporting. Differences may be due to the following reasons:

A. Differences in time span—objectives are generally written to be completed in a year, whereas goals may cover a longer duration of time.

B. Amount of detail—as a consequence of having a shorter time focus, objectives may be more detailed.

C. The differences between the job description of a manager and the functional mission of his department—the job description is a basis for writing objectives, whereas the functional mission is a basis for departmental goals.

2. MBO is an extension of planning in that employees without the responsibility for managing a unit are asked to prepare objectives.

3. Since the planning and goal-setting procedures are linked to MBO, the MBO reviews are also reviews of goals and action plans.

4. MBO can be used as a means of focusing effort on improving the basic systems approach to management without which good planning is not possible—the point made in Chapter 1.

Group processes. Work groups in the nontraditional structures of organizations, as outlined in Chapter 9, should be given responsibilities for setting goals and/or objectives. It is virtually axiomatic that a project organization and a task team by their very nature would have goals and objectives, since these tend to be single-purpose organizations. An admonition that these groups should have objectives should be totally superfluous since they could hardly operate without them. On the other hand a formal MBO program, totally integrated with the goals and planning procedures of the group, brings more people into formal planning.

MBO can make a great contribution to the operation of the team or product line slice of a matrix organization. Since matrix organizations, as opposed to single-purpose organizations, tend to have a degree of permanence and to pursue sequential goals, there is a need to sharply define and redefine the objectives of the organization and those of the key individual in the organization on a periodic basis. Again, the MBO program must be linked to a planning system, ensuring that the contribution of the group supports the mission and goals of the larger system.

There is a great, as yet untapped, potential for using MBO with semi-autonomous work groups. These are groups of first-line workers who have been given a high degree of discretion in planning their own work. In some instances, the organization of assembly work has been entrusted to groups of workers. Along with the prerogatives for planning and organizing should come the responsibility for setting group objectives. Although certain individuals in the group may be given the task of putting the objectives into writing, the adoption of the objectives should be a group process. Moreover, the review of objectives should also be done with the participation of the group. Without question, this system would strengthen the cohesiveness of the group and enhance its performance.

Performance appraisal and compensation. The purposes of performance appraisal, which have been stated many times by many different writers, boil down to these four:

1. An assessment of capability. This is the basis for a multitude of actions such as new assignments, transfers to other locations, promotions, and the like. Some companies organize data on individuals to have an inventory of skills and capabilities.

2. A basis for monetary reward. Merit increases are based on the appraisal of performance.

3. A source of motivation. If people know their performance is subject to formal evaluation, they will work harder.

4. A means of counseling and developing. Appraisal gives people information which helps them to increase their strengths and overcome serious deficiencies.

Let's look at how MBO can be used to achieve some of these purposes and, in doing so, become integrated with the appraisal and compensation system. First, MBO gives some insight as to a person's capability. What kind of objectives he writes, how difficult and how creative they are, and how well he attains them tells you something of his mettle. How well he has done in the past doesn't automatically mean that he will do well in a new assignment but gives some basis for making a judgment.

On the other hand, performance on objectives is not the only measure of a person's contribution. There are many aspects of a person's job which are not covered by objectives (although the important ones should be). Furthermore, there are incidents and conditions unanticipated at the time of setting objectives. How well a person performed under new conditions or in a crisis may not be reflected by reviewing the progress toward and the attainment of objectives. New circumstances may place some objectives beyond reach, leaving the person to be judged on how he has made adjustments.

Important actions with long-range payoffs such as building knowledge in subordinates and creating a team environment—actions that strengthen the underlying system of management—may not be stated as objectives. Yet the ability to build must be judged to get a measure of a person.

The correct approach to using MBO as a means of evaluating a person's capability is to stress that it is an important input, but only one input. Since objectives are written to cover the key effectiveness areas of a position, it would be foolish to overlook the results. But you should tell your subordinates that MBO will not be the sole basis for evaluating capability.

The same reasoning applies to merit increases in salary. If the decision to give a merit increase is based entirely on MBO, two counterproductive tendencies will emerge. First, there will be too much game playing in trying to get objectives approved that are virtually in the performer's hip pocket. He will be discouraged from writing objectives with stretch. Second, he is motivated to orient his performance fully toward the attainment of objectives. And as I have just concluded saying, there are intangible and long-range aspects of the job that are exceedingly important and may not be reflected in a one-year objective. As with performance appraisal, you should inform your subordinates that how well they meet their objectives is an important consideration in deciding on merit increases but it is only one consideration among others.

Individual and organization development. MBO is ideally suited to the purpose of counseling and developing people and groups of people. For example, a problem-solving objective for overcoming interdepartmental conflict could be written. Personal objectives are specifically for the purpose of self-improvement. All improvement is actually self-improvement, but the organization can provide opportunities for self-improvement both on the job and off by financial support for courses. A person may be given an assignment which forces him into new areas of knowledge. Furthermore, changes from one department to another and changes from line to staff can engender changes in attitude and breadth of understanding.

Conclusion

This chapter has stressed that an MBO program can become the mucilage that holds other programs together because it is a sensible and practical procedure for planning and follow-up. You can talk about building and you can stress the importance of involving today's employee in decision making, but without a mechanism for ensuring ongoing implementation, little is likely to be achieved.

The viability of MBO as a system of planning and reporting depends on its philosophical underpinnings, described as the four cornerstones. Inculcating a philosophy which attaches great value to self-control, knowledge, a track record, and communication is an essential step toward building a strong organization. The view here is that an organization is actually a subsystem of a larger system and has subsystems within it. Properly conceived and properly managed, the systems at all levels should display attributes that are defenses against Murphy's Law, such as knowledge, a sense of responsibility, and effectiveness.

An organization as a system reacts to good planning, in accordance with the third law of motion (for every action there is an equal and opposite reaction). The action is good performance; the reaction is a system with still greater capability.

Index